I heard that Woody Allen was once asked by a journalist if he was ok with
living on in the hearts and minds of his fans, to which he replied,
“that’s fine, but I’d rather live on in my apartment”,
which made me chuckle.

THE RAGING STORM

THE RAGING STORM

THE ALBUM GRAPHICS OF STORMSTUDIOS

STORM THORGERSON & PETER CURZON

Published by de Milo and StormStudios 2011

Design by
Peter Curzon and Storm Thorgerson
Text Storm Thorgerson
Graphics Peter Curzon

Dedicated to Sally and Barbie our wives who have had to put up with a lot of design narcissism
and to the memory of the late Peter Christopherson valued partner in Hipgnosis

Copy edting David Gale and Marcella Edwards

StormStudios are Dan Abbott, Rupert Truman, Peter Curzon and Storm Thorgerson
Lee Baker, Jerry Sweet and Laura Truman

Thanks for support above the call of duty Del, Trudy, Brian, Di, Theron, Alex and Morag

Print consultant Vic Lime
Proofing by Hilite
Printed by LEGO SpA, Italy
Typing by Angelique Kendal

ISBN: 978-0-9570054-0-2 Hardback
ISBN: 978-0-9570054-1-9 Softback

A catalogue record for this book is available from the British Library.

Several images from this book can be purchased as fine art prints via:
www.stormsight.co.uk

So I says to my friend I am doing another book and he says of the same old crap I suppose and I say tartly yes or as my mother might call it: The Same Old Brilliance.

Now says he there's an unbiased view if ever I heard one.

You wouldn't say the same of Picasso but there lies the problem says my friend (soon to be demoted) you are a million light years from Picasso.

Yeah okay yeah I admit of course but the principle stands like hell it does says he turning away.

So, despite my ex-friend, I herewith submit a collection of the same old crap, being our most recent endeavours in the field of music design, or more specifically album covers for Rock 'n' Roll bands (God preserve us), executed during the last three years and previously unpublished in book form.

Its all new folks!

We have been fortunate during these difficult times to have been working fairly continuously and have consorted with a variety of bands including Shpongle, Muse, Mars Volta, Steve Miller, Biffy Clyro, Disco Biscuits, Rival Sons, Pendulum, The Wombats, Powderfinger, Goose, and Pink Floyd amongst others.

We have adopted a random order for the book seeing no good reason to do otherwise, and have included text to describe the reasons for and mechanics of the work, written in conversational manner with anecdotal detail and a bit of technical information.

We have been brave (as we see it), to opt for a landscape format despite stackability issues. It is a departure and is better suited to much of our output. When it is open it reminds us fondly of gatefold vinyl, and we of course like vinyl, because our images can be bigger.

And largeness matters when trying to represent music which can be played loudly through the house, in cars, gigs, across the country via radio etc., etc. Large emotionally as well as acoustically at a time when imagery can be shrunk to postage stamp size through the computer, and much to our chagrin it often is.

Many apologies for unwitting errors and forgetfulness - no disrespect intended. Letters, emails and texts of complaint to Mrs Anna Evangeline Thorgerson please.

I hope, dear reader, you enjoy perusing the work half as much as we enjoyed making it in the first place.

ST - LONDON JUNE 2011

A PERSONAL OBSERVATION

YOU CAN'T BEAT A GOOD IDEA

BY DAVE BROLAN
PHOTO RESEARCHER EDITOR AND WRITER

I wonder if Storm himself works to such a vague but direct brief: 'I want you to write something for our next book, Dave, it's all new work, If you don't want to then piss off.'

I agreed, mainly because it is next to impossible to say no to the impossible man, it's a word he doesn't seem to hear, personally or professionally, always repeating it in a shocked tone and with a puzzled look, "No?" as if it's the first time he has heard it. I agreed also because I need a design from him that is being held to ransom, plus I am mildly qualified for the task he hints at, as an outsider looking at his body of work and as someone who looks at music-related imagery all day.

I suppose the correct thing would be to dissect the new work, contrast it against earlier work, highlighting its importance and originality, perhaps its artistic merits or its underlying cleverness and wit. All of which I could easily do, but Storm does it better if the mood takes him. Typically I find that type of analysis by anyone else dull and unhelpful. I like things or I don't, and can appreciate something without liking it, as I have an opinion on everything. With Storm, I like that there is mystery to his work, there might be an explanation behind the imagery but what does it matter? As with music, does it really matter what the meaning or what the message is? I don't think so, everything should be accepted, enjoyed and interpreted by the individual as they choose. The important thing is that the work connects to the music.

A quick look at the catalogue of the last ten years and it is clear he has worked as hard as ever, and remained constant through the changes brought about by the technical advances in the record industry. We have reached a point where the traditional physical album and the cover looked like they were becoming extinct, brought about first by the CD and then with downloadable music. Now things have turned around and vinyl has made a remarkable comeback with the need for cover artwork as important as ever. An old art is being learned by new designers, and although techniques can be learnt, visual subtleties cannot, and Storm has remained constant here too. In his work everything is very big and everything is very real, with minimal computer wizardry. Whether it's the story of a thousand beds on a beach, the simplicity of a prism, a car driver with a hood over their head or even our beloved teddy bears half buried in the ground like some perverse puzzle, the image he presents is always clear but not its implication, meaning or intention.

My brief is expanded a little 'You can, Dave, be humorous and sarcastic, or not, but don't be too sycophantic' which I take to mean that I should be... just a little sycophantic. This doesn't help though as I know that his response to anything I write will be more sarcastic and humorous than anything I write, and I will fail to meet the required level of sycophancy. In a rather fine restaurant, which also displays fine art prints of some of his images, we talk about various aspects of his work and his personality. The two things, as I see them, are inseparable.

It is fascinating to see the studio team at work. In Storm's own words, 'the creation of an album cover is a collaboration', and it involves his co-designers, photographers, graphic artists, illustrators, prop builders, random members of the public, band members or artists and, reluctantly, the management - whatever and whoever is required to produce the best result. It always starts with the music and what the band are trying to put across, and this has always been very important. Fortunately, he says, people like his work and allow him the freedom to indulge his creative and artistic needs, doing more or less exactly as he pleases.

I have seen Storm in action - in fact he always appears to be in action in one way or another. At a recent gallery exhibition of his work, his entire time was spent rearranging the carefully arranged (by him) works on the wall. A punter walked in, wearing a faded and rather tight *Dark Side* t-shirt, and was admiring a large print of *Division Bell*. Storm was sitting anonymously nearby and suddenly barked at the man to take down the print and swap it with the one next to it. "It looks better like that," he announced, and it did. The startled but dutiful fan looked very pleased with himself as he realized he had just collaborated with Storm. He, like the rest of us, became a part of the ongoing process.

Storm admits to possessing an enormous ego; when I told him the National Portrait Gallery in London would like to display one of his images, he asked 'Why don't they display them all?' He had a valid point but despite this he is also extremely modest about his achievements and always quick to acknowledge the input of his devoted colleagues. In the direct line of fire are Peter Curzon, Dan Abbott, Rupert Truman, Lee Baker and Jerry Sweet , while Laura Truman dodges the bullets and keeps the studio and its leader in order. This team, he says, provides 'A pretty personal service for what I think is a personal matter. If a band wants me to design their cover, they call me and they discuss it with me, simple and straightforward - I prefer to work directly with the musician and it's been a pretty good working principle for the most part.'

He is happy to accept input from the band, in fact he welcomes it, be it Muse suggesting a chalkpit as a more suitable location for the *Absolution* shoot, or the Pink Floyd members taking a few moments to look at the six or seven different ideas for *Dark Side* before unanimously choosing the prism without any further discussion. Not everything is his choice but he's happy to go with it, and a band has rarely made a drastic change to the work, 'What they do is fiddle about with the details, which is great.'

Previously, Storm has said that he is neither a photographer, illustrator, designer nor graphic artist, but rather someone who comes up with ideas and explores different ways to realise them creatively. Whatever the opposite of a micro-manager is, that is probably what Storm is. I witnessed one frantic exchange of mad, wonderful and creative ideas between Storm and his studio team, again over a fine meal. An important meeting was looming with 10cc to show ideas for a new cover. Designer Dan Abbott presented the sketches of the ideas that had been discussed. Nothing was quite right and the race was on to find a better one. Ideas were exchanged and drawings, scribbled when Dan made a casual remark about the band being seen as clever clogs. Storm homed in, instructing Dan to get rid of all the earlier roughs and start a new page. 'We'll have Van Gogh's chair but instead of a pipe we'll have a pair of clogs, we'll draw mathematical equations on them and photograph it - quickly sketch it out, they'll be here in 15 minutes!'

I left them to it and the following week I called round to the studio and tripped over a pair of large wooden clogs inside the door! The finished cover of course, was excellent.

Storm explains that the album cover is an expression of taste, as is the music, so it is most important that the band like the cover, and less so the label or management, regardless of cost. 'If a band like what we do, then it's authentic and an extension of them.' When Storm and Po (Hipgnosis partner Aubrey Powell) suggested shooting a cover for The Nice in the Sahara (the only desert they knew of), the label were horrified, but Keith Emerson loved the idea, which came from the music, and Keith understood that. This is a recurring story too, the artist usually gets it and recognizes a creative companion, a visual interpretation of their music.

It always begins with an idea, 'A good idea is hard to beat' but the way each idea is executed will be very different, and the idea itself not always obvious, from a cow to a burning man, a brain-shaped tree or an eyeball, there has been no effort to maintain a theme with any of the long-serving bands he works with, but perhaps there is a common approach.

If you ever say you like a cover of his then be prepared to explain yourself, he will almost always demand 'Why?' I personally enjoy his work because it always provokes a thought, 'Why did he do that? How did he do that?' (Storm has yet to learn Photoshop). I suppose the whole point is 'What is the music like?' I usually like the cover even if I don't like the music. Storm is a great salesman. More record companies should hire him for his selling skills, just to annoy him.

Storm gruffly rejects the idea of an album cover of his ever being better than the album itself, explaining that the cover exists simply to protect the record, not to help sell it. Cover artwork developed from a necessity to add information so one would know what is inside. Storm has taken full advantage of this blank canvas and created a whole new genre: album cover as art. Most, if not all, of his works stand alone as works of art although that is not his intention at the start. A large print of Steve Miller's *Bingo* that stares down at me as I write looks superb, almost three dimensional, and the colours stand out in a way they do not on the CD. It also does its job as an album cover perfectly well, even at CD size.

All of the artwork is to varying degrees personal. Storm is a visual storyteller, the story may not be clear to everyone, or anyone, but he is telling a story even if that story reads like a puzzle. That he originally wanted to be a filmmaker explains a lot as there is a cinematic quality and a big screen scale to everything. The brain is very quick at deciding if something is interesting and worth spending time on or not, and Storm has mastered the ways of seducing the brain into looking at his imagery and returning to it again and again. He'll explain it reluctantly but prefers you to tell him what you think, or to just enjoy it as a companion to the music.

So it's all about the idea, and about thinking, and also about getting away with it, pushing ideas as far as possible. His work makes you think and any conversation with Storm will have you on your toes. Like a hyperactive five year old he will ask 'Why?' to almost everything - it's exhausting and challenging but in the best of ways. A question is answered with a question, and usually a better one.

Death now figures in Storm's conversation and in his approach to work. (He is 67). He has been predicting his professional and premature demise for many, many years now, even though he gets fresher and healthier-looking each time we meet and he is more productive than ever. His current output is breath-taking: new bands, old bands, galleries, museums, books, and always new ideas with a sense of determination and urgency that has probably always been there anyway, just not turned up to eleven until now!

An advantage of being an old and ill sod, he says, is being able to tell labels, management and other possible time wasters to "fuck off", something I doubt he had trouble with in his youth and good health. The point is now everything has been finely focused, so that each job is approached carefully and executed with an enthusiasm that produces results comparable to, and often exceeding, his more familiar covers.

In creative terms, Storm is all the things he claims not to be and very good at all of them, he leads a brilliant and loyal team, he is an impulsive, impatient, pain in the arse, a captivating dining companion and dazzlingly unique.

Storm's work over the last decade is as strong as previous decades and most likely the next. He is an evolving, mindbending genius and and I sincerely hope that this is satisfactorily sycophantic for the the old grump!

Dave Brolan
Musical Imagery Specialist!
London 2011

DESIGNS

BIFFY CLYRO
PUZZLE 2007

One advantage of age (and there are very few I can assure you), is that it provides time to create a history - a trail of work which can be accessed and assessed. I think Biffy Clyro came to us via this. One disadvantage of age on the other hand, is that a young band like Biffy might view me as past it, too old to rock, or so my paranoia informed me... but it was not the case. They didn't seem to give a fig, and were more interested in talking, in talking about themselves and their album *Puzzle*. It transpired that the puzzle in question was grief, what it was? and how to cope with it, there being loss, anger, some guilt and much sadness. These sensations get all muddled up and confused, so that is a puzzle to sort as much as is coming to terms with the loss itself. Why was the one dear to me taken prematurely?

All very puzzling.

I have of course no answers for this (not being a grief counsellor), but can well imagine the confusion. Most cultures have various forms of ritual devised to help cope, so we thought of something ritualistic, vaguely Japanese, despite the band being Scottish, which accounts for the body painting. The posture is a grief posture derived from asking several therapists if there was such a thing, and in the background is an event that alludes to the story of the particular loss. The puzzle is not only the pattern, but the piece on the floor. How can the fallen piece be three-dimensional having come from a two-dimensional surface, the body painting? The man is naked, not just to show the body painting, but also to imply vulnerability - not only the vulnerability one feels when grief-stricken, but also a quality of Biffy Clyro, wherein they seem capable of playing hard heavy rock and yet are unafraid of exposing their vulnerability in melody and lyric - a rare and interesting quality in a bunch of geezers from Scotland. They're a great band, I hope we did their music justice.

MUSE
STRINGY LOVERS 2009

This pic is a cousin to 'Teddy Bears' (pg 69) inasmuch as it was approved and purchased by Muse but not used. With no further fanfare here it is. An enormous advantage of doing books is the ability to release and display neglected pieces even if just to encourage other bands to use them. And it is also our pleasure, of course, to show them to our valued readers.

One of the preoccupations of a designer, be they of books, brochures, posters or album covers, is the actual physical item - in our case, squares. What can you do with a square ? (Just don't let him in the house).

'Ashra' was an early exploration where the dimension area of the square forms the basis of the design. Before you become indignant, 'Ashra' is just and only an image of a girl drinking from a water fountain, I swear it.

'Stringy Lovers' is an inelegant name for an image striving for elegance as well as for union, but it concerns lovers who are impeded by obstacles and who cannot quite reach each other or consummate - they are held back by unnamed forces represented by strings or tethered ropes. The lovers stretch out towards each other and are so nearly making it that it breaks your heart. Despite this Mills and Boon nonsense the design is, we like to think, greatly enhanced by the diagonal lines of the strings/ropes which increase the dynamism of the whole affair.

Like proper serious artists, like an apprentice or a student, old hand or a young buck, us designer types can get preoccupied, if not obsessed with particular things. The design adjacent is a culmination of a long love affair with a big black object. I have never been sure whether this big black object was a sculpture, a building, or the flight recorder of a gigantic aeroplane? But I have been long enamoured of the idea of a big black cube plonked in the middle of nowhere in particular. The big black cube had no apparent function, and by and large probably no relevance, I just liked it. It appeared in numerous guises over several years, sometimes with sheep. Sometimes as a series, but mostly as just a big black box type thingy.

And I'm jolly glad to say that my long enduring friends, the very lovely Pink Floyd, managed to find a use for it one day. We were asked to design a calendar of images and designs that had been utilized on Pink Floyd singles, of which there were more than we thought. Not known as a singles band - unlike the Stones for example - there are in fact an entertaining number of variations from Venezuela to Japan, from Australia to Belgium. The front cover of this calendar could not of course favour any one single over another, and therefore called for a new design... it is an aspect of singles in Western countries that they be taken from albums. The single therefore is a breakaway, a small piece of the main thrust, a segment or trailer of a much larger event, a 'chip off the old block', as it became known to us.

The album that is therefore represented by the big black cube as an unknown fathomless entity, the single from which is a small part, an extracted piece, and in the case of this image an uniquely hewn cube, cut from the larger cube, a cubette one might say. It is seen being carried away by a workman to live a life of its own, as the epynomous single. The big black cube, now representing a record, is therefore made with vinyl, in which the grooves can be detected and a degree of shininess, reflecting in part the countryside surrounding it.

An interesting quality of a cube seen in this way is that one tends to presume solidity and three dimensionality although one cannot see it. I think the blackness tends to enhance this sense of solidness, and the shadow it casts suggests its 3D-ness, but I'm not going to tell you if it is solid or not, complete or not. Only those on a need-to-know basis, need to know. I'm not playing hard to get or difficult or bloody minded, its just that one doesn't need to know because it just looks like a huge mother of a lump of black vinyl sitting mysteriously in the countryside, its function undeclared, and its intentions unknown.

Rupert did a great job photographing it, and since his model, the workman was my son Bill (my beloved son Bill) (My favourite son Bill) therefore this picture was known as the 'chip off the old block' for yet another reason, there being more strings in the Floyd bow, more arrows in the Floyd quiver, than is at first apparent.

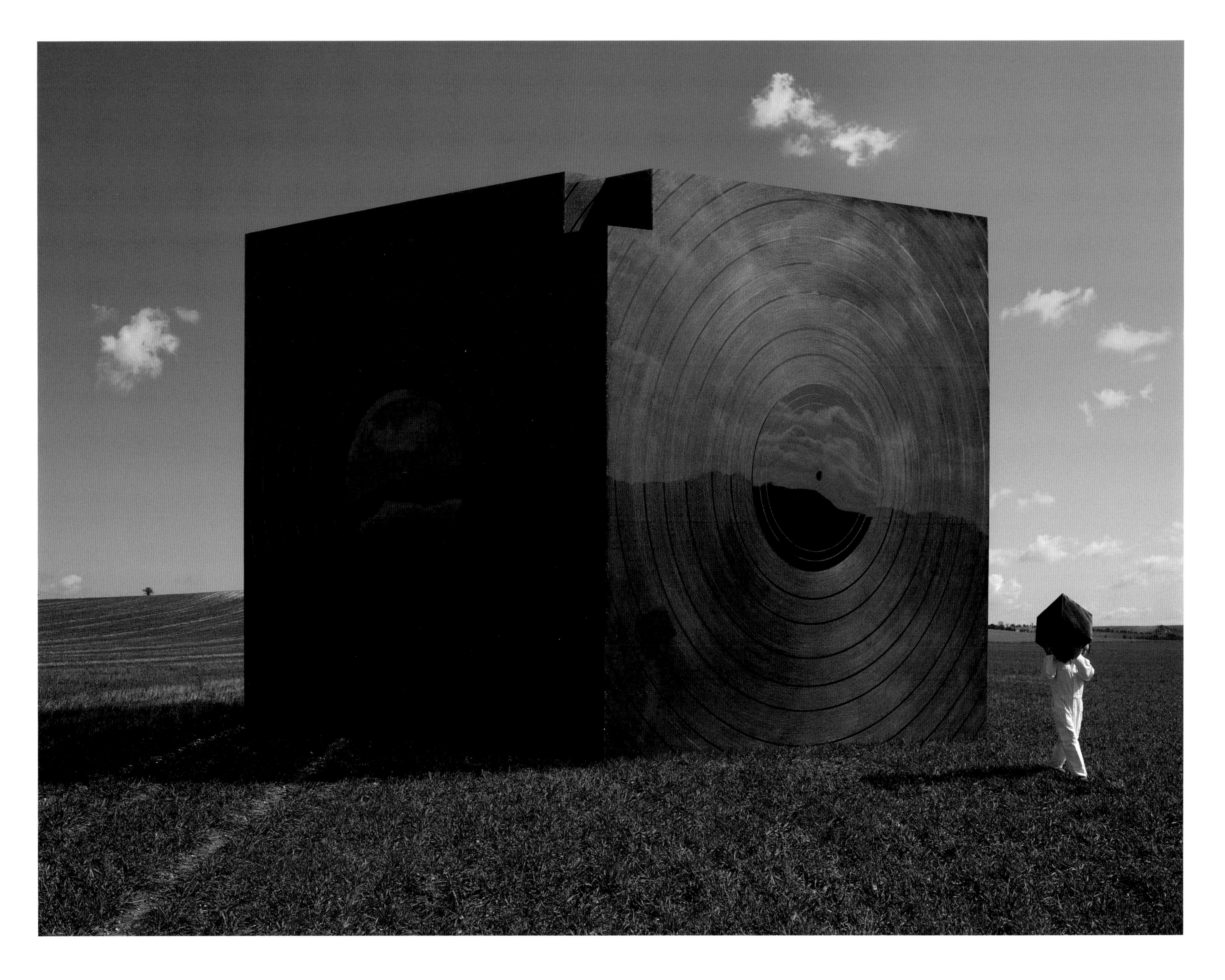

SHPONGLE
INEFFABLE MYSTERIES FROM SHPONGLELAND 2009

I should have seen the writing on the wall. I should have seen the writing on the wall. Shpongle, a trance techno band, comprising one Simon Posford, and Raja, are chalk and cheese... Simon known affectionately as Mrs Posford, is a charming and reasonable man, and his colleague Raja, seemed not unhappy to call himself a traditional Indian ruler. Shpongle's record company was called Twisted Records (I should have seen the writing on the wall), which was run by Simon Holtam, who was married to Serena. Now, the other Simon, Simon Posford, was seeing a girl also called Serena, from LA, but not the same Serena, so what we have here is 2 Simons, 2 Serena's and an Indian ruler... I should have seen the writing on the wall.

Because of the Indian tinge to some of the music, I suggested an idea set in India about a trainee Saddhu. I further suggested that to save costs, we do a picture for the CD, the DVD and the boxset, all in India, and all different - who wants the same design on different products? Apart from being dull, it tends to confuse the packing factory. Shpongle and Twisted, being more or less one and the same, agreed to this proposal and said, 'Lets do it now, in August', the hottest month in Rajasthan, which was where we proposed to shoot. 'You can hack it' said one of the Simons, probably the simpler one.

The trainee saddhu is endeavouring like a jumping yogi to levitate and float across the ground. In my mind I saw him bouncing across a lake, like a skimming stone, bouncing from spot to spot, leaving in effect a trail of rippled circles across the water. When he gets older, and better, he will no longer need to bounce but will float. It means though that his arrival on the near shore is in a wet loincloth, dripping onto the stone floor below. He is a novice but he will improve.

There are a few of these garden lakes in hotels and cities across Rajistan, and this one is situated in Anwar, about 100 miles from Delhi, en route to Jaipur, where we took another picture entitled 'The Stairway To Nowhere', which is in fact an old observatory. It is a marvellous thing, but as Dan and Rupert who were in Rajasthan reported, it was stiflingly hot, never mind the frigging visuals.

They were in actuality bound for Pulwer, which is a religious centre with white buildings, temples, hotels etc., surrounding an inner lake, but where, it later transpired, it was unacceptable (irreligious) to take photographs, so it was just as well that they found Anwar. This left the cover of the boxset to do, and I found a place called Bundhi, where there was this extraordinary descending stepped building (pg 129), in effect a large hole in the ground with steps everywhere. There are a few of these in Rajasthan, but I am unsure of their significance. I was, however, blown away by the resemblance to Escher, thus becoming, unbeknown to the Indians, a real live Escher. It turned out in fact to be a rubbish dump, the smell of which was brutal, and it was infested with rampant flies and a plethora of bushes, which annoyed the hell out of me because it interrupted the Escher qualities, so I had the redoubtable Lee clean it up and restore it to its original form, though its function was still unclear.

What was most unclear, however, was the schedule of Twisted records, and the two Simons and the two Serena's and a Raja. The album did not in fact appear until a year later, and Rupert and Dan could have visited Rajasthan in the cooler months of January and February, which would of course have been less twisted and less mysterious and definitely less ineffable.

DISCO BISCUITS
PLANET ANTHEM 2009

Disco Biscuits come from Philadelphia, and are a jam band. I didn't know what that was, and got confused with confiture, thinking that a musical jam was usually as it were made with assorted and different musicians, instead of with the same musicians, ie. a band. However, I think a jam band is a band that plays extended numbers, or different tunes on different nights, or different variations on different nights, and occasionally with different musicians. Either way, their spokesman, one Aron Magner, was quite droll, and was telling me that their music had a sort of new quality to it, you might not be sure what you're getting, it might be different from what you're expecting, it had therefore an intrinsic newness (I suggested that, after Milan Kundera's book *The Unbearable Lightness of Being*, that they call their album The Newness of Being). He wasn't greatly interested in the title, but agreed about the newness, like a present unopened on your birthday or Christmas, one of the pleasures being the unwrapping, not knowing what it is you're going to get. You might know that it's a bicycle but not know what kind, you might recognize the music of Disco Biscuits, and know the tracks, but not what the tracks sound like, being a jam band and all that.

So presents wrapped in brown paper and string, became a theme, which in turn became wrapped women, because you would know what they were, but not what they looked like, nor what nationality, race or colour. At the same time of course, there might be an issue of bondage. Is this some form of punishment, or S&M? I can imagine some women might not like this picture, my wife certainly didn't, though the women in question don't look as though they're suffering and seem quite proud and at ease, a metaphor rather than a real thing, though done for real. I can assure you, dear reader, that the good women were fine, and thought it all highly entertaining. I thought it peculiar, rather than oppressive.

The picture for us is also about the piece of white material whose shape we found elegant, but why is it there? This is a quiz dear reader, answers on a postcard please to your mother. Returning to the theme of newness, not experienced nor sullied, led to the thought of virgins, which is of course again why they are women. In medieval times in parts of Europe, it was customary to verify the marriage contract by a crude display of a sheet hanging from the nuptial window, for all to see. If the sheet was red, the bride was a virgin and all was well, and if the sheet was white, she was not a virgin and the marriage might be in jeopardy.

PS: I don't know about the lightness of being, or even the newness of being, but the light in South Africa, where this shot was taken, is gorgeous, and sometimes so clear and beautiful as to take your breath away. I guess the purity of the light in this picture reflects by chance many of the themes in it.

EAR MAIL

THE PLEA
DREAM STADIUM 2011

You can never tell the twists and turns of the avenues of fate. How would a band from Donegal, represented by a man from Belgium, ever come to a Norwegian living in North London? Not for us to question, huh? (It came about, in fact, through a friend, Jill Furmanovsky from Zimbabwe, spirit catcher and portrait photographer extraordinaire). The Plea are brothers who are not atypical in their love/hate relationship with each other and they have a spirited bolshiness about them, which will stand them in good stead - you need a bit of this chutzpah to sustain a life as a performer in Rock 'n' Roll, I'll wager. I asked one brother about his Rock 'n' Roll influences, and he said "so and so" and then his brother said in sarcastic disbelief, "total bullshit, not so and so but such and such", being in effect the complete opposite... they played distinct songs against a wall of guitars, big cascading sound in thumping rhythm, with clear melody to the fore.

Sufficiently stimulated, we composed several designs, two of which I particularly liked and are shown here. They're about a reflection fighting with itself, the reflector and the reflected - an impossibility that is eerily appropriate since it's not only about reflections or brothers but possibly a spirit from an underwaterworld. Then there was the diving board, the longest diving board in the world, along which a man was running in order to enact the greatest swallow dive in the galaxy. The swish of that dive that you can only speculate about, seemed to us very representative of the sound of The Plea.

They unanimously chose, however, 'The Tunnel' from which schoolboys are emerging, from the darkness to the daylight, observed by four shadowy figures on the bridge. The boys are carrying lighted orbs, which I saw as 'the great spheres of knowledge'. This is a design about education, hence the schoolboys in uniform. It is the possession of knowledge, especially in a Rock 'n' Roll context, which marks the grown up emerging from adolescence into the light of young adulthood. The Plea also had a song called 'Out Like A Light' which may or may not have been about the same thing.

My stepdaughter says laconically that boys never grow up, least of all Rock 'n' Rollers. Being a bloke myself, I find this a little strong, and am much enamoured of the idea behind this picture, which we all thought turned out rather well. It's spooky, atmospheric, reminiscent of *The Midwich Cuckoos* or *Children Of The Damned*, a sort of funky image of a story but with undertones of possible perversity. Are the watchers on the bridge looking back at their past, recalling their early adolescent years, or are they more devious?

There was a heated debate before we took this picture, while searching endlessly for a usable tunnel - not so easy to find - about trouser length... "About trouser length?" I hear you exclaim. Yup! Trouser length. The manager insisted on long trousers, I said that they could be either long or short. He blamed the band, the band blamed him, all the fun of the fair and, you might ask, why? Somewhere lurking in the background is paedophilia which had no place in the derivation of this picture but there were large scandals at the time in both the Irish and the Belgian churches. However, it ended up as long trousers, because it was fucking cold and the boys naturally arrived wearing them, which was fine. Between you and me I have no idea where paedophilia comes in, but I know where it goes out, namely the window. Hrmph!

At the time of writing neither the band nor their manager have seen it. They know what it is, but not how it is. Us at the studio think it's splendid, as does our typist, Angie. The Belgian manager, Renaat, is in some ways refreshingly direct and said 'I so much like a design of yours Storm, called 'Guitars On Trees', can I have that as well?' Yes he could (see pg 136).

RED HOT CHILLI PEPPERS
STADIUM ARCADIUM

We were very excited by the Red Hot Chilli Peppers ringing our studio and asking us to design the cover for 'Stadium Arcadium'. We were even more excited by the initial proposition of a trilogy, a three album set. And still more so when speaking to their producer, the renowned Rick Rubin. And, if it is possible to be even more excited, by the music itself - a plethora of great songs, or so we thought, but it all turned ugly. Not just pear-shaped, but hugely disappointing, which is in truth such a pity when feeling truly thrilled at the outset by a great project.

We talked to the band, listened to the music, read and re-read the lyrics, thought we had done our homework, devised several designs, some of which you see here, and felt pretty good. I particularly liked the 'detective groups' with oval mirrors like some bizarre contemporary dance, but it was not to be. I was rung up by Flea - I think - no, by the guitarist John, during a driving lesson (which I had to retake on account of a minor inconvenience) to be told, thank you but no thank you.

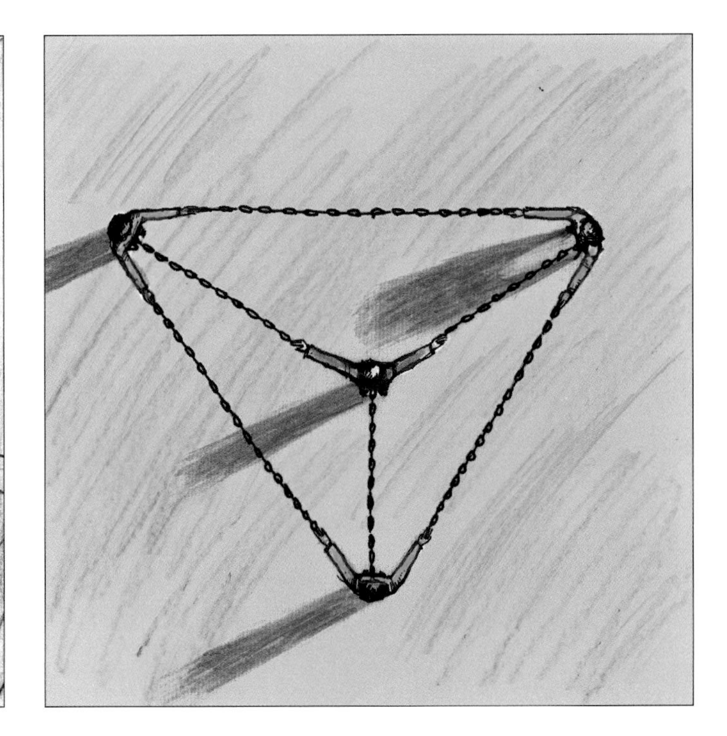

I don't know about you, dear reader, but rejection in any form, artistically, financially or romantically, is not a lot of fun. It may be a fact of working life (it is), but it is unpleasant all the same. You may have difficulty in believing this, but what gets my goat is not the rejection so much as the replacement or use by the band of a design inferior to those we submitted. I hear you say it's just sour grapes, but the design that was finally featured on *Stadium Arcadium*, was dull to say the least. Speaking freely, it being a free country so I'm told, the design was derivative and moderate at best.

Due to a strange twist of fate, it later transpired that someone I knew in San Francisco who worked in a very lovely San Francisco Art Exchange, was on holiday with her boyfriend in the Caribbean - it's alright for some - at the same resort as a couple of the Chilli Peppers, and the boyfriend went surfing with the Chillies, and my name cropped up purely by chance, not during surfing of course, and apparently the Chilli Peppers conveyed their apologies.

I hated them, but I'm softening.

BIFFY CLYRO
THAT GOLDEN RULE / THE CAPTAIN / MOH / GOD AND SATAN 2009-2010

There are many things in God's playground that one doesn't understand, so it should hold no surprises should it come to pass, but I haven't fully grasped why Biffy Clyro and 14th Floor Records decided to release so many singles in what is generally described as a declining market. But I am not complaining, mostly because they employ us to design them, and it would seem imprudent if not churlish, to bite the hand that feeds. And anyway Biffy Clyro are a great band, but I'm first going to digress.

Biffy were asked to interview me once, this has nothing to do with the singles, for a magazine running a feature about Rock 'n' Roll bands and their designers. We met at a hotel bar, as you do, and they proceeded to interrogate me. It was in fact very funny, and we spent most of our time laughing, and I told them about a recent idea I had for a logo, whose derivation was outlandish, and they said, 'Oh yeah?' And I told them that their inscrutable, meaningless, peculiar name had come from a time when they were at school,when they were 15 and fantasizing about starting a band, which would of course be a rock band and nothing like Cliff (Richards). They were scrawling this with a Biro, and were writing Cliff Biro, NO! Never Cliffy Biro, which got spoonerized into Biffy Clyro, and they looked at me incredulous! How did you know? they said, and that is in truth where the name came from, but I digress.

There were 4, maybe 5 singles from *Only Revolutions*, 'That Golden Rule', which was photographed on Skye, 'The Captain', which used a flag from the album cover shoot, and the hull of a boat, which happened to be near by the great flag shoot (pg 97), 'Bubbles' about a trail of Red Herrings, 'Many Of Horror', later a hit called 'When we Collide' by somebody else, was a dark tale of lovers meeting in death, but none of the above worked as well, I believe, as 'God And Satan'.

The lyrics of 'God And Satan' displayed an ironic degree of reasonableness about disputes. The singer wanted to ask both God and Satan the same question in order to hear both sides. Our simplistic interpretation of this was to have Satan as a black figure, and God as a white figure sitting at a table, waiting, as it were, to be consulted by the vocalist, one Simon Neil, who is arriving with his horse. Despite the simplicity, I've always enjoyed this image, mostly because of the indeterminate blurriness of the figures on one hand - one cannot of course see deity clearly, for fear of godly blindness - which was was done 'in camera' as us professionals call it (pompously) - and the ordinariness of supreme beings on the other relaxing on chairs in the calm of a sunny landscape

So, the scene is in daylight, and Mr Satan is wearing black down to his gloves and socks and is shaded by an umbrella, and therefore is underexposed and of course short-focused, and God is dressed in white and lit with a flash, and so he is overexposed and short focused. The blurred edges are also employed to remove the thought of compositing, for I was keen that this imaginative scenario was as real as possible, and not simply photoshopped. It puts me in mind of an exhibition we held in London, where a little girl of 8 looking up at Shpongle's *Ineffable Mysteries* (pg 23), which features a floating Saddhu, told me that it was not real. I said 'How do you know, you haven't been to India' she said 'People don't fly, even in India - he's sitting on a box which you've taken out in Photoshop'. I slunk off, unraveled by an 8 year old!

PINK FLOYD
POSTER 2010

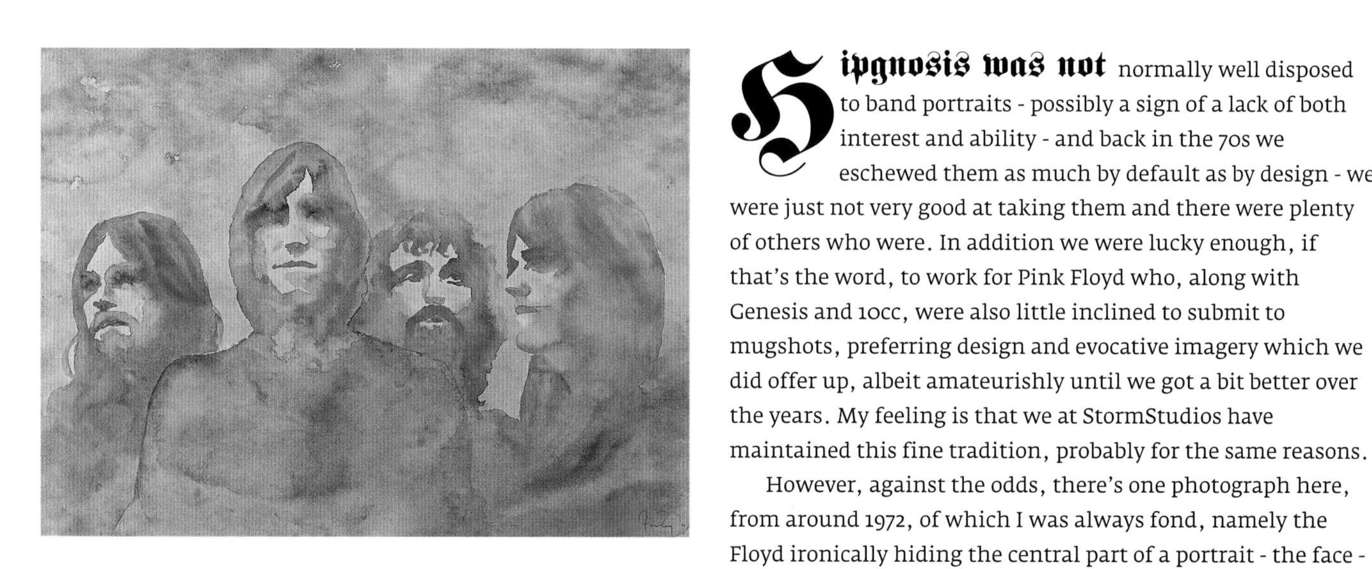

Hipgnosis was not normally well disposed to band portraits - possibly a sign of a lack of both interest and ability - and back in the 70s we eschewed them as much by default as by design - we were just not very good at taking them and there were plenty of others who were. In addition we were lucky enough, if that's the word, to work for Pink Floyd who, along with Genesis and 10cc, were also little inclined to submit to mugshots, preferring design and evocative imagery which we did offer up, albeit amateurishly until we got a bit better over the years. My feeling is that we at StormStudios have maintained this fine tradition, probably for the same reasons.

However, against the odds, there's one photograph here, from around 1972, of which I was always fond, namely the Floyd ironically hiding the central part of a portrait - the face - as a protest at having to endure yet more PR and band photo rigmarole. There's also the watery world as painted opposite by Dan Abbott into which the band are plunged in 2010 plus a patchwork photo border of pretty tiles of band miniphotos in historical order. In total we have irony, history and artistry all in one and, despite our portrait phobia, here it is.

PINK FLOYD

THE CRANBERRIES

WAKE UP AND SMELL THE COFFEE 2001

Most of our designs emerge from the music, the lyrics and occasionally from words of wisdom from the band themselves. A few come from titles like *Technical Ecstasy* and *Smell The Coffee*. Some even come the other way round; the title comes from the design, *Wish You Were Here* for example. For The Cranberries *Smell The Coffee* album, the full title was *Wake Up And Smell The Coffee*... so I imagined lying in bed upstairs in the morning with the aroma of coffee wafting through my nostrils. To be precise, I visualised little coffee granules bouncing around and waking me up in a lively fashion. Alert and ready to face the day, as Dolores put it.

Since cranberries are red berries these granules developed from brown amorphous shapes into red bouncing balls, which were at first conceived on a minuscule scale (in order to gain access to my nose, which is not as big as you might like to think), but then grew and expanded considerably, in order to gratify our unchecked egos. The granules became balls, which became large gym balls, and the bedroom, now too small to contain them, became an open space, a beach. We knew the perfect place: on the southwest coast, called Burnham. You could drive onto it easily.

Since it is our solemn mission to do things for real, we consulted our props company, Hothouse, who suggested building a scaffold tower with an adjustable sloping pen at the top, from where a collection of inflated gym balls could be released and permitted to bounce down the beach under their own steam. The balls, propelled by their fall from the tower, would head directly towards a bed, in which someone would be woken up by the approaching horde. Such a complex and risky enterprise called for a test in case it went horribly wrong on the day. This 'insurance' test was conducted on a grass airfield near London and was a great success. It was in fact a complete mind-blow, an unforgettable sight, even more so from the bed in the path of the oncoming mass.

The real on-the-beach version was done a day or two after the test and was also a great success, another mind-blowing sight, being 'cleaner' or clearer for vision than the grass on the airfield and occurring without a hitch. Regrettably, owing to Rupert's and my utter amazement at seeing such a thing, we forgot to take a photo! So we did it again and again, much to the annoyance of the crew who had to go and retrieve the balls from down the beach after each take.

This beach version was the one used on the actual cover. The grass test has lingered unused for some time, except perhaps in Japan, which is too far away to count, and I now prefer it anyway, so here it is.

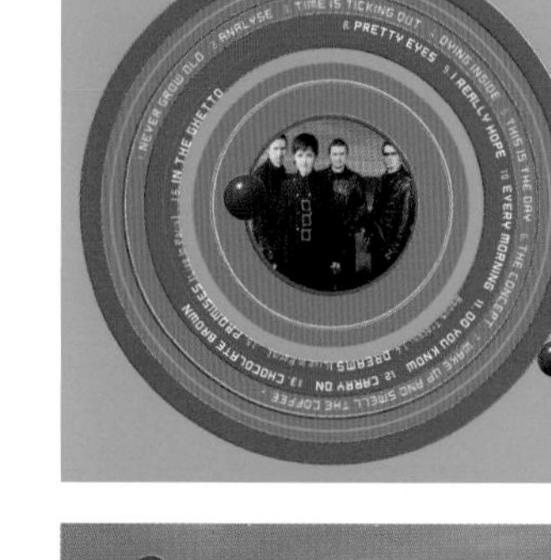

I wonder if musicologists think there is a particular quality to a town that lends a corresponding quality to its music. If this is the case then along with the Detroit sound, the Philly sound, the West Coast sound and so forth, comes the possibility that growing up in such a town may unduly influence your musical aspiration, presenting you with a reputation to live up to. This would be at its most compelling in Liverpool - it can't be easy to be a band emerging from the town that fostered the world's most famous Rock 'n' Roll band. But that's where the Wombats come from.

The Wombats might be described as 'indie', with eclectic, occasionally busy, unexpected sounds, an ordered cascade of cacophony laced with catchy tunes and surprising, idiosyncratic lyrics, all underscored with guitars and drums. The songs are often about blighted relationships, about people with minor disturbances, and this may account for why they chose this cover of the picnickers, and why they also chose to be in a picture in which you cannot see their faces.

The idea, which is intended to be slightly annoying, is based on a conviction I have that, like the 'Stroop effect' wherein seeing a word makes you read it, seeing a person, makes you want to see their face. In our picnic the assorted participants are hiding their faces with a picture of a therapist's couch, indicating in some way their frailty, vulnerability or disturbance, their need for therapy.

We shot the original picture of a picnic in a park - life is not a picnic now is it? - in sunny Cape Town because winter in the UK, especially in Liverpool, is particularly un-picnic-like. For those who are geographically minded, the picture was initially taken in Kirstenbosch then moved computer-wise to a beach in Bloubergstrand, just north of Table Mountain, as you can see. The Wombats, consistent with their mild and engaging perversity, decided they wanted to be in the picture themselves and insisted on keeping the same idea despite the fact that you can't see their faces. They and their friends congregated in London and replaced the original grouping in Cape Town. Much to my surprise, all of this comping seemed not to matter much, either because the retouching was so expertly completed by Lee 'Bombat' Baker or the idea is strong enough to carry itself wherever it was located.

I, of course, like to believe the latter. I think in retrospect that the notion of the band being in a picture when you can't see the band is quite appealing. It reflects both their quirkiness and in some ways their honesty. We met the songwriter Murph in Lime Street at the beginning of the project and he is indeed a revealing but modest character. What I'm trying to say, despite the picture being moved here there and everywhere, is that the picture is actually very Wombat-like.

Roger, aka Syd, Barrett of Hills Road, Cambridge, and Cambridge High School for Boys, was a good friend and part of a group or gang of us who ran around Cambridge aged 16-18 circa 1960/61. He was good-looking, humorous, played the guitar, could paint and write songs. He always had pretty girlfriends. In fact you could say he was rather annoying but I was very fond of him and have been reluctant in subsequent years to submit to interview about his notorious decline.

The whole sorry story of Syd's derailing is basically too harrowing to recount and the reasons too complex to unravel. However, a mutual good friend, Andrew Rawlinson aka Willa, whose intellect at the time was frightening but in later years more stimulating than frightening, suggested a possible explanation.

In no way wishing to assert the absolute veracity of this theory, I found it both plausible and inspiring - inspiring in the sense that the poster herewith comes directly from it (via *Spellbound* and the sets of Dali). Andrew suggested that Syd was creatively spontaneous and would create/produce paintings, artworks and particularly songs and their lyrics, without much effort. They seemed in effect to pour out of him, but there was a potential downside, namely the absence of a work ethic. Syd had no idea how to 'work at it'. He was not accustomed to trying hard, or sitting down and solving a problem, or thinking it through, instead stuff just came to him. At the point at which this may have ceased, when the supply of creations may have dried up, coinciding with leaving Pink Floyd, he would have had no way to rectify the matter, no ability to draw on inner reserves, no work ethic. Instead he would await the re-arrival of his muse, and if that did not happen, he would retreat further into himself, continue waiting and produce nothing.

I envisaged this scenario as a sequence of imaginary doors, like a stage set, in which a figure was continually opening doors expecting to find something - a song or a painting, some art - but instead finding only another door through which he thought he had simply to go again to find another creation but instead found yet another door. At the end a lone figure is seen running, or is it escaping? Into nothingness? The configuration of doors is in an S-shape: 'S' for Syd, 'S' for sadness. Whatever other descriptions or diagnoses of Syd's decline may be offered up, and there are many, the feeling derived from them all is one of sadness, of a talent denied.

Like a comet, briefly flashing through the sky, brilliant but doomed.

YOUNGER BROTHER
LAST DAYS OF GRAVITY 2008 / VACCINE 2011

Falling down on the job is hard for me to take personally, probably for other people too. Failing to do it right, delivering sub-standard work, or any variation thereof, is anathema - makes me feel really bad, duly disappointed, guilty and frustrated. Such was the case with Younger Brother aka Benji Vaughan and Simon Posford, an electro-techno-trance outfit awkward to deal with but with great sounds, and fortunately a good sense of humour. Benji's lovely wife Lucinda does reflexology, which puts her amongst the stars, in my opinion. I just love foot pampering.

Getting back to the matter in hand, *Last Days of Gravity* was an album cover that I screwed up. I could shift the blame onto lack of funds, prop house inadequacy, indifferent photography, poor location but this would not only be untrue, but there would be no point. It was my cock-up and such a pity because I thought it a promising idea, namely a large automaton in the form of a pair of scissors. It had a mind of its own, strutting about town randomly cutting things up; cars, lampposts, people. I thought this was macabre and funny. The image would show the giant scissors striding down the high street, leaving a trail of cut up objects, cars in half, people in strips but I guess I had not thought this through enough and thus had not the wherewithal to cut a car in half nor the butcher's skill in cutting up a person or a dog, never mind the savagery or immorality.

In order to render any of this wild idea feasible, we had instead to make large photos of the objects and cut those. This might not have been so bad if we had been able to make the huge photos more credible. Most particularly, this idea would have been salvaged with a larger pair of scissors. However I felt so mortified by the inadequacies of the result that I told Younger Brother I would do the next album cover completely free, well, more or less free. Let's not go crazy here.

A year or two later I was able to make amends and wipe the slate clean by doing *Vaccine*, which worked much better. This idea came unwittingly from my itinerant son, who said, sarcastically, when driving through the blossom-laden London streets, how insidious he thought blossom was. 'It gets everywhere', he said, very seriously. The concept of 'nasty blossom' appealed to my warped sensibility and seemed an inversion not unlike a vaccine, which is a small dose of a disease or poison that permits the body to protect itself from the real disease or poison, in the same way as listening to the album might protect you against other unfriendly or poisonous forms of music.

And there it was, a vision of flying blossom attacking a hapless victim in the street, like a trail of bullets from a machine gun. The blossom-like bullets streaking through the air were unlike bullets, they didn't penetrate the body, because that would be silly, but they stuck to it like jelly. Insidious blossom, attacking and suffocating a person, is a reverse metaphor for a little bit of poison that does you good but at the same time is dreamlike and illogical.

Last, but not least, it transpires that the word 'vaccine' comes from the Latin for cow - 'vacca' and the French 'vache'. This is because the pioneer of vaccination, Dr Edward Jenner, used cowpox to combat smallpox, which at the time was killing half of the population of England, and he was successful. Injecting a young lad with cowpox led to the prevention of the spread of smallpox. The young man in question was called James and the cowpox came from the blistered hand of a milkmaid, Sarah, who had in turn caught it from a cow named Blossom. Would you believe that?

STEVE MILLER BAND
LET YOUR HAIR DOWN 2010

Continuing the delightful relationship with Steve Miller (pg 67), next up was *Let Your Hair Down*, which was one of the many roughs Steve had responded to on the floor of his hotel room in Berkeley. I remember him saying two things in particular; one was in answer to the question 'What is your album all about guv'nor?' Steve said, 'Having a party'. I pressed him for more. 'It's about having a good time, Storm: a rocking album, an album in the groove, music to dance to.' Looking for something more meaty I said something fairly tactless, like 'Is that it?' And he said, 'Yup, Storm, that's it' then, in what I took to be in a friendly but sarcastic fashion, 'Yes, Storm, of course you know what having a good time is. Or don't you?' I didn't say another word.

Later on, in thinking about music that gives you a good time, I thought we needed an image or a design that is not about having a good time, but about giving you a good time, there and then. I guess, simply put, an image that makes you smile a little when you look at it. Not a design about other people having a good time but addressed directly to the viewer, to you, hoping that looking at the image will give you a good time. Not for long, of course, because the still image does not have duration.

It also does not have sequence, which, if I may digress, is the key difference between the audio and the visual. It means that consecutive songs or episodes in a narrative which might last, say, 40 minutes, can therefore work on a completely different level to a single static, immediate image. In a similar vein *The Division Bell* for the Four Mop Tops, as Nick Mason likes to call them, aka Pink Floyd, is not about communication, but is a piece of communication. *Let Your Hair Down* is not about having a good time, it is intended to make you smile, thus 'giving you a good time', albeit briefly.

For an exhibition called 'Right but Wrong', featuring extended album art, we used the *Let Your Hair Down* image as its poster and advertisement. It seemed to work insomuch as many a person was seen to smile. The second thing I remember Steve asking was 'I like this but I don't get it. Why does the rabbit need a ladder to get up?' I said 'No, it's a hare, and the ladder is not for going up but for coming down, as in 'Let your hair down', which we all know is an expression for having a good time. It's both metaphor and not real, because the bald man has no hair'.

The bald man is a good friend of our photographer Rupert Truman and is a very humorous chap. He subsequently described himself, after the shoot, as an international male model, which as he freely admitted could not be further from the truth, but he was cooperative in subjecting himself to the presence of a Belgian hare on his head. It is often said that one should never work with animals - they fail to read the script - and this hare lived up to expectation and continually stood, sat, or lay in the wrong position. Our master retoucher, Lee Bunny Baker, skilfully composited several different positions in order to provide for what is in fact a real hare but not real all at the same time.

Being rather silly, this image makes me smile but it has a surreal edge, which is doubly appealing once you get the verbal connection. Letting your hair down is precisely what Steve hopes the music will encourage you to do.

The hare was returned safe and very alive to its keepers, and the delightful Wilton's Music Hall in East London remains very much the same - still in the wrong era. The album is about to be released as I write these words, and you can't get more current than that! (I'm sure there's a joke here about bunnies and rabbits and hares and currents and buns, but I can't get to the bottom of it, thank goodness).

Extensive conversations with the aforementioned Disco Biscuits resulted in agreement and disagreement, agreeing to what was known as the *Wrapped Virgins* (page 25), and disagreeing with *Picasso In The Sand* (see adjacent). Dan Abbott Esquire drew a beautiful rough of this idea, which evolved from footprints, particularly footprints in the sand, leaving a trace of where you had been, but subject to decay when washed over by waves from the sea. This 'notion from the ocean' felt like music, the notes of which decay once played in order to make room for the next note, and so provide a melody or such. Since we are talking art here, not footprints or even shoes, but music and pictures, we decided that what was about to be washed away in the sand would need to be art, would need to look like Picasso for example, immediately recognizable and not too hard to imitate.

I endeavoured to persuade Aron Magner, the spokesman for Disco Biscuits, that this was an idea as close to his music as I could get. This was a picture intended NOT to last - a sort of impossibility, since it would last being an album cover - but it refers to the notes in music which do not last. Mr Magner would have none of it, although to his credit he agreed to pay for it, although to his discredit he hasn't as yet. And so this is what we have in reality, quickly drawn Picasso's in the sand on a beach in South Africa, about to be washed away, erased, forgotten forever, by the approaching surf, such is the transitory nature of the sounds of music, an intrinsic difference between audio and visual. Apart from the theorizing, which I found completely valid, and was thus most aggravated by Disco Biscuits demotion - I think the picture appeared on the back of the CD - I found the image very satisfying, personally speaking that is. You may, dear reader, share the view of Disco Biscuits, in which case, you can go and join them in Philadelphia.

PS: I hope I can describe this as it happened, but one of the funniest things I have ever seen was Dan drawing Picasso in the sand. He was wearing a newspaper hat, clutching sticks like paintbrushes, with his trousers rolled up to his knees, drawing furiously in the recently-dampened sand, which he claimed to be perfect for the purpose, only to find that our idea was incredibly accurate and that his drawings were indeed being washed away by the waves. We saw him 50 yards away, jumping up and down, shouting at the sea, cursing it for ruining his drawings, for no sooner had he drawn a Picasso nude in the sand, than the sea came and washed it away. Rupert and I and the very lovely Brendan thought this hilarious, and laughed and laughed, failing to show any sympathy with the struggling artist.

LOGOS
VARIOUS 2007-2011

A logo is something little trying to say a lot, which is probably a good deal more than I can manage in this paragraph. I suspect that a degree of graphic simplicity, a dash of elegance, brevity and depth combined with appropriateness and a modicum of cuteness are also requisites, although the most important thing is that the outfit for whom it is intended like it, and those below did, thankfully.

'Wind Up Bird' - is Mirelle Davis, a one woman consultancy agency for Rock 'n' Roll promotion whose chosen title is humourous i.e. this is a bird who is not easily wound up. On another level, though, when wound up, she is ready to go. I have no idea of the truth of this, but she certainly liked our slightly literal translation - a bird made of watch parts which was brilliantly assembled in a spontaneous burst of energy by Dan.

'Genesis' is a book company, specialising in limited edition handmade Fine Art books, often with elaborate components. They spent quite a long time deliberating on the form of the figure stepping out of a large book, and finally settled on a more graphic representation.

'20/20' was done for ourselves to mark a series of fine art prints. 20 prints of 20 different images.

WIND UP BIRD

deMilo
MANAGING ART

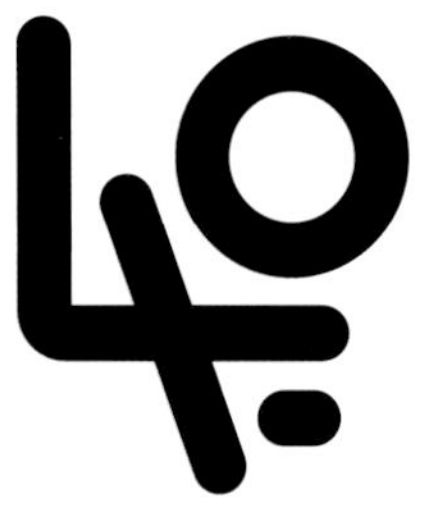

WHY PINK FLOYD?

Pink Floyd's 40th anniversary clearly required the four logos you see here, executed by Peter, who also did the 'Space Cowboy' for Steve Miller. This was the one where the lasso spun by a cowboy - it can only be a cowboy with a lasso - is also forming the orbit of a planet or the rings of Saturn. Again, I thought, appropriate, graphic and engaging... Mr Miller is often referred to as the space cowboy, even by his good self.

Theatre designer Rob Roth asked us to design him a logo, so Peter executed a nifty little man with his hands on his hips forming the R's of Rob Roth. In addition Dan drew him a biblical scene: a panorama with heavy purplish grape clouds sending down bolts of lightning upon the sinful masses fleeing across the landscape, all done in the style of a mezzotint or an old engraving which one might find in a Bible. It was inscribed 'The Grapes Of Wrath', which caused Rob Roth to burst out laughing, as did his mother when shown it. God bless mothers, huh?

ROB ROTH

God Bless the gifts of God, aka modern technology, for the internet, although it is not always clear if it is beneficial. Simon Neil, the intrepid singer and guitarist for Biffy Clyro, replied to my question on email, what's the song all about? 'Saturday Superhouse', that is. He answered with three words, 'Anger, Sanity, and Grief'. That was it. I don't know why just these 3 words but I didn't question it since they came from the source, Neil. And being a designer the source is important, the most important single entity in the chain of creativity... no surprises there then.

It had an immediate effect, namely a vision of three figures sitting rather formally in a waiting room, possibly medical. The three figures sit on straight-back chairs, representing the three words that Simon had emailed. The right-hand figure was about to be drenched in water (tears of grief), the central figure was consumed by fire (anger) and the left-hand figure was sitting at ease with his demons (sanity). These demons appeared in the stereotypical form of black animals, namely bats, snakes and a dog... and that was it, all of sudden, at once, there and then, which doesn't happen that often - kinda wish it did, would make work easier... but it don't.

One of the rewarding aspects of how we work is playing with fire, or rather hiring a man who plays with fire (a pyrotechnic). He set fire to our figure (a dummy, of course, you dummy) with relish, but we were disappointed. He looked crestfallen. 'What's the problem' he asked, 'a bit squibby' we said, and he replied, his eyes opening wide, 'You want bigger?' We said 'yes', and then suddenly an enormous plume of fire leapt skywards towards the ceiling of the studio, and it was 'fantastic! 'Will that do? he asked sheepishly, 'oh yes!' we replied. 'Oh yes!'

The animals, including a snake, seemed to be no problem for our good friend Dusan, but you wouldn't catch me anywhere near one. He was most intrigued by the animal handler, a woman who told him that she lived with two crocodiles. Dusan thought this was impressive but went and hitched up with a poker player from Scandanavia.

I've always been fond of this picture, enamoured by the real fire and the formality of people in a waiting room, adding, I thought, to the sense of metaphor. It was pointed out to me however, by my fine art printer, that in fact this picture was about an error... the water was being thrown to the wrong geezer. Oh dear, I had never noticed, nor thought of it! But of course... and now it is an error of an error.

There were other singles we did at the time, but not, I think, as well. It is sometimes important I like to think, that one is self-critical, hoping that it is neither pseudo-modest nor self-effacing, but 'Machines' (pg 103) is too well executed for its own good and hard to see that the chest is hand-painted and not a tight fitting t-shirt. 'Living Is A Problem...' (pg 16) did not have enough money to pay for enough different models to be thrust up against the bars, their faces distorted under pressure, and 'Who's Got A Match', (pg 16) is a 3D/2D trick about anger but is a trifle heavy-handed and 'Folding Stars' a trifle simplistic pg 102... but I'm being hypercritical, a luxury of age and false modesty.

UNUSED
ROCK HUGGER 2011

The Sacred and the Profane - gotta be at the heart of Rock 'n' Roll - aspiring to spiritual exaltation whilst transported by sex - girl hugs rock, naked flesh scratched by rocky encrustation, girl in frenzy hurls herself at standing stone - you can nearly sense the discomfort (a picture to feel as much as to look at).

The rocks are the real deal, not any old rock; called 'standing stones' they exist in Wiltshire near Stonehenge and are replete with spirituality, pointing the way, like leylines do, towards some nodal point where energies collide and where, at the right time of the year and right time in your personal life, Fate may lift you skywards and transpose you to a better place.

And to think we sullied this spot with burning flesh, woe is me. Mind you, fleshly libations were in order and young maidens being sacrificed and penetrated may have been the norm when the standing stones were originally arranged. Memory being like gruyere, I think this idea was intended for Marsha Swansion, a singer songwriter whose determination to make a record whilst being ignored by labels was to be greatly admired. *The Rock Hugger* was a testament to her rawness and desire to lay bare her thoughts and feelings honestly, but she preferred the piano room as being more musical and her critical eye as more self assessing or 'therapeutic'.

This idea would never have materialised but for the enthusiasm of Omega, one of our favourite models, who said "I'd love to do that for you." so she did and so we did.

Gawd knows, Rock 'n' Roll bands are a law unto themselves! It could be said that there is nothing quite so quirky, wilful, egocentric, child-like, demanding, insensitive, incautious, unthinking as a Rock 'n' Roll band, especially a successful and rich one. Not that I would ever say that.

Muse, a well-known band from England, were not keen to use us after *Absolution*, though I don't know why. Personally I thought *Absolution* was rather good, but what do I know? Muse's manager asked us to submit some ideas anyway, as a safety measure, and it turned out that they liked what we called the *Four Horseman Of The Acropolis*, which in turn was a variant of the *Four Dogs* at a table which we had first proposed to the Red Hot Chili Peppers, for whom yapping dogs (anthropomorphised naturally) seemed appropriate, but weren't.

The four dogs were changed into four men, which is quite a change, although I know many men who are dogs. The four men were sitting in an alien landscape around a sturdy wooden table with their symbolic nature represented by suitably decorated apparel. There were a few miniature magic horses hanging around, as you tend to get. This set of thoughts was derived directly from the music, which comprised three songs that seemed to evoke galloping ('Invincible' and 'Knights Of Cydonia' being two), along with a propensity to musical grandness - majestic passages followed by thumping rhythms - with words like 'epic' or 'biblical' coming to mind. Biblical horses became the Four Horsemen of the Apocalypse, obviously, but hold on... Muse are a contemporary band so our four horsemen needed to represent not the evils of a medieval world - War, Hunger, Famine and Pestilence - but more contemporary evils. So what would they be?

In our considerable wisdom we decided that they would be Paranoia, Intolerance, Narcissism and Greed, so Mr. Paranoia wears a suit of eyes,always watchful, Mr. Intolerance wears a suit of patterned religious symbols, Mr. Narcissism wears, of course, an outfit of many mirrors for he can never see enough of himself and Mr. Greed, a suit of gold, obviously. They are at a table to negotiate some pressing issue, either the future of the Earth or the price of the miniature horses owned by Mr. Greed, who is, of course, asking too much. Mr. Intolerance wears blinkers and, since these people are otherworldly, possibly discussing the fate of the world whilst not being of it, the Earth hangs in the sky above.

An epic meeting, to match the epic music.

I always thought that the magic undersized horses were a particular feature, central to the generation of this idea, but the band had half of them removed. The band also preferred another location to the one you see here. They also wished to colour the landscape in an elaborate fashion, detracting, we thought, from the reality of the location, which is in Bardenas, Spain. I was not overly pleased but the situation was resolved by the purchase of the copyright, which seemed fair, not only of course because my soul can be easily bought for money, but also I think it presumptuous for me to tell a band they can't have something when it's their record. What you see here is my preferred or alternate version.

PS: The location in Bardenas was extraordinary because a couple of miles away, by chance, was a Spanish Air Force testing area, where jet fighter planes were blowing up mock targets: buses lorries etc. The air towards the horizon was full of clouds of black fumes, explosions and the sounds of bombs - all very warlike, very biblical. In addition, this location was used by Terry Gilliam when making *Don Quixote*, a film he never finished but about which a telling documentary was made.

Their name may be Godsmack, and by God I would quite like to smack them, but I want to talk briefly about 'anal sunshine', which seems more common around Rock 'n' Roll stars than amongst more ordinary folk. The intermediary, told us that the Honourable Sully Erna aka Godsmack would like us to try our hand at designing an album cover, but would not let us hear the music. It was not, said the man in lofty terms, Godsmack policy to let the music out before it was complete. I don't know about Godsmack, I was certainly gobsmacked with the perversity of such a policy - to attempt to represent the music on an album cover without being alowed to hear the music is what I see as perverse.

It nearly happened once before with The Cranberries, when Dolores' husband was simply trying to be over-protective, and momentarily wouldn't let us have the music for fear I suspect that we might lose it. So Godsmack wouldn't let me hear their music. I should have smelt a rat there and then. I mean, dear reader, I put it to you... how could we possibly, how could anyone, do a fair job of visually representing the music, if they cannot hear the music. Sounds straightforward enough, except when you come to people who think the sun shines out of their arse, ie: some Rock 'n' Roll musicians.

The irony of 'anal sunlight' as we might call it, is that it only shines on that which you cannot see, and clearly Sully couldn't see behind him. He was blinded by the brilliance of his own ego (anal sunlight), and consequently turned down our suggestions. Now, you might, dear reader,think this is all a great whinge, which it is, and simply sour grapes, but the illogical aspect is only part of the story - it's the demise of good ideas (rejected roughs), that is upsetting, topped only by the subsequent use of seriously naff ideas on their covers. It is of course the bands privilege to reject - we have no God-given right to acceptance - but deploying moderate or uninteresting design in our stead has gotta be aggravating... we are not made of stone.

Yet again in the graphic tales that we weave, it is the monstrous egos of successful rock musicians, that defies imagination, and gets my goat. Or as they say in Dortmund 'Holt meine Ziege'.

One of the interesting questions for us designers when considering a box set, such as *Oh By The Way* by Pink Floyd, is which way up is the box? If you're on the business end you might consider how much to charge for the box, if you're on the music side, you might wonder what is in the box, if you're in the press department, you might wonder how best to promote it, and if you are a fan or prospective purchaser you might wonder what is the point of the box?

In their fondness for delicate craftsmanship,the Japanese pioneered the mini vinyl, a miniature version of the vinyl album reproduced the size of a CD (and therefore containing a CD). Being quite taken with this Japanese invention we suggested - God help us - a box of mini vinyls, mostly due to our overbearing egocentricity, it being another fine way to reproduce our work. So all 14 Floyd studio albums were encased in this box, plus a couple of coasters, the boxes sturdily made with a snug lid, and the mini vinyls reproduced as faithful facsimiles.

Where was I? Ah yes, I was considering the front and back or back and front of a box, not the bottom and top but very much the front and back - a set of coordinates which, of course, depends on which way you hold the box and which, in turn, most likely depends on labelling. My proposition was that there were in fact two fronts and no backs and that I needed, therefore, to design a double picture or diptych. Since the box contained all the albums not just a single one, there was no overriding theme to represent, other than the band themselves. This was not *Dark Side*, or *Animals*, but the entire body of work.

One idea I liked was a nude male model, posed like Rodin's *The Thinker*, his body painted with Roger's lyrics, but this was trumped by the 'mirror room', which was done in two versions, for the two fronts - one cream, one lilac. The rooms were extremely similar and the central feature in both was a mirror, which reflected the other side of the room, down which in turn was a corridor to a window against which stood a shadowy figure. Mounted on the wall next to the mirror were two framed portraits. In the reflection were two more framed portraits, making in total four portraits of the four members of the band. The two framed near the mirror were similarly positioned to those in the reflection of the mirror but in fact on the far wall, in an attempt to ever so slightly confuse the viewer, who would not be sure what was in the mirror and what was not.

There were also items scattered about the rooms that belonged to the Floyd, such that the 'mirror room' was clearly a Floyd room. When we later made fine art prints of the *Oh By The Way* diptych and hung them opposite each other, not too far apart, it was quite unnerving, because they looked as though they mirrored each other, whilst containing real mirrors within them. This entire procedure, apart from messing with your head a bit, was also an attempt to echo *Ummagumma* and *Echoes*, not a picture on the wall, nor a window, but a mirror, all three of which are often envisaged as portals into other worlds, as is the music itself, naturellment.

Back to my original preoccupation: the two fronts allowed diplomatic relations to be maintained within the band in terms of who was favoured where, as it guaranteed that they were equally distributed. Hopefully this would satisfy the Floydian egos. The one fly in the ointment was that the record company, in my entirely unknowledgeable and unbiased opinion, severely over-priced the box. "Not his department," I hear you say, but it doesn't mean that I don't have an opinion and my opinion is that Floyd fans might have conceived it as a ripoff and didn't buy it, and thus there are, I suspect, many thousand boxes in small warehouses in Tirana, Botswana and Kettering.

But I could be wrong...

I have been before, once in 1986 and again in 1993.

While in conversation with Steve Miller, I found that a favourite expression amongst musicians having a good time and 'dancing' to music is 'in the groove', often used when referring to the rhythm or the beat. The expression does not refer to a particular rhythm nor beat, or to specific timing, but about how well the timing or rhythm is being executed. It refers to a feeling not easily measurable or quantifiable. It is also, of course, a phrase used by musicians to consolidate their own relationship and probably exclude outsiders, because a non-musician, such as myself, hasn't a fucking clue what they're talking about. Anyway, I like the expression and think that it is always used positively.

It so happened that we were approached by a Belgian techno band called Goose. Why such a name? There's nothing technical about a goose, it's a word of limited allure in English but in this case it derives from the movie *Top Gun*, which was big in the 80's when Goose emerged. Although they were beginning to extend the boundaries of their music there was still a lot of focus on the rhythm, often the incessant rhythm: the repeat beat of techno.

We met the band in an Italian restaurant in North London as you do, and presented roughs, which included two woodpeckers! One of the birds was admiring himself in a mirror, the other was being psychoanalysed by an owl. Goose didn't like these. We also presented a sculpture of a goose made of celluloid i.e. 35mm film, given that their name came from a movie. We also presented upside down legs with either long socks or legs painted like socks, with yellow toe ends, looking like geese, but they didn't like that either. Time to throw in the proverbial towel? Not quite...

The design for 'in the groove' they loved. It was a unanimous decision, largely because they had read somewhere about our aberrant tendency to do things for real. Dan had completed two drawings - one a curvy groove and one a dead straight groove. They favoured the latter, and asked how we were going to do it. I said that I was going to build an actual groove half a mile long, well, a quarter mile, which they felt was great, cool, wonderful and unmissable. We had already included the hovering pyramid to represent the 'needle' that plays in the groove of a vinyl record but I had no idea at that point how I was going to excavate a quarter of a mile of dead straight groove in the middle of the countryside, lined with vinyl and on a Belgian budget.

Fortunately, Peter and I are familiar with the Fens, a large area of reclaimed land in East England, used in the war for numerous airfields, and used in peacetime for extensive farming. It's a complex network of rivers, canals, ponds and flatlands, irrigated by ditches. We commandeered a ditch and placed 'vinyl' boards (hardboard with grooved rubber covering) along a 500 yard stretch. Rupert took a photograph of each section then Lee composited it in the computer. This is a real vinyl ditch, though not real all at the same time, but we think it looks great! Straight as a die, arrowed across the field in the middle of the countryside, an endless vinyl groove, pure and linear, a piece of shiny land art, black and mysterious, a homage to all records including, of course, Goose's album.

The shoot took place on a beautiful hot day, much to the annoyance of the crew who had to move 20 or 30 boards continuously, leapfrogging along the ditch in the heat. But what price art, huh? Well, if you're Belgian, not a lot.

The pyramid or 'needle', a separately made prop, was held manually above the ditch, representing the cosmic needle (not the cosmic egg - (pg 100) playing the cosmic groove. It stretched way into the distance, visually representing the expression 'in the groove', with geometry and scale. Maybe we will do a curved groove one day, which would be an all wooden affair: a long wood-lined groove carved out of the hillside with a wooden ball rolling down it.

Can't wait.

BOOK COVERS
THE BLACK STRAT / COMPROMISE / THE MAKING OF DSOM / MIND OVER MATTER 4 2007 - 2010

If one is interested in design, and not haberdashery or espionage, then one could be forgiven for thinking that book covers might be like record covers, or not a million miles away. But they are not, they are quite different. Book covers tend to be changed quite a lot, whereas record covers very rarely are. Book covers are very type-conscious and inclined to include hyperbole... "This is the best book I've ever read in the entire universe"... When I say type-conscious, I mean not just big letters, but embossed, golden, radiating, shiny, gross colours, etc. and so forth - got to see it on the shelf, a myopic philosophy if ever there was one! But records can also be type-conscious, but more discreetly, and boast little or no hyperbole.

More surprisingly is the willingness to change a book cover seemingly at whim, through pretend anniversaries, special editions, additional chapters, updating, etc., etc. but mostly in a dubiously ethical desire to present the book as if it were a new book, another book, in case the gullible punter could be persuaded to buy it twice. The direct opposite exists in Rock 'n' Roll where, in fact, album covers remain unchanged for centuries, even when they should be changed because they were terrible in the first place. Ho hum.

We found that in re-doing *Mind Over Matter*, we invariably extended the book by a noticeable amount to include images produced in the intervening years, twixt one edition and the next. And so we compromised and did in fact change the cover as per book tradition, but clearly made it Floydian.

I was sitting in my local restaurant when I was approached by the Polish manageress, the lovely Agnes, Queen of the North London Polish Mafia. She showed me a Polish travel magazine of all things, wherein was a picture of The Wave - a stunning rock formation on the Arizona/Utah border in Vermillion Buttes. I thought this most spectacular, and resolved to use it one day, because it was the most explicit geological representation of audio/sound I had ever seen. Literally the rocks look like waves, whose striations run in curves like water patterns. The local Indians claim that this is where their gods shouted and the land changed to reflect the godly word, and I don't doubt it.

We made seven suits styled to represent different Floyd albums, which were then worn by figures standing around in this extraordinary place. The central pairing are shaking hands as in *Wish You Were Here* - in fact, I wish I was there to witness this vision, but my trusty pals Peter and Rupert, along with Joshua Richey, had the pleasure, whilst I remained at home, impaired and full of envy. It was a seven mile round hike to get to the Wave carrying props and camera in soaring temperatures. They of course complained loudly until they got there and reported that it was truly inspiring - proving the old adage of reward through endeavour, good things are hard to get, or some such.

Next up was a book cover we designed for a Floyd book by John Harris, about the making of *The Dark Side Of The Moon* whose prism we rendered again, but this time made out of words, since it was a book (of words) and not a record (of sounds) commemorating the incredible longevity of the album in the American charts - namely 14 whole fucking years! 9 more than its nearest rival, one Johnny Mathis, would you believe?

Thirdly is a book design for *Compromise* a play written by our good friend John Woods, a psychotherapist, about the conflict between ethics and behaviour. It is generally understood, and agreed, that it is totally forbidden for the therapist to have sexual relations with their patient. In the play a younger therapist discovers that his mentor has had sexual relations with a patient, who in turn has come to the younger therapist under false pretences. Not to mention adultery and a degree of mendacity in his own marriage. A lot of compromise ensues, including the book cover which initially featured the body painting of howling wolves or angry dogs upon the back of the nude, but the author rejected this canine element as too angry. I compromised and removed the dogs, but later regretted it. And of course have never let him forget it - we continue to be friends hanging on by our not-so-canine teeth.

PINK FLOYD
THE BLACK STRAT
A HISTORY OF DAVID GILMOUR'S BLACK FENDER STRATOCASTER
PHIL TAYLOR

A
LAND
MARK ALB
UM THAT STAY
ED 724 WEEKS IN
THE BILLBOARD TOP
200 - THE LONGEST EVER FOR
AN ALBUM - AND DESPITE NUM
EROUS ATTEMPTS TO ELUCIDATE
THE MYSTERIES OF ITS SUCCESS
THE UBIQUITOUS POPULARITY OF
THIS RECORD REMAINS AN ENIGMA...
roger waters david gilmour richard wright nick mason
ABBEY ROAD

In the entrails of the great recoupment campaign mounted by EMI in Sept 2011 in an ambitious attempt to retrieve funds which were, I believe, paid to Pink Floyd several years previously, one may find a CD called *The Best Of Pink Floyd* (see pg 77), a horrid title, one of insignificance and tedium, which was finally improved and replaced by a suggestion from Roger namely *A Foot In The Door* - a self effacing reference to pop history and Floyd's position in it.

I thought it funny and embraced it as a clear improvement on *The Best Of*, which I guess is not saying a lot.

At the same time the inscrutable Japanese requested a different cover from the UK one - the tiled floor across which strode a teacher - because of imports it was alleged, but I believe it is simply down to inscrutability and a desire to be different.

But who are we to disagree? We commenced work on *A Foot In The Door*... subversions, inversions and in this case reversions, all are grist to the design mill - a simple but adroit reversal gave me a door in the foot, which if made in miniature might possess Alice-type vibes or even those of C.S. Lewis portals to magic places with eyes beyond, just visible through the door thus providing 'doors of perception' an easy idea to shoot with allusions to Lewis Carroll and to Aldous Huxley and cheap to boot (no pun intended).

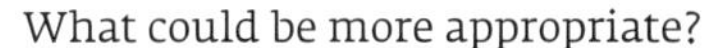

What could be more appropriate?

Well, wrong again... totally inappropriate, because the Floyd gave it the royal boot and turned it down flat, or so I hear - strange, especially since the finished piece closely resembled the accepted rough - clearly but shamefully these boots were made for walking, right outta here.

40

Small dreams sometimes come true. During emotionally fraught times in the mid 70's, I was introduced to the music of Steve Miller, particularly *Fly Like An Eagle* which I played numerous times to provide solace for me and my young son. I thought Steve Miller was brilliant and wanted to work for him but did not do so until 2010. It was even better than I had hoped.

Due to an intricate web of connections, Peter and I ended up at a dinner party of gay couples, at which Steve Miller and his wife Kim were present. A gentleman by the name of Rob Roth, who is a theatre designer for musicals such as *Beauty And The Beast*, proposed doing a Pink Floyd extravaganza without Pink Floyd. I think this surreal notion would have appealed to the band, but unfortunately Rob Roth did not, because he made a 'political' error, which we won't go into right now. Rob was a great fan of Pink Floyd and tended to wear a lot of white, including white socks. We came to know him, affectionately, as Crazy Rob Roth. He decided to employ us to design a logo (see Logos pg 46) and said he would introduce me to his friend Steve Miller, which is how we met, at a party, to celebrate Rob's partner's birthday.

I was so tongue-tied and excited to meet Steve Miller after all those years that I kind of pawed his arm like a demented fan. He must have thought I was extremely peculiar. A month or two later, however, we met again in San Francisco. We showed him a bunch of roughs of the many ideas that we had come up with and it was a great meeting. I think he was really quite impressed. I base this supposition on the fact that he crawled amongst the roughs spread out across the floor exclaiming, "Oh, I like this! I like that!" He ended up selecting four pieces, the first of which was known to us as 'rhyming showdown.'

I've always been secretly envious of musicians and their ability to play together and commune through their music. I fantasize that this is a blissfully enjoyable experience although I have met many musicians who do not lead blissfully enjoyable lives. This communing, be it via jazz or rock, seems to consist of exchanges - exchanges of melody lines, riffs or licks, and deploying variations thereof, and expanding or shortening as desired. Musician A plays a sequence of notes and musician B responds, either on the same kind of instrument, or on a different one. This exchange seems to go on in many quarters, and certainly did so at a Steve Miller concert which we attended in Oakland.

Our visual equivalent was staged like a gunfight, where the exchanging protagonists were facing each other as if in a Western, the camera seeing it from a very typical 'filmic' point of view, close to the hand and holster of one, whilst taking in the other beyond. The exchange between our cowboys was a friendly affair and consisted not of bullets but of items whose name rhymed: chair-bear-pear. The other gunslinger was about to respond with items of a similar rhyming shape, namely variously sized circles. The whole procedure took place in a cowboy town, but in Spain rather than America, in fact in Tabernas, where *A Fistful Of Dollars* was made.

What you see is what you get. The 'gun and holster' i.e. the snooker ball and the plethora of round shapes were made in England and brought with us. The distant cowboy is literally throwing chairs and bears. I find this image quite odd, even though it comes from my brain. I still think it's odd. I think it is also odd to find your own work odd, although not quite as odd as Steve deciding to call this album *Bingo*. I suppose that's about the corresponding numbers, the similar shapes that connect and the objects whose names rhyme - all acting to echo and represent the music exchange which forms such a fundamental part of rock music. Maybe *Bingo* meant 'Got it!' or 'That's good!', like 'Ker-ching!' or 'Eureka!' What do I know? I don't really know why I find this image unsettling, not like me, not that like images I tend to make, and also not like me to be unsettled... by my own work, which feels absurd.

But it is me.

YELLOW ROSE

Muse kindly gave me tickets for a show they did in London, some of which I passed to a friend of my wife for her two children, a boy aged 16 and a girl aged 12, who both absolutely loved it, the girl in particular. She wrote me a thank you note saying how great she thought Muse were, and that "it was the best day of her life... yet." I tell this tale to illustrate how good Muse are live, and how it seems appropriate to design something for them on a large scale.

They were returning from Exeter in south-west England which is their home turf, and we met them on a train coming back to London, in which we had a cover meeting. This sounds fairly extreme in writing, but seemed not especially out of the ordinary in reality, a bit daft perhaps, but not out of bounds as it were. We traveled down from London, in order to travel back. The meeting was productive, or so we thought. And two ideas were accepted, one was called 'Teddy Bears', and the other 'Stringy Lovers' (pg 18).

'Teddy Bears' as you might adduce concerns teddy bears, a theme to which I am inclined to return. It's clearly some childhood trauma that I can't, or won't, recall. In this instance, it was a field of half buried teddy bears, and it was unclear as to whether the teddies were rising out of the ground or being submerged in it. It was either an army of zombie teddy bears on the march, or a teddy bear graveyard. In effect a typical 'glass half full - glass half empty' dialectic. How you interpret is more about you than about it. To me personally it was about childhood, and growing up. Either way it was a panorama, an image with epic qualities, and therefore, up Muse's street, especially when I told them we would do it for real. You're going to actually bury 150 teddies? they asked in disbelief. Half bury I corrected.

I knew a friendly farmer and his very lovely wife in Bedfordshire, who didn't mind too much that we completely wrecked a field by taking 150 teddy bears each about 2 foot high, and burying them one by one (not ordinary teddies, but ones bought from Hamley's, London's most venerated toy store). This was a difficult and arduous proposition especially because we had to do it at short notice for release reasons, and therefore in the drizzle - a particularly English phenomenon which always occurs when you don't want it to, in this case, in August. At the end of the second day, the sun peeked through for about 3 milliseconds, we took a quick shot, dug up all the teddies and headed home rapidly, tired and bedraggled.

We thought the result was fine, very moody sky and the image looking now much like the rough, and we had been quite quick, much to our own surprise, let alone the clients. It then went all pear shaped.

Despite the urgency, rapidity of execution, acceptance and so on and so forth, Muse demoted my beloved teddy bears, from an album cover to a single cover, for a song called 'Uprising', which was in fact not wholly inappropriate, and 'Stringy Lovers' was put on the shelf, not I think because they didn't like the image, but rather didn't like what the lovers were dressed in. The teddy bears would have looked fantabulous - he said modestly - as a billboard, a spooky image, comprised of objects of affection subjected to an uncomfortable and ambiguous experience... an army of zombie teddy bears arising to seek revenge, or perhaps a rebirth... or alternatively a prospective burial.

What got my goat, not my bear, was that the design used for the album *The Resistance* was an illustration of a surprisingly uninteresting nature, not normally given to criticising covers designed by other folk, for fear of ungracious behaviour or critical reprisal (see RHCP pg 28) but this illustration looked very like the work of a novice who had just discovered the computer, plus some drawing software. It was amateurish, with little artistic flair or conceptual interest (I hope Muse never read this... listen, guys, I love it, really I do).

PINK FLOYD
ATOM HEART MOTHER
40TH ANNIVERSARY PRINT 2010

Anniversaries don't cut much ice with Pink Floyd but they do with management and with us if it engenders new work, even if variations on a theme... what's ok with Van Gogh (9 x sunflowers) or Cezanne (27 x his favourite hill) is ok with us...

So *Atom Heart Mother* would be 40 in October 2010 and could do with a revisit to commemorate it, but the imagination was bereft, nothing in the locker, the mind was a blank. The due date loomed closer, the mind was still a blank, the anniversary passed, no picture to commemorate.

No image no fun - perhaps this was because the original was so very fitting, truly a lucky break via Warhol and our good friend John Blake, for it was just a cow, a cow with attitude certainly, but still just a cow - perhaps it didn't warrant reworking.

The main thrust or reason for the original cow was its seeming irrelevance - it had very little to do with the music, but lots to do with Pink Floyd - it was ironically and strangely appropriate, so that viewers were not put off but tended to ask 'why a cow?'

Then fate took a hand and conjured up an idea, in New Zealand of all places. Whilst Peter and I were motoring with Peter's friend Spencer, we talked about our missed opportunity and an old idea of a wire sculpture duck cropped up and Pete said, 'wire cow' or rather 'why a cow?', and Bingo, there it was! - a sculpture of a cow made of wire, in the same position in the same field as the original, slowly disappearing. The record fades from memory due to the passing of time thus it became a very fashionable though unusual 41st anniversary thingy.

Beach Catalogue

TAKEN BY STORM

FILM

BY RODDY BOGAWA
FILMMAKER

It's a tall order to write something for Storm so I'll try and stick to the 'hard facts, ma'am' in order to convey the feel of some of our time spent together. I've made a film about his life and work, as well as being involved with loads of other side projects and events (read: shenanigans). Sometime in mid 2007, I had dinner with a friend and musician, Chris Brokaw, who did the original score for my last feature film. Chris had just come through London and mentioned visiting his friend Dan Abbott at Storm Thorgerson's studio. I remember joking with Chris that Storm Thorgerson was a great name for a Norwegian black metal singer but then Chris mentioned that he was a record cover designer who was part of *Hipgnosis*. I immediately knew the work, having spent several teenage years utterly obsessed with some of their imagery.

Chris told me that Storm, along with Peter Curzon, Dan Abbott and Rupert Truman, was still designing record covers and that they had just shot an image for a band where they dug up part of a beach, built a stairway down into the sand, installed wooden doors to frame the steps and simply photographed this construction. It struck me as completely arcane to work like this, with computer manipulation being what it is these days, despite the fact that I still shoot in 16mm film. I couldn't shake off the idea that StormStudios still worked in this manner and it reminded me of installation work like Marcel Duchamp's Étant donnés or Robert Smithson's land art.

I had been writing a feature length narrative script but somehow this image haunted me for several weeks. I went online and bought an old out of print book - *Walk Away René* - about the work of the original Hipgnosis team back in the day. When it arrived, I had a freak-out flipping through, not having realised just how many record covers in my own vinyl collection they had been responsible for: Pink Floyd, Led Zeppelin, Wings and Peter Gabriel and also more obscure ones that I hadn't connected with the company - Sweet's *Desolation Angels* or *Electric Warrior* by T-Rex, for instance. Who were these guys who had shaped so much of my teenage psyche?

Despite the need to get on with my feature project, the imagery in Storm's work just wouldn't let me go. I've made all my films in 16mm - doggedly working in a medium that everyone says is teetering on the edge of extinction - and the story of Storm's imagemaking spoke powerfully to me not only about my own life and my relation to music and images, but also in terms of how technology had changed culture.

I'd collected vinyl for most of my life; I still have incredible connections to that physicality. So I shelved the narrative script and started thinking full-time about Storm's story. I emailed the Studio with about eight different proposals with little response other than, 'Sorry, Roddy. Storm read it the other day and seems interested. He didn't write you?' This lasted maybe three or four months and I made numerous variations on the project idea: one with lots of academic speak, one that talked about the art world, one with loads of pictures, one with no pictures. Meanwhile, I had started to try to get funding, and amazingly I raised some startup money from an arts foundation. Of course, I didn't mention in my application that I hadn't even talked with Storm.

Finally I sent off a proposal that was a stream of consciousness about my Dad in his VW bug driving me and a friend to see Pink Floyd at Anaheim Stadium and that I still wanted to make a film with Storm. That night, I got a five-line email back from him: 'Dear Roddy, am in Ibiza on holiday. Read your proposal. Doing a talk at BAFTA in London in two weeks. Want to come?' That was it. I packed up an Arriflex, ten rolls of film and booked a ticket, not knowing if I even had permission to shoot.

When I arrived at Storm's studio, he was incredibly busy and said 'Sorry I can't talk to you, you must go with my assistants'. I spent the afternoon driving around buying up every head of cabbage we could find from the local grocery stores. That night at BAFTA, as Storm projected images of his work on the screen while on stage a naked woman was getting body-painted with eyes, his assistants passed out several hundred cabbages as Storm instructed the crowd of several hundred to hold them in front of their faces and his photographer took a shot of the scene from the stage. In retrospect, I can say that this was a complete mind fuck and at that instant, I had a deep inner feeling that I was now sucked into Storm's cosmos and that this was a much bigger story than I had originally envisioned. The next day I hung around in Storm's studio while he did work and spent several hours with him cleaning out his upstairs storage space lugging out an old drafting table and organizing prints in flat files. Maybe this was some kind of test or maybe he wanted to get some work out of me while he got to know me, but at the end of the day we had tea together and he turned to me and said, at last 'Okay, Roddy. Tell me what you want to do.'

My ideas for the film were rooted in memory. I had a very simple plan - to do a portrait film about Storm and how he worked and to take him back to some of the sites where he created some of the most iconic images. I think the turning point maybe was when we were in

Los Angeles for a show he was having and he asked me to drive him somewhere to get his hair washed. I told him 'Sure but you have to let me shoot it.' We couldn't find anywhere near the gallery except for a woman's hair salon (believe you me, Storm can talk his way into pretty much anything), and as I filmed him getting primped and blow dried, I think he realised I was interested in something more than just a glamorised history.

After that trip, Storm called me up and asked 'So what musicians do you want?' My original idea had consciously avoided or conceptually written that out, but once I started interviewing the musicians that Storm had worked with for decades, the whole film changed. On one trip to London, I shot three cans of film with Robert Plant and then jumped in a car and interviewed David Gilmour on the Astoria, his houseboat recording studio. It was utterly surreal and there was a sense that this was a film that would document something that was so much a part of everyone's identity. Most musicians are so used to talking about themselves in front of HD film cameras that when they saw me setting up the 16mm camera, they were totally focused and spot on. David Gilmour recognized the camera as an Arriflex SR 2 and we talked about cameras for ten minutes before the interview. I think it was Robert Plant who said 'You're fucking shooting film? So you only want diamonds from me.'

Storm talks a lot about his intense commitment to his art and work ethic as part of a bargain in relation to the efforts of the musicians and to 'the punter' (fan to us Americans), who pays for these efforts. Interviewing these musicians closed part of this loop. Aside from all the trappings of the music industry muddled as it is with commerce, ego, drugs and so forth, it was clear there was a profound sense of admiration for Storm both artistically and dare I say historically. There was also a belief in the moment where music and the imagery created by Storm aspires to something greater. Many of the musicians talked about this with me including Cedric Bixler-Zavala of The Mars Volta and Simon Neil from Biffy Clyro as well as Dominic Howard of Muse. This points perhaps to another closing of the loop - that to some extent they may have become musicians because the power of music and the imagery of Storm's work affected them in their adolescent years. Steve Miller, who was one of the last interviews I did, told a story of how how he commissioned four images from Storm, one of which was of a guitar-shaped swimming pool being filled by a brigade of Country & Western and 50's characters. Miller decided there and then to write a song based on the image!

I've joked with people that my film has been made over thirty-three years because really I've known about Storm's work since about the age of fifteen or so. It's a story about his life and inherently about his work and the cultural and social importance of his art but it's also about our collective identities, and the growing emptiness that technology leaves in its wake. Storm's images, his insistence on the real rather than Photoshop, are more important now than ever. They affirm the value of our being together and enjoying each others' company rather than sitting alone in front of a computer screen.

Roddy Bogawa
New York, 2011

As part of the great recoupment campaign of September 2011, EMI, Floyd's only label - such fidelity - proposed amongst many other things a Best Of album which was, in effect, *Echoes* Part 2. It was called, *The Best Of Pink Floyd*, the originality of which is enough to put a grown man to sleep (it was later re-christened *A Foot In The Door* thank God, but that's another story), (see pg 64).

So firstly there was *The Best Of*... now I guess the Floyd are getting on - not that you'd believe it if you saw Roger doing his Wall show this year - but they rejected the roughs you see here.

You have some strange robot sculpture thingy, then a special feast - a chintzy meal reminiscent of the end of *2001: A Space Odyssey* table and butler, set in some impossible location - on top of a mesa in Monument Valley perhaps. This record is like a fine meal, similarly unforgettable... Best of all to me was the submerged ear, like an iceberg, with simply more to it than you imagine, further depths not apparent on first listening or on first viewing. This was no iceberg but a giant ear in reference to *Meddle* specifically, and to music in general, encrusted with coral as in the song 'Echoes'. There is a man astride, standing at the pinnacle, at the top, at the top of his game. The best, the best of Pink Floyd.

Pink Floyd preferred instead a tiled floor of old covers over which strides a teacher - a newly constructed floor of album tiles upon which people could walk, stand, play, dance etc. etc... and thus we made the real tiled floor which was distressed a bit to avoid looking too new and purpose built. It was a floor that some enthusiast had laid which we found out about - lucky us.

PINK FLOYD THE WALL
pinkfloyd
PINK FLOYD THE WALL
PINK FLOYD THE WALL

THE CHAKRAS
BUILD ME A SWAN 2011

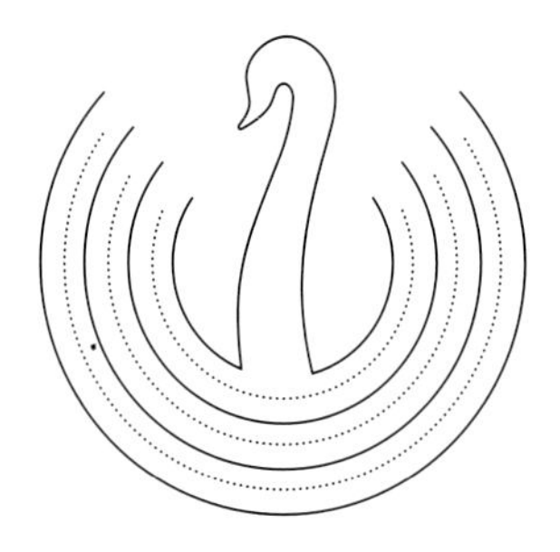

Mantra or principles by which to negotiate the violent seas of a working life No. 12... 'work begets work' or so I believe, and I don't mean moneywise, though we are commercial artists earning a living, and money matters of course, but not perhaps as much as one thinks (yes it does you idiot!). Work leads to further ideas which lead to more pieces of design which in turn give rise to other thoughts and hence more work.

Via an unlikely source in Belgium we designed The Plea (pg 26) and from there to The Chakras. Not my favourite name for a band, nor theirs, I trow, but a nice bunch of chaps from Ireland nonetheless.

We met and talked - they told us about their album with useful interjections from the manager (I mention this only because I think it a rarity). We told them how we usually worked. We then met a fortnight later, submitted roughs from which they chose nudes walking from the sea carrying swans - an everyday sight.

The album was called *Build Me A Swan* and swans are symbols of the creative muse, as are women. They were keen on the risqué element and were forthright in their admiration of the female body. The choice was unanimous.

So far so good.

We recruited the ladies, checked the weather forecast, and headed for the beach at Burnham to meet the tide on the turn - always important on a shallow beach (good for walking). Surprise surprise the weather was shit, if not evil - cold, rainy with no sun. Not a glimmer, and in July when it is supposed to be summer! We shot anyway. The girls were magnificent, enduring the worst conditions imaginable without a stitch on.

But it left me in a quandary, for dull light was anathema but the shimmering reflections were great.

We tried a second beach which was sunny, but too steep and short for poised and comfortable walking. I could not decide at first, the overcast conditions altered the idea I'd seen in my head, but fortunately the shallow beach provided a very glassy film of water fanning out in front of the camera like a sheet of mirror. What to do? In the end I plumped for the reflections as being more unusual, and what you see is what you get... swans of creativity carried by sirens emerging from the sea of the unconscious, the vast repository of ideas and creativity.

To be frank, I had thought they might choose the tree of keys but no, they were adamant, nudes it was, and nudes it is.

THE MARS VOLTA
AMPUTECTURE 2006

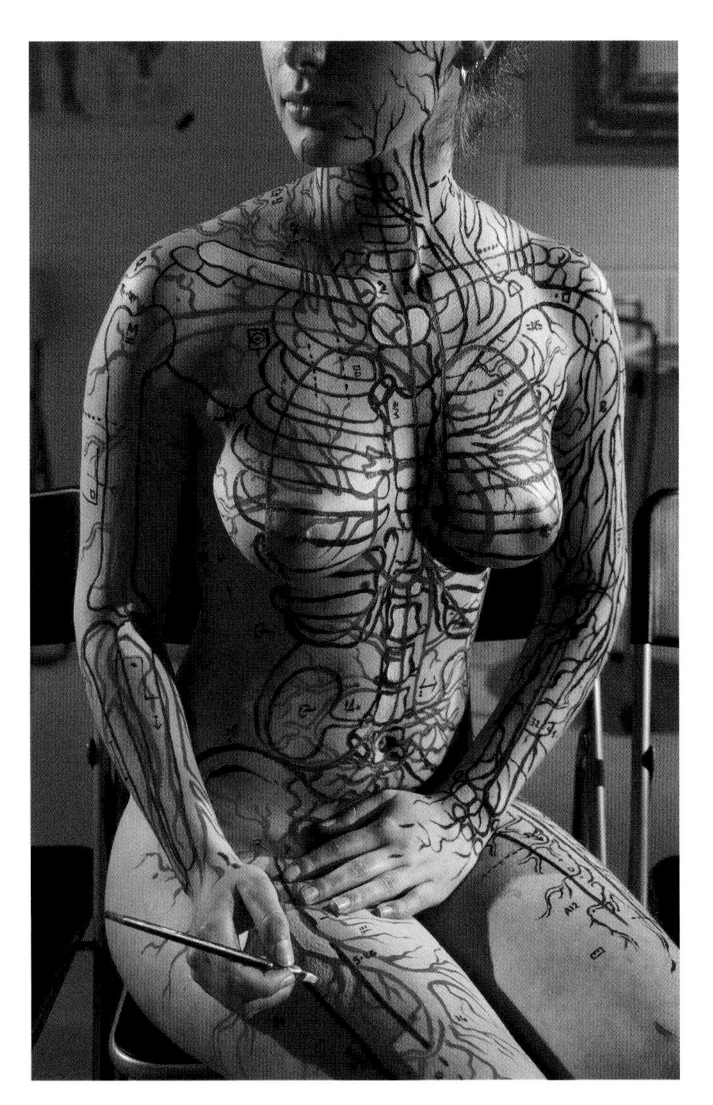

Another sorry tale of rejection, but with a happier ending. This time it was not the rejection of an idea, but the rejection of the finished art for an album called *Amputechture* by The Mars Volta, sometimes known as 'the insane duo with hair' from Juarez/ El Paso. The latter, as you may know, is a border town, and like many such places is divided in more ways than one. Imagine an impoverished Mexican garden backing onto a wealthy American garden with a large heavily electrified, camera-ridden fence running between them - gotta be weird.

We submitted eight or nine ideas and Omar from Mars Volta said he wanted them all, particularly what came to be known as the Aztec Mask', a large ethnic head made of mirrors and coloured tiles, floating across the fields and threatening a Catholic nun in black habit (or a hapless gypsy girl in white). This was based on a request by the band, who had heard about a Polish nun imprisoned for her visions, or maybe dreams, in which she claimed a God spoke to her. This is an unheard of punishment in the modern day, a throwback to crueller medieval times, and it appealed to Mars Volta, who happened to be passing through Poland at the time. We built a large mask looking much like the rough and photographed it floating across the countryside, haranguing a nun, like an insistent vision.

But The Mars Volta turned it down, whether it be for the colourising, the composition, the lateness, or caprice, was not at all clear. Our normal conduit, the lovely Kristen, had been herself recently fired, again for no apparent reason, and told us that this was the way MV worked. We might never know. In my frustration, I completed another picture called 'Body Map', consisting of a nude painted with her nerves and veins exposed, as if you could see inside her. I'd hoped that they might go for it. They didn't. Instead they chose an existing painting by Jeff Jordan from California. It could have been any old Jeff as far as I was concerned. I think we were as upset by the lack of communication and explanation, the apparent 'dismissal', as we were by the rejection of our treasured design.

Three years later Omar came to play at Dingwalls, a notorious club in Camden down the road from the studio. My PA and I cornered him and I was about to berate him furiously for his intemperate behaviour when much to my surprise, he was friendly and apologetic, telling us that he was very paranoid at the time and subject to too much intoxication. To my PA's amazement, let alone my own, I was immediately mollified. There is something so vulnerable and engaging about Omar, that it's hard to stay angry.

There ensued a spectacle which must have looked very weird to a passerby: a mutual hugging in which a thin Puerto Rican with too much hair was embracing a white disabled geriatric. I hope we meet another day... same place, same onlookers.

PENDULUM
IMMERSION 2010

"Love is strange" sang the Everly Brothers. "Musicians are strange" say I (in the nicest possible way) but you meet all sorts, don't you? Being a musician may not be the strangest of professions but they certainly need some ego to get on stage at all and strut their stuff in front of thousands, although they may need rather less in everyday life. Who would be a dentist? spending a life in other people's mouths? Who would be a miner in the bowels of the earth? Who would be a surgeon in the bowels of a patient? Who would be a politician where lying and corruption seem second nature? I'm not sure where I'm going with this but I'm trying to understand what happened with Pendulum. It's not helping.

Drum and bass band turned rock group, the brainchild of Rob Squire from Perth, western Australia, Pendulum are currently respected and popular. Rob is a quiet, shy man, reluctant to talk much about his music or himself, which is of course OK. I am, on the other hand, inclined to chat and talk, according to my friends, more than I might need to. Rob and I both have rampant egos nonetheless, and clashed, if that's the word for egos rather than titans, in the strangest of ways.

Jennifer Ivory at the record company, one of the few intelligent souls to inhabit that dark and gloomy world of record labels full of short-termism, short memory, scant scruple and small brains (nothing like biting the hand that feeds, huh?) asked me, on behalf of quiet Rob, if it would be alright to amend our design,our image. I no more understood this request than I did my acquiescence to it. I agreed, probably succumbing to a combination of female persuasion, the attraction of a topical/trendy band, the possibility of currying favour and a dash of disbelief, little imagining what was to come.

Rob selected a rough design showing male and female nude swimmers underwater in a shaft of light. Behind them drifted clothed figures, all male and all female, representing their past loves and the romantic baggage we invariably bring with us to a new relationship. The image would be staged underwater all at once, which was, I have to say, a pretty difficult affair. The figures of the 'past lovers' were clothed and unlit, to lend them a ghostly quality of drifting through the void or memory, whereas the loving couple in question were in bright light and naked and therefore seen more clearly.

Several of my friends and my friends' children were corralled and the event was staged in an Olympic swimming bath and photographed through a subterranean window - a proper film set at Pinewood being too costly. We were all quite pleased with the results of what was a fairly strenuous exercise, since swimming underwater with clothes is quite demanding. The image looked alright and, more importantly, nobody drowned.

We put it together and sent them a scan of the finished art, and they turned it into the most awful quasi-Avatar, fantasy poster that you ever did see - it was a travesty. I 'died'

They added a coral reef and a whale! A whale, would you believe! Also fish and godly light, rendering what was a real event totally unreal. I was horrified, in fact I would say that we were traumatised, but I had agreed that they could do it, foolishly believing that they would never make such absurd alterations. Wrong again and how!

But clearly the band and their fans had no issue, since the album went to number one and all was well with the record label. I suffered quietly in the background but the story wasn't over. I imagined that Rob Squire and cohorts would not appreciate my negative and irate reaction and would dispense with my services forthwith, but wrong again.(cont pg 146)

Talking of Avatar, I was appalled by the film on two counts - firstly it was a blatant rip of Roger Dean not only in my opinion but attested by an avalanche of protest on twitter, secondly they chose, at the time of writing, not to compensate him. As I believe Roger was heard to say in pain 'they stole my DNA' - not just a simple rip but a wholesale theft. We staged our own protest in Auckland with the 'fuck Avatar picture' of Kiwis holding kiwi fruit like 3d glasses (see pg 111).

That work begets work is one good reason to keep working. There are others of course, but I think this one is particularly relevant for us arty types. We were constructing a variation on the *The Dark Side Of The Moon* prism design, destined for a calendar and made this time out of fruit! The black background would be composed of dates, lots of dates, being a calendar 'n' all, and for the 3 elements of the design i.e. white beam prism and spectrum. We needed to build a tray with dividers in order that the compartments could contain a variety of fruit, such as blueberries, cranberries, oranges, gooseberries, baby lemons (never knew they existed), and physalis for the prism itself.

This worked quite well, even though Peter thought it a bit naff (just wanted to get that on record). Both he and I realised that the compartments we had created for the fruit could also contain liquids, which was a much better and entirely different proposition because the liquids could be paints and could flow into each other, ripple, or anything else that liquids get up to.

For some reason our carpenter Nick suffered a minor aberration and built the initial tray to hold only five of the colours in the spectrum, which is taking a liberty since we had already cut it down to six in the original design, from the seven provided by nature. This gargantuan error was fortunately spotted and corrected before shoot day. The paints were poured into the compartments in their appropriate colours and the effect was totally brilliant and nearly as exciting as *Only Revolutions* (page 97), because the liquids slowly leaked into each other, bringing to mind the marbling effect used in the endpapers of old books. Bizarre patterns, magical swirls and spumes of colour like clouds in a constellation began to appear in the most glorious psychedelic fashion.

This constantly changing colourscape was duly recorded by Rupert from his vantage point in the gantry. He took photos looking down upon the wondrous scene and ended up giving us an enormous choice upon which to exercise our predilections. Editing, in fact, took twice as long as the job itself but I'm only going to show you a couple here for fear of overdoing it. One simple, one busy, one pure, one exotic - controlled random it's called, where what happens is broadly contained but locally out of control.

It's a wonderful thing. Dan thought it might even be an innovative artform but I think not and nor do I care because it was a hell of an experience, let alone a marvel to enjoy later.

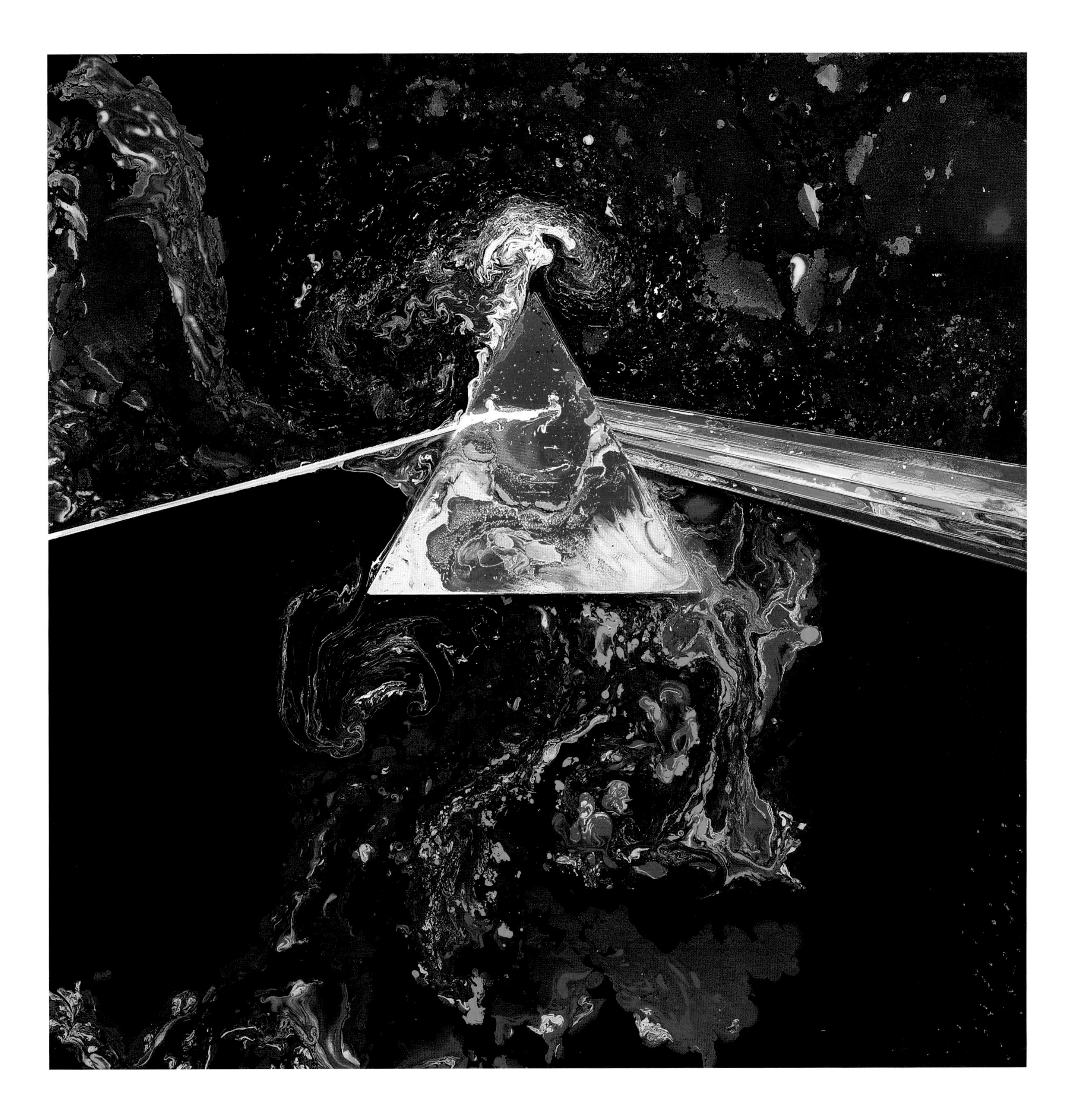

ANOTHER ANIMAL
ANOTHER ANIMAL 2007

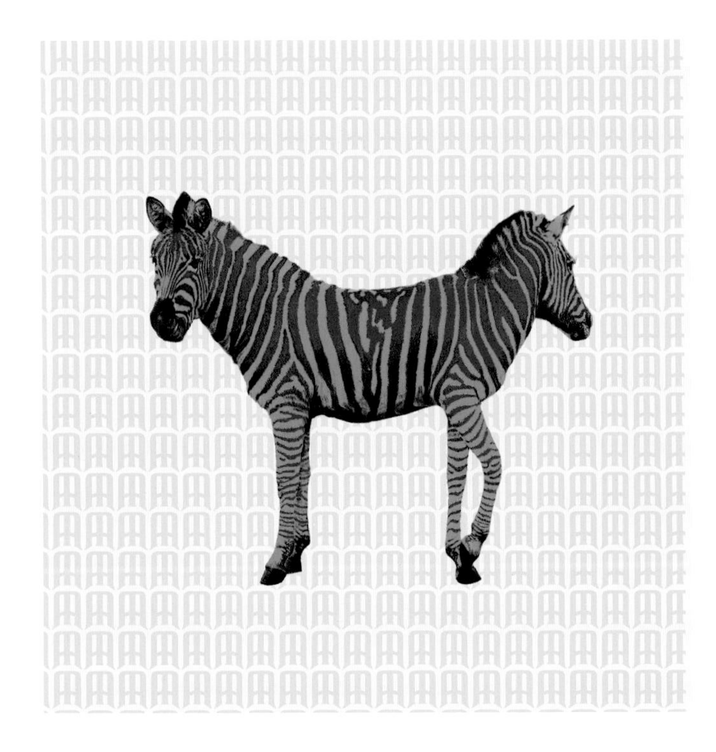

Is it proper, can it ever be proper in commercial design, to submit an idea to a client and then withdraw it? This may not be a question that grips you unless you are a designer. We sometimes find ourselves in this quandary having submitted a few ideas, in desperation to secure the job, but then deciding that some are clearly better than others. Or more particularly deciding that one idea is better than all the others. Such was the problem with Another Animal who themselves were slightly improper, being an off-shoot of Godsmack, or rather part of Godsmack who did their own album while waiting for a Godsmack album.

Another Animal selected the 'Push Me Pull You Zebra', and not 'Handy Chicken', though we did use that in the package. The real issue for me was that they did not take 'Dogfish', herewith reproduced as the original rough. It was an idea I much preferred, but what was I to do? I wanted to tell them that they couldn't have the 'Push Me Pull You Zebra' and had to have 'Dogfish', but they didn't want the Dogfish. It was their album, and we *had* submitted the Zebra.

Against such issues as nuclear war, global poverty, an imploding sun, a tsunami, melting icecaps, ravaging AIDS, my original dilemma may pale (of course it does you complete idiot!) but to us then and there the problem took on a great significance. I particularly liked the circularity of our 'Dogfish'. As it approached land it became more dog-like, and was of course chasing a cat which is disappearing into the bush, whilst in the river the 'Dogfish' is being watched, catlike by a Catfish. But the 'Dogfish' is not a dog and the Catfish is not a cat but a fish, nothing is as it seems, just like Another Animal, who were not Godsmack but were.

PS: If you know your pop history this design also feels like an early Genesis image, or so I like to believe, though executed in a different illustrative style.

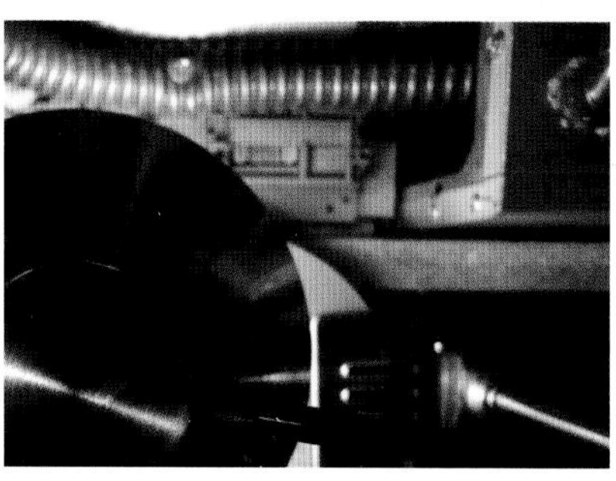

Memory being what it is, a slippery thing at the best of times, I cannot recall for whom this was initially designed, but Peter assures me that it was for Skunkworks - a band temporarily fronted by Bruce Dickinson when on artistic leave from Iron Maiden. One can readily see how the retro machinery in our picture might go with the word Skunkworks, but I'm not sure why the idea would have seemed appropriate.

There is something about retro that makes it attractive, be it Victorian machinery in a pumping station or 30's gadgetry. I wonder if it is because it is from the past and therefore cosy - the brain likes to see the complexity of machinery, provided that it is unthreatening. The grimy steelworks of Pittsburgh or the machinery of war might always seem more threatening and hence less attractive.

Our retro machine is a gigantic probe, probably several storeys high and wide, made of sundry and disparate items, dials, pipes, pumps, fan belts, grilles etc., in profusion. They were accumulated by all of us, then designed by Peter and Jerry and put together by Nick Baker who had made a valued contribution by purchasing an entire car engine to add weight and a degree of solidity. Rupert's lighting added the final touches - we especially liked the spots of light on the ground

We thought The Wombats liked this image, but they preferred the picnic, (pg 37) by which time we were so enamoured that we funded it ourselves hoping to sell it in the fulness of time or at least get it used. So, dear reader, if you've got a few grand it's yours!

I think we were not only keen on the visuals of our retro machine, but also on the ambiguity... at first glance it may look like an image that's about threatening a woman - since machinery is often a male preserve, it is a male threat. But I think it is more about man's paranoia, his fear of woman more than his antipathy, i.e. the only way that a man can understand a woman is via an enormous machine - a scientific probe which can scrutinise the inner recesses of the female mind that many men claim to find so elusive.

There were two issues much discussed back at camp - namely the nudity - was it necessary? And at what was the probe actually pointing? Finally the nudity seemed valid for reasons of vulnerability, and it was felt that the vagina was the best target, possibly over contentious but still the most likely focus of mystery.

Following on from *Planet Anthem*, a title I never could grasp, Disco Biscuits turned down the 'Newness Of Being' and 'Picasso In The Sand' (see page 45), but commissioned a succession of EPs whose covers we designed on the theme of wrapping to accompany the album cover design. That's wrapping not rapping, or Wapping, after Christo, not after Eminem. Firstly we wrapped a tree in green cloth, with a lady nearby in her lingerie, as if the tree had nicked her dress. Secondly, a red-taped lady wrapped tightly, standing in a town hall, reflecting the red tape of bureaucracy. Thirdly, an object in open countryside, wrapped in black material. No one was entirely sure what the object was underneath. Lastly, a couple kissing under yellow plastic, by a canal. I think I recollect that an alternative picture was taken of a couple under yellow souwester, fornicating in some unlikely position, which from the outside looks the shape of a motorbike. I dread to think what they were actually doing down by the canal, although I remember it made us laugh, I think, because the couple underneath the yellow plastic were in fits.

The great thing about wrapping is that you can't really see what's going on, and your mind is left free to invent. I don't know if Christo particularly enjoyed this aspect.

THE STEVE MILLER BAND
WATER GUITAR 2010

Boys like to dig holes... Masquerading as design ideas, I have dreamed up several holes - one like a pyramid where the conical-shaped hole reflects the cone of dug-up earth. What you take out you can put back in a hole. Another was slightly macabre, a burial plot shaped like a volcano.

It is hard to know what is going to suit a band; just because we think a design might be appropriate doesn't mean a lot - second-guessing musicians is a fruitless exercise and we might submit 6 or 7 suggestions/roughs, only for a band to prefer the least expected, which is of course one reason for submitting the same idea to different people - one person's goose is another's gander so to speak.

The Dark Side Of The Moon came from something else, previously designed as a record label.

The 'water guitar' shown opposite was first tendered to a little-known Scottish band called The Casuals. They rejected it. We thought Steve Miller might like it, being a guitarist 'n' all, and also because the album in question featured material from his formative years in the 50s. We knew we could dress all the participants in 50's gear, all those flared skirts, wide belts, tight sweaters, bright colours and bobby socks and so we resubmitted it and he liked it.

Being half crazy for doing it for real, we located a willing farmer in Wiltshire and dug a large hole in his field in the shape of a Fender Stratocaster as favoured by Steve Miller. The shape was obtained from a photo of the guitar in the vewfinder and string laid out to fit the outline, and then a mechanical digger was deployed to do the dirty work. The resulting hole, looking just like a guitar, was then filled with water. The models were arranged as you see, pouring their 'emotions', their watery tears, into the guitar to represent in a simple way the emotions guitarists bring to their playing. Our favourite dog model Chester is actually swimming in the water and was added in reference to Steve and his missus' great fondness for dogs, and to add substance to the reality of the water and thus the whole exercise.

Some musicians are uncomfortable or unwilling to easily express gratitude, notably the more successful/wealthier ones, but Steve had no such difficulty. He said thanks so much I love it... in fact I'm going to write some new music for it... what more could a boy want? Brilliant.

BACK CATALOGUE
DELUXE.../ OUTBACK... 2009

It is not always clear if an idea will work. But there is a lot to be said for doing it, as many a sculptor will attest. Back Catalogue, was originally suggested by Finlay in a rather sheepish fashion, when doing a poster for EMI, circa 1996, to promote Pink Floyd's back catalogue i.e. all their old records. Finn suggested painting the album covers of said catalogue on the backs of six nude women. 'Sounds naff to us' we said, but we did one anyway, because the record company thought it 'commercially viable' as they put it. It was of course great fun for me to do, and it turned out rather better than expected. EMI liked it, people in general liked it, even my wife liked it. It seemed chatty, friendly, mildly erotic and kind of uplifting and so with unsurpassed inventiveness, we did it again, and again, and again, and it was great fun again, and again, and again. On each version, we changed the location, we changed the girls and we changed the images that were painted on their backs.

So herewith Deluxe Back Catalogue, which was taken in the middle of London, albeit in a more Egyptian looking location than English, which for reasons of colonial heritage was a club in Pall Mall, the RAC Club, which boasted an exotic swimming pool, reminiscent of a Pharoah.

We then decided that exterior locations were called for if we were to do it again. I blame Rupert, who I'm sure was the first to say, 'Let's go to South Africa'. Fortunately we were doing another job, Disco Biscuits, (page 25), and we persuaded a couple of print publishers to cough up some dough to finance the visit. We took our body painter, the now infamous Carolyn, and a film maker, Bob Bentley with us on our expedition to Cape Town.

No longer doing Pink Floyd's back catalogue, but now exhibiting our own, which is more extensive, and of course, more ego-centric, enabled us to firstly do *Outback Catalogue*, located in the rolling hills outside Cape Town, and also *Beach Catalogue* (pg 72), in a mild parody of a swimming costume brochure, and taken on a wooden slatted seat we found at Blaubergstrand, just North of Table mountain. Finally, instead of *Back catalogue*, we employed the services of 6 gorgeous black ladies and called it *Black Catalogue*, due to our deep and clearly clever sense of humour, which has yet to see the light of day.

In each case the tableaus were painted on the backs of the women. This takes about 5 hours, and requires complex stencil work etc., because it has to be done at one time, or in one part of a day, leaving enough time to do the photograph, otherwise the paint gets worn off by the following day. So the whole exercise has to be completed in a single day, which includes a lot of waiting around from the photographic department, but it was all right for the art department, who of course spent a lot of time looking at naked women.

My thought is that these pictures are friendly, that the women are enjoying each other's company, that it is a little erotic, but not very - and more for what you can't see than for what you can. I also think it features the backs of women, a less often depicted beautiful and elegant feature. I think I might do it again.

BIFFY CLYRO
ONLY REVOLUTIONS 2009

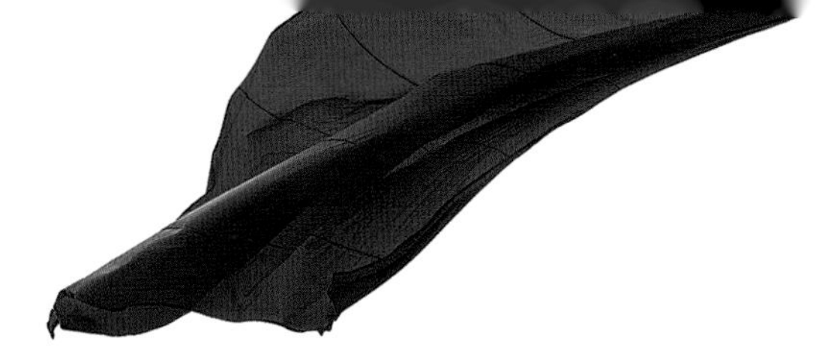

I was sitting in a hotel in Glasgow, showing roughs for *Only Revolutions* to Biffy Clyro, and pointing out that various small details could be changed or amended if one wanted but not the larger issues, for example, the table on fire in this image for *Only Revolutions* could be axed, but both the bass player and the drummer - twins by the way - leant forward quickly and said 'We don't want to take that out, we like it, absolutely out of the question'. I said meekly 'I'm just giving you an example guys', but they said 'yes, yes, but we like it and we want you to keep it, so dont take it out!' This design soon became the preferred choice for *Only Revolutions*, a title borrowed from a book which told the tale of a broken relationship between a man and a woman from both sides, on opposing pages. The title had a reference to records obviously, which tend to revolve, and also for the politics between neighbouring states (could that be Scotland and England?) and of course for the eternal battle between the sexes.

Not wishing to exceed the bounds of ego decency and restraint, I have to say that this design is a treat - it is graphically and emotionally very satisfying and was an exhilarating experience to work on. At the outset I was talking to Dan about revolutions - is real (social) change only feasible through revolution? - and how the participants were often represented by flags and how those flags became very important and symbolic. And he said 'gags that become flags', and talked about how prisoners of revolution would be gagged, and how these bits of material might become the flags of revolution but just much much bigger, emblematic rather than actual. Such a great idea Dan, mostly because I could see it in my mind immediately, humungously large flags blowing in the wind, billowing and undulating in extraordinary shapes (not completely unlike the student gown in *High Hopes*, which the Floyd manager kept reminding me).

Firstly we had to find a large flag, and since London is a big place like New York or Tokyo, you can in fact find anything you want, ANYTHING. Sure enough a flag maker was uncovered in East London who sent us a polyester cotton flag like a parachute, and it was so enormous that when we tried to stretch it across our apartment block it went right over the roof and down the other side. Much as we like big things, this was ridiculous, so we had to order a replacement a bit smaller, in fact 3 flags, one blue, one green, one red.

We took the flags to our friendly farmer in Bedfordshire, whose farm was on a hill. A scaffold tower was delivered to the same hill farm and we tied the flags onto it one at a time. The weather was crap, grey, spots of rain, and windy, the sort of weather which makes a photographer go home early, but for us it was perfect, in so much as the wind blew the flags into incredible shapes, literally folding and unfolding like giant tethered waves, which I of course watched from the comfort of the car, whilst Rupert and Dan held flags and took photos... at one point Dan was blown over by the rippling undulations of the enormous blue flag. I kept uttering gutteral noises of delight at the sight of the unbelievable shapes that were being made naturally - just incredible! What you see here is a flag being blown by the wind, and apart from joining a corner of the flag to the end of the gag around the mouths of the warring couple, there is no further computer trickery here.

Not only were the visuals spectacular, they were accompanied by amazing sounds as the material flapped and undulated in the wind. It was like an audio event of its own. My big regret was that we didn't film it in extreme slow mo. The couple facing each other are carrying a rolling pin and a knife, ready to 'murder' each other, and the flags I always saw as representing their inner emotions which they feel unable to express easily. It is as though the man's flag in blue is attacking the girl's flag in red. Dreamy. The table on fire is the table around which they can no longer sit to negotiate, any more than can revolutionary forces and the governments they oppose.

All of which was immensely gratifying and the icing on the proverbial cake was that we all loved it, the record company and none more so than Biffy Clyro whose powerful yet elegant music was suitably portrayed by our enormous flags billowing musically in the wind on a hilltop in Bedfordshire.

In 2003 the Musée de la Cité in Paris asked us to stage a Pink Floyd exhibition in their premises. It was called *Interstellar*. To cut a very long story short, the exhibition was OK but the experience was diabolical. We did manage to design one piece, called 'Mirror Balls', that has survived, literally and artistically. The idea of one perfect mirror ball sitting on top of another - no disco ball this, but one perfect electro-plated mirror sphere without joins, cracks or distortions - provided for an endless repeat of reflections at the point where the balls met.

In between balls aka the planets/stars was an unending repeat reflection, mirror in mirror, an infinity, just as there is between the actual stars or in inter-stellar space. This repeat, or infinite regression, echoes *Ummagumma* and of course *Echoes*, and so seemed eminently suited to expressing that which is sometimes referred to as 'Le secret de Pink Floyd'. All of this has even more relevance given that this design started out as an idea for a logo based on the infinity symbol, for a company called Timeles.

I was impressed with some of Anish Kapoor's mirrors and white spaces and concluded I would be 'inspired' by him to do the mirror balls. You could say I was paying homage. Or ripping him off if brutally honest. Some years later he ripped me back by doing not two mirror balls, but 50, for his exhibition at the Royal Academy. They stood as a gigantic Christmas decoration in the courtyard. Kapoor's mirrors were not as perfect as ours and I thought the structure looked a little cheap, so nyah! Mind you, his mirror thingy in Chicago is pretty fucking spectacular, and I had the rare pleasure of seeing his red, fluted trumpet thingy on green hills in New Zealand, which is even more fucking spectacular.

Our two modest mirror balls worked very much as expected and encouraged several variations, so you see here an arboreal version - set in an English wood; an architectural version - in a glass house in Syon Park; an aqua version by the side of the Thames, and an autumnal version photographed in a neighbouring park. I feel these versions, all mounted in real places, offered different possibilities in terms of the reflections, shapes and colours.

The initial version for the French exhibition was done by the side of the river Cam in Cambridge, with the mirror hemispheres (the backside is not visible and therefore does not exist) lying on the grass vividly reflecting the blue sky and white clouds of a summer's day. Children gathered round, unable to resist peering into the bright and vivid depths, distorted by curvature not by imperfection.

The architectural version reflects the glass window in all its geometric splendour. The arboreal reflects the tall trees, making the mirror spheres look a bit like Elizabethan breeches. The one by the Thames seems to float on water, while the autumnal one is a delightful riot of colour at the same time as being difficult to delineate.

All of which goes to support my thesis that herein lies 'Le secret de Pink Floyd'.

WOLFMOTHER
COSMIC EGG 2009

I think it is usually bad form to slag off another party in print, be it a newspaper, magazine or book, on the grounds that the maligned party have little chance to reply. However, I am going to be very hypercritical and justify the following tirade by saying that Wolfmother did not give us much chance to reply, respond, augment or explain when we were being shuffled off and brusquely terminated - I see 'tit for tat' is clearly my new policy - and I include both the manager and Mr. Wolfmother himself. The story goes like this...

The manager knew me from old, knew me well, and asked me if I would like to do a Wolfmother cover, because I would be' just right' for the project. He complimented my work, he eulogised the record, assured me that Mr. Wolfmother (Andrew Stockdale) was greatly in favour of us doing it. He also remarked that though it was to be called *Cosmic Egg* they didn't want anything cosmic or eggy. He said it twice.

Wolfmother is a one-man band, and he, Andrew, lives in Australia near Brisbane, and it so happened that Peter was visiting Brisbane (see Powderfinger pg 118), and therefore we agreed a personal visitation at no expense to them. Peter met Andrew at a party, I think, and had a brief discussion during which Andrew talked about black and white photos of himself - a bit like 'Electric Warrior'. Peter was understandably confused since this sounded different from what we might normally do and yet we were, apparently, so 'perfect' for the project. We discussed the matter online and decided that Andrew had probably had a beer too many.

We set about designing stuff with some vigour in response both to the music and the encouragement from the manager. In the nicest possible way the music displayed traces of numerous predecessors but it was performed with verve and gusto. We suggested an umbilical guitar connected to a dancing flying figure, the chord coming from a wolf. We suggested a hole in a lake - a surreal notion at the best of times - but somewhere totally real, namely a lake in California with a raised plughole. In winter the water rises and the surplus escapes down the hole, whose function as a plug you cannot detect. I thought this was a very bizarre image, this magic hole in water. We also suggested a thief in the night, a dancing figure across the Australian desert in moonlight, carrying the Mona Lisa. And then we suggested...

Anyway, we were privately chuffed at this creative splurge and thought, "Nice, job done". Clearly wrong again. Despite all our brainstorming endeavours, they were all rejected out of hand and Wolfmother chose a picture of a cosmic egg - what a surprise! A pedestrian but florid illustration of an enormously large egg floating, I think, in the sky above a lyrical landscape. Conceptually bland, dull as ditchwater. Why they bothered us in the first place is a mystery. Why I believed the manager's enthusiasm is a mystery. I make that two mysteries too many!

I have written several times in this book about rejection, about our ideas being turned down seeming close to a litany of complaint or even a high handed attempt to elicit sympathy as if we might be above rejection or have been unduly hard done by (which we aren't, and haven't been). I think it interesting which bands which ideas and what reasons lie behind decisions and I wanted to show the designs that otherwise wouldn't be seen. What gets my goat and cheeses me off, big time (if only there were an expression involving goats' cheese) is that some really nice ideas bite the dust.

And that hurts Mr Wolfmother, that hurts.

BIFFY CLYRO
FOLDING STARS / MACHINES 2007

Just because we are designing a single cover, as opposed to an album cover doesn't mean we treat them as lesser. 'High Hopes' (Pink Floyd) 'Butterflies And Hurricanes' (Muse) 'Saturday Superhouse' (Biffy Clyro) are all approached with the same attitude as an album and finished with the same degree of care. Herewith two others to illustrate the point...

Both covers are for Biffy Clyro and both are executed with body painting. On the left is 'Folding Stars' taken from the *Puzzle* album so *Puzzle* references seemed appropriate - the same 'empty' set and the same 'pose of grief' for our figure who is now covered, or immersed, in sadness or in tears of grief represented by the waves of water painted in the Japanese style of Hokusai. This adds to the ritualistic aspect of the idea, the Japanese being fond, possibly over-fond, of ritual. I recall it was quite impressive how quickly and deftly our favourite body painters Carolyn and Carly rendered this from scratch, no stencils or masks needed.

'Machines' above is quite a straightforward idea after Superman, whom you may recall pulls open his shirt to reveal an 'S', and becomes Superman and assumes super powers. In this case our character reveals only a chest of machines... he opens his shirt to to display complex machinery. I was indisposed when this picture was taken; on seeing it I was amazed by the sense of it really being there, in so much I thought it was at first merely a t-shirt he was wearing, not body painting at all, making, the design in fact more disturbing when one realised it wasn't (a T-shirt).

So hats off to Larry or rather to Carolyn, and caps off to Carly.

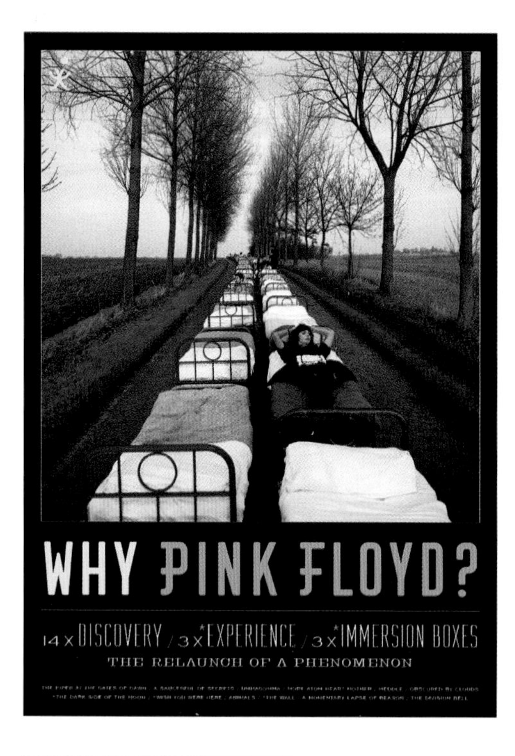

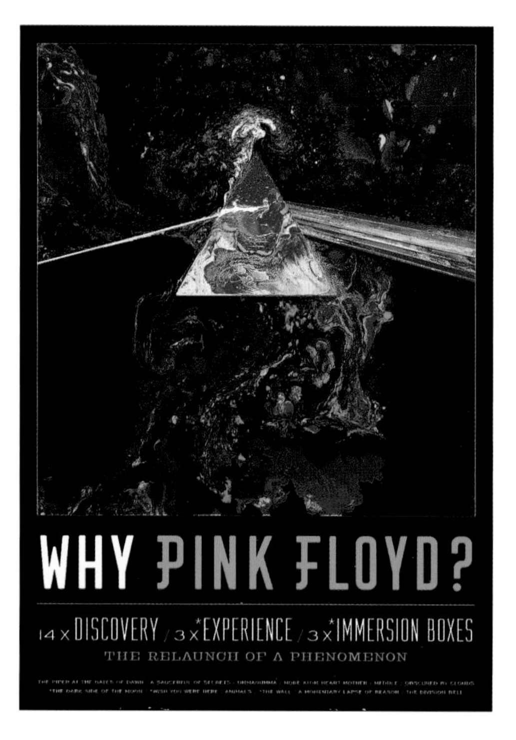

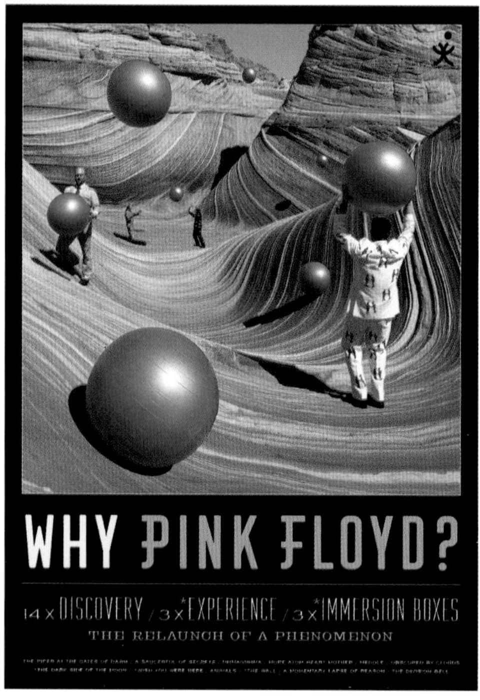

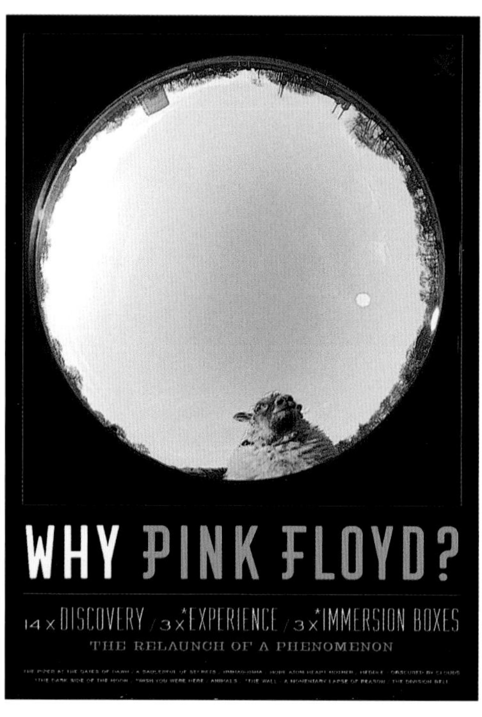

In EMI's great recouping campaign of September 2011 the company determined to advertise and sell the Pink Floyd back catalogue (i.e. *all* their old albums) in various new guises at extremely competitive prices. The *Discovery* range was intended to counter 'illegal' internet borrowing and home copying which deny the company income. Expensive box sets can also be made competitive by the inclusion of rare recordings, live tracks, demos and physical objects like marbles and scarves. These are items which simply cannot be passed down the digital wire. EMI also issued a number of intermediary double CDs called *Experience*.

This massive undertaking would be difficult to sustain or justify if it were not presented and marketed with considerable energy. Not that Pink Floyd gave much of a toss, being a) not in great need of dosh and b) it being a label matter - no new creativity was involved, after all. Fans would appreciate the archival element and the band would approve demos and live tracks etc., but actual band interest wasn't very noticeable.

The label and managers, in their infinite wisdom, were searching for a tag line to hang it all on and had finally emerged with 'Pink Floyd 2011?', certainly dynamic enough to vie with paint drying but susceptible to improvement. Peter suggested 'Why Pink Floyd?' which couldn't be worse and was, in fact, much better as it contained several meanings - like 'Why bother at all?', 'Why is Pink Floyd relevant today? Let alone yesteryear?', 'Why were they successful?' and 'Why is Pink Floyd called what it is?' and so on and so forth.

In addition it's short and easy to read and lastly it seems to sit comfortably alongside numerous Floyd images already in existence. It doesn't look unintentional, forced or trumped up either, and we wouldn't want that now, would we? There is a surfeit of trumped up stuff already in the music business, and so say all of us.

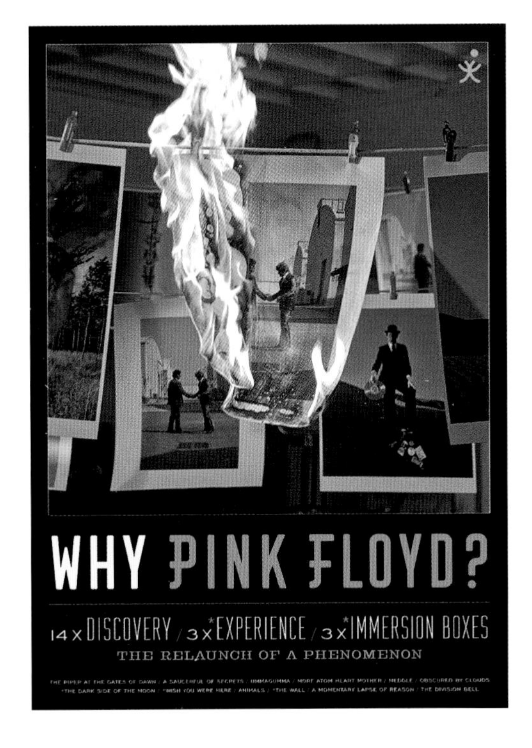
WHY PINK FLOYD?
14 x DISCOVERY / 3 x EXPERIENCE / 3 x IMMERSION BOXES
THE RELAUNCH OF A PHENOMENON

WHY PINK FLOYD?
14 x DISCOVERY / 3 x EXPERIENCE / 3 x IMMERSION BOXES
THE RELAUNCH OF A PHENOMENON

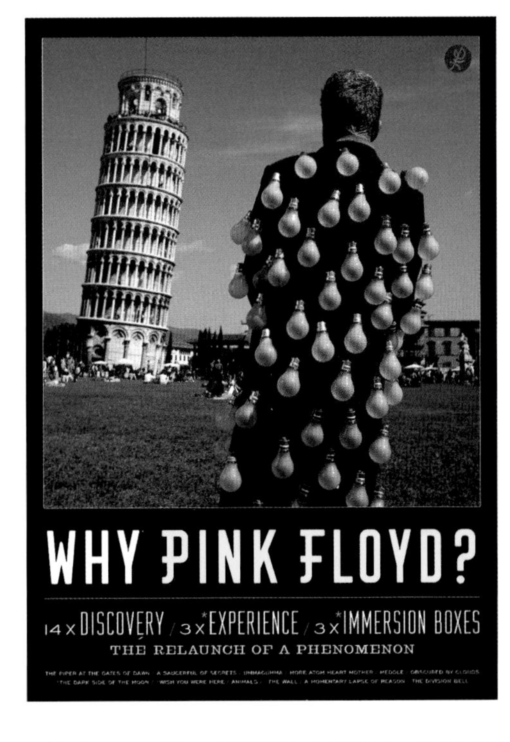
WHY PINK FLOYD?
14 x DISCOVERY / 3 x EXPERIENCE / 3 x IMMERSION BOXES
THE RELAUNCH OF A PHENOMENON

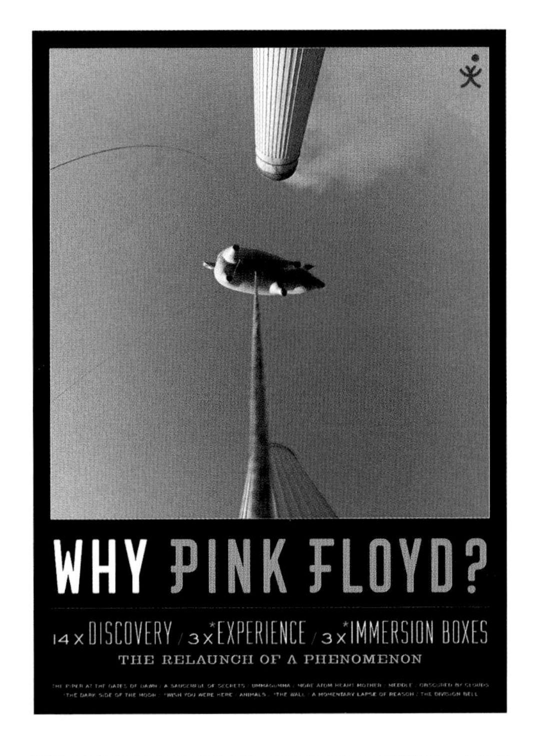
WHY PINK FLOYD?
14 x DISCOVERY / 3 x EXPERIENCE / 3 x IMMERSION BOXES
THE RELAUNCH OF A PHENOMENON

WHY PINK FLOYD?
14 x DISCOVERY / 3 x EXPERIENCE / 3 x IMMERSION BOXES
THE RELAUNCH OF A PHENOMENON

WHY PINK FLOYD?
14 x DISCOVERY / 3 x EXPERIENCE / 3 x IMMERSION BOXES
THE RELAUNCH OF A PHENOMENON

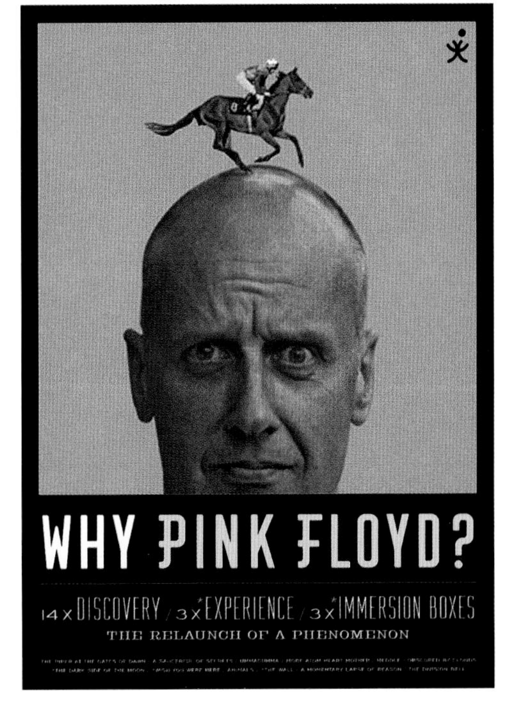
WHY PINK FLOYD?
14 x DISCOVERY / 3 x EXPERIENCE / 3 x IMMERSION BOXES
THE RELAUNCH OF A PHENOMENON

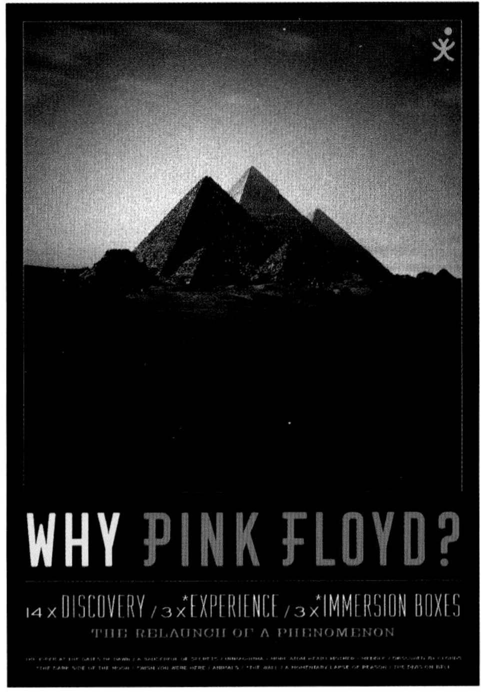
WHY PINK FLOYD?
14 x DISCOVERY / 3 x EXPERIENCE / 3 x IMMERSION BOXES
THE RELAUNCH OF A PHENOMENON

There I was sitting in a restraurant at a West End hotel with Luke Thornton (please don't tell on me), peering at a woman seated at a neighbouring table who must have thought me weird until we recognized each other. She was and still is Katia Labèque, who plays classical piano duets with her sister Marielle. We hadn't seen one another for 20 years and were both delighted. She soon told me that she and Marielle had started a record label, KML Records, despite these hard times for the CD format (not unlike Steve Miller's Space Cowboy records). It was probably a crazy idea but a testament to their love of music and records - tangible items not virtual downloads. She hesitated then asked if I would do a cover for them. Since my efforts some 20 years previously were a tad ordinary I was pleased to have a chance to redeem myself and started work on B for Bang.

KML's remit was good music (classical, ethnic and jazz), however obscure, played by accomplished musicians and admired by Katia and Marielle who would also play from time to time. B For Bang was a loose knit collection of virtuosos, not widely known, who got together only occasionally when they weren't busy on other projects. Since their music was avant garde and experimental, positioned between jazz and pop with classical overtones, they elected to play well-known material, namely Beatles songs.

The content was recognisable but the approach was not and it seemed clear to me that the listener would, or should, have his ears washed clean by new renditions, metaphorically speaking. Perhaps the listener would even need fresh ears in order to respond to fresh interpretations.

The cover, of course, was *visual* not audio therefore we used not ears but eyes. A large sculpture of a glass eye being thoroughly washed by a brigade of cleaners with mops, soap 'n' suds was called for. Perfect but too costly, so Dan came to the rescue and drew a delightful illustration in watercolour crayon and computer.

We added a balloon on the very verge of going bang being pricked by an impossibly long and ineffectual pin. We also mused on the well known phrase about the futility of trying to reinvent the wheel then made a rough featuring this unimprovable item - a reference to the intimidating challenge of re-doing Beatles tunes. I love the shapes and the unforced, Dali-esque overtones. Must do this for real one day.

In 2000 we inaugurated the business of fine art print making which led us directly to mounting exhibitions - a gallery wouldn't need us in person but would need our work. This led, in turn, to talks, lectures and so forth. Being rather shy and disinclined to public speaking I did manage to do it once I had aids like modern slide projection via computer. Talking about imagery that is displayed is much easier and then later we tried our hand at practical demonstrations where feasible.

I wanted to highlight the collaboration without which most projects would be difficult if not impossible. Our relationships with prop houses, body painters, carpenters, set builders, labs, retouchers, researchers, other graphic designers, illustrators - the list is long - are vital. In order to illustrate the importance of this I dreamt up a stunt where the audience were invited to collaborate, and if they didn't, the result was greatly impaired.

Thinking of a cheap but manageable prop looking a little like a face or a brain led me to cabbages - cabbages? We bought 600 cabbages (an act of surreality in itself), and asked members of the audience to hold them in front of their faces.

This insane enterprise was initiated at a talk I gave at BAFTA and was highly entertaining, surreal, absurd and funny, especially when a minority in the audience objected, refusing to handle a cabbage - what's wrong with the lowly cabbage then?

10
9
8
7
4
3

An auditorium of cabbages has its charm and directly involves the audience, therefore I've repeated the scenario several times: boxes in New York, melons in Mexico, stars in Texas (the Lone Star State) but in hindsight the most successful was in Auckland, New Zealand. I was concluding speaker at a graphics conference and was complaining loudly that the movie *Avatar* was a pinch from my friend Roger Dean. The audience agreed and showed their approval of my diatribe against the director James Cameron with whoops and shouts.

They were then more than happy to join in a pastiche of 3D glasses (and thus *Avatar*) by holding to their eyes horizontally-cut kiwi fruit whose innards, by chance, closely resemble human eyes - 'kiwi glasses' in Kiwi Land was too hard to resist. Kiwi photographer Matt Grace then took the picture.

It was a hoot and came to be known as the *Fuck Avatar* picture in solidarity with Roger, who will no doubt be shunted around by Hollywood money and not receive the compensation that we all agree he should get. Those in agreement especially include the Kiwis of Auckland who kindly indulged my whim and helped me make a picture which is illustrative, surreal, odd, funny, geographically relevant and replete with social commentary... thanks guys.

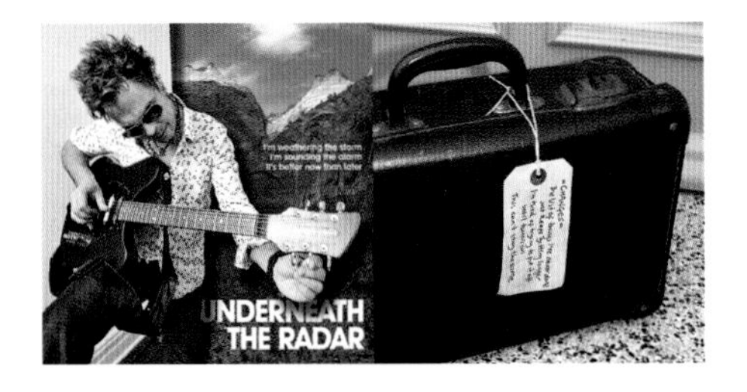

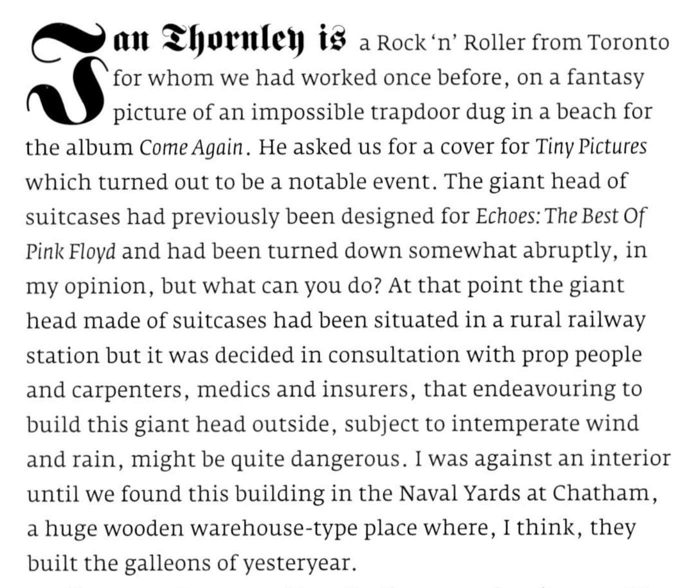

Ian Thornley is a Rock 'n' Roller from Toronto for whom we had worked once before, on a fantasy picture of an impossible trapdoor dug in a beach for the album *Come Again*. He asked us for a cover for *Tiny Pictures* which turned out to be a notable event. The giant head of suitcases had previously been designed for *Echoes: The Best Of Pink Floyd* and had been turned down somewhat abruptly, in my opinion, but what can you do? At that point the giant head made of suitcases had been situated in a rural railway station but it was decided in consultation with prop people and carpenters, medics and insurers, that endeavouring to build this giant head outside, subject to intemperate wind and rain, might be quite dangerous. I was against an interior until we found this building in the Naval Yards at Chatham, a huge wooden warehouse-type place where, I think, they built the galleons of yesteryear.

There was then a problem finding enough suitcases. We thought mischievously that they could come from Heathrow Airport Lost Property (at the time the new Terminal 5 had just opened with a huge loss of luggage it was a national joke). It was not until we hired them from the National Theatre - God knows why they would have such a lot of suitcases - that we had enough to build a head of any size. We like Big Things, especially big heads, probably because that's what we are.

In line with our mantra of doing it for real, approximately 200 suitcases of different size, shape and colour were deposited in the warehouse and assembled on a frame built by our carpenter Nick Baker, he who made the trays for *Liquid Dark Side Of The Moon*. The cases had to be old and assorted, for the look of the thing.

So what you see is what you get: a large number of old suitcases arranged in the shape of a head. The lady is there with her pet dog to consult the great God of Lost Luggage as to where her other suitcase might possibly be. Ian Thornley liked the travelling connotation, for his songs were often about travelling physically and metaphorically, in fact he felt like a 'well-travelled man'.

My take is much more about the baggage we carry with us, and that we come to relationships burdened with our baggage, the luggage of our past. It also provided an image that was a bit spooky, a little more threatening than I had originally intended perhaps, but still susceptible to jokes about a head case, nut case, or a suitable case for treatment and so forth.

As is often the case, when we build large sculptures or installations, the proprietors or the property owners are not keen for us to leave it there and so, sadly, no sooner had we put it up than we had to take it down, and return all the cases to the National Theatre.

Maybe the God of Lost Luggage, like the tree head in the *Tree Of Half Life*, only exists temporarily, being in the mind of the viewer, sitting unwanted on the property of an impatient owner, clearly not an owner of a lonely art.

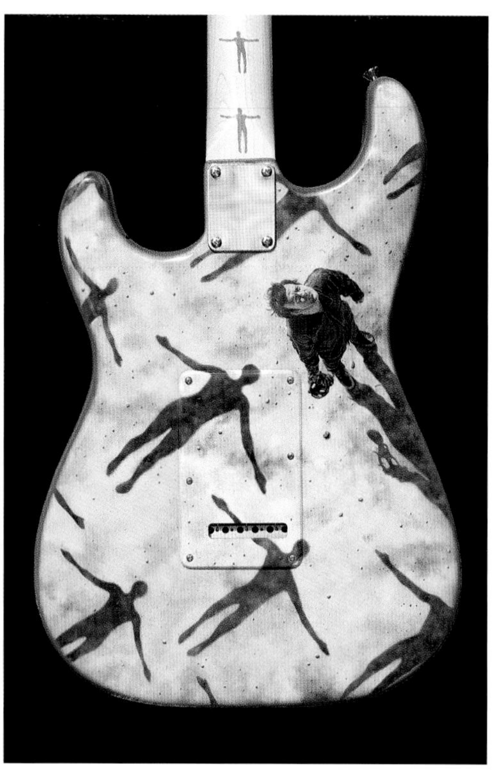

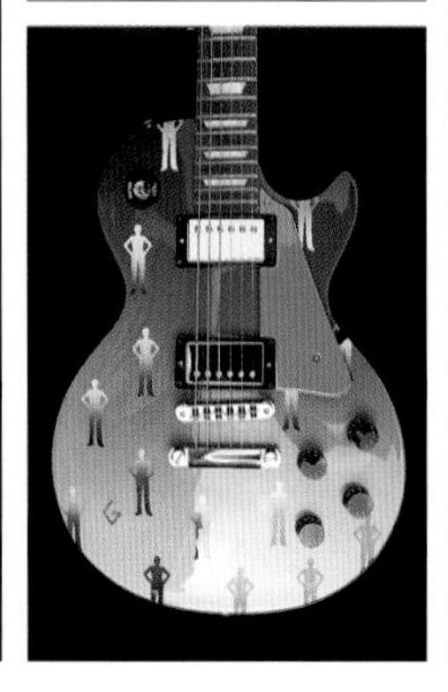
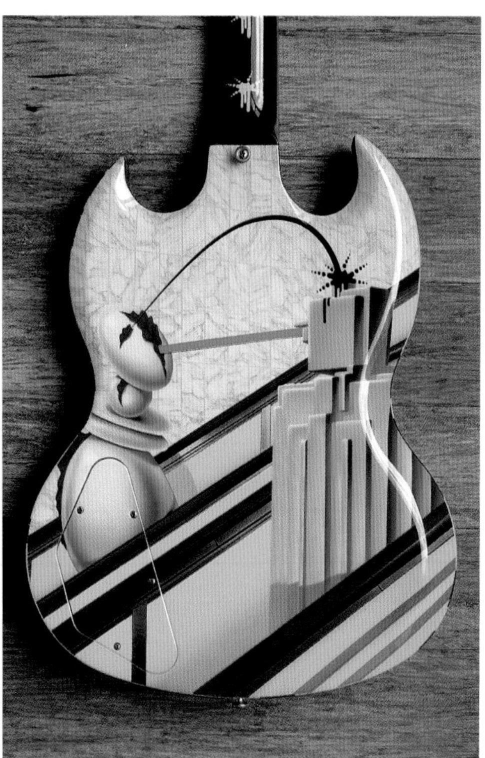

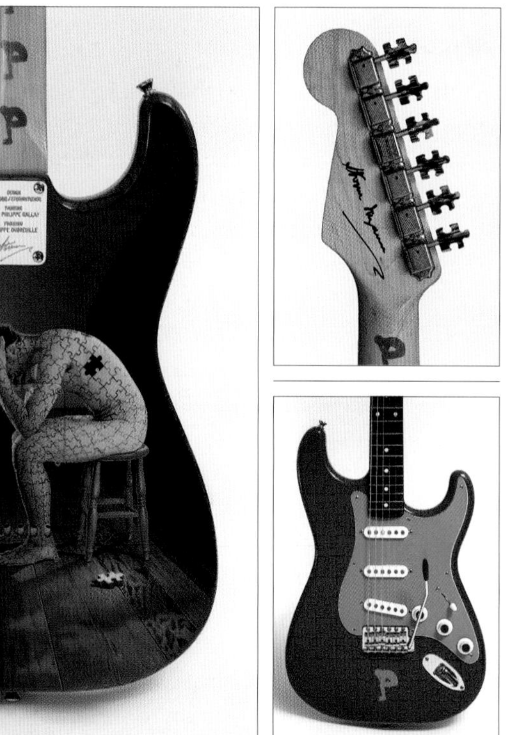

GUITARS
VARIOUS 2010 - 2011

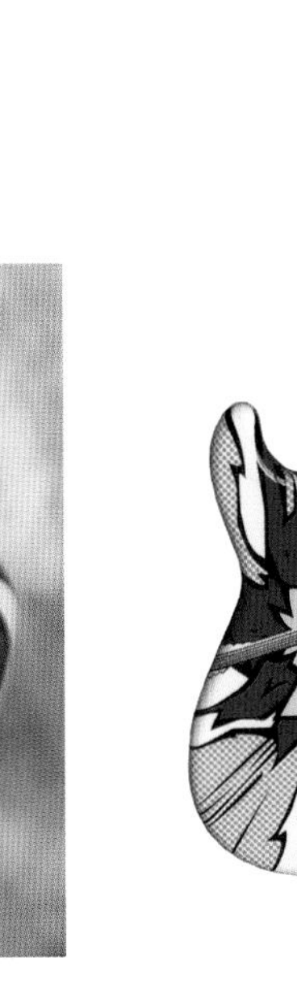

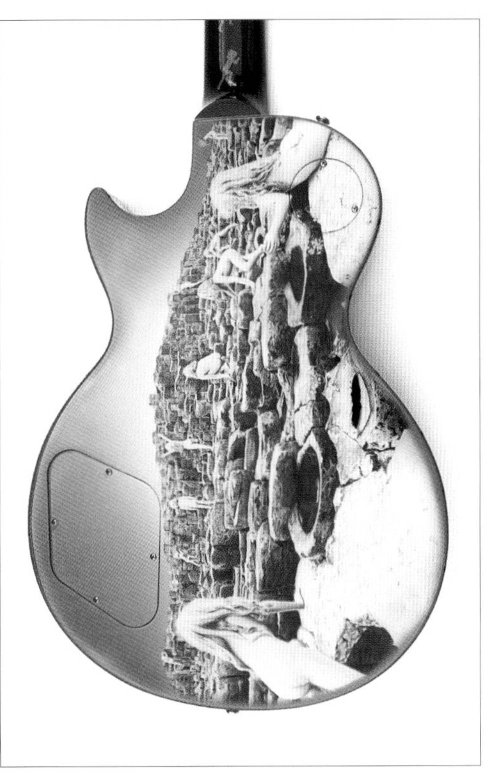

When we were asked to 'design' some guitars re-deploying old cover designs we'd done years ago I wasn't terribly keen on on the idea, to put it mildly. A proper guitar was too 'crinkly', too fussy or interupting all those bits (scratch plate bridge strings knobs tremelo etc etc) to get in the way thus disturbing imagery - oh no, not for me but we tried anyway being game for anything... and luckily two factors emerged to help our cause;

Firstly we uncovered a template, an approach which looked ok viz the the use of patterning on the front, thus 'working round and 'bypassing' the knobbly bits whilst, putting the main image or front cover on the back of the guitar which was relatively flat and undisturbed.

Secondly via a complex set of connections we located two fabulous Frenchmen - Phillipe Dubreuille, master finisher and guitar maker who knew Jean Philippe Gallay, obsessive painter, who rendered our designs in exquisite, breathaking detail, and lending familiar images a whole new quality because they were now detailed paintings not photographs, a sort of hyper-realism.

So each guitar was an individual one off creation, original, playable and looked smashing... we were blown away on seeing the first one completed, so much so we embarked, now rejuvenated, on a whole set - here are a few of the others.

THE STEVE MILLER BAND
BOX SET (BIG DISCS) 2010

The grand plan for Steve Miller was to do two albums, namely *Bingo* and *Let Your Hair Down*, followed by a box set in vinyl, containing both CDs and vinyl versions and assorted goodies. The big discs or records were a development of an idea I had had for Pink Floyd for *Set The Controls*: a large frisbee disk with a big hole in it, a bit like the Rings of Saturn except that the planet in the middle was missing. What appealed to me most particularly, was the shape; when a disk is turned away from direct flat view as a circle, it takes on a much more elegant shape, like an ellipse.

At the same time, the perspective gets more interesting as it is no longer flat but recedes from view. Lastly, the angle feels a bit edgy, if not unlikely or even impossible. It's slightly magical in the sense of seeming to defy gravity. So the use of very large vinyl records not only fulfills all these taste issues but is also a homage to vinyl. What could possibly be more suitable for the front of a box of vinyl records?

I'm often inclined to describe the manner or method in which we create an image, but in this case, I won't. It feels unnecessary in this instance because what you see is what you get: very large records in an empty terrain, perhaps thrown like a discus by the God of Vinyl, coursing through the air, landing at an acute angle and stuck there by the force of entry.

The location is Holkham Bay in Norfolk, England. It's a spectacular place between the land and the beach, flat as a pancake and presumably flooded at high tide. The actual sandy beach beyond the dunes in the background was used in the film *Shakespeare In Love*, where the very lovely Gwyneth is seen walking away towards the sea, fully clothed for a change, with Shakespeare's voiceover setting the scene for the beginning of *Twelfth Night*.

Peter Curzon, my long-suffering colleague, has an old school friend in Brisbane and a best friend in New Zealand, which seems quite a long way away to have a best friend, but who are we to question the toss and turn of circumstance? Thus when we were approached by Powderfinger, who live in Brisbane, we thought 'Ah-ha! If we can but persuade the very lovely Powderfinger to pay for the flight for a direct conference, which is so much better than internet exchange, then Pete could stay with his school chum and also visit his best friend.' This plan worked very well and gave rise to the design and making of a cover that I believe the band loved. We certainly did.

On visiting Powderfinger in their studio at Byron Bay on the Gold Coast, near Brisbane, Peter of course necked a few beers, Aussie style, and spent some time in conversation about the record, about the band, and more particularly, about the way they worked differently on this record to previous ones. They were not always sure what was going to happen when they got into the studio. They tended to bring chords, or half ideas, a riff or two, a lyric and then spend some time exchanging info, talking, playing to each other, evolving the songs and instrumentation in a random but controlled fashion - random because they didn't know what was going to happen and controlled because they were in the studio to do it.

Random control is a big favourite of mine as far back as *Drastic Plastic* (Be Bop Deluxe) and *Smallcreep's Day* (Mike Rutherford). We'd also recently explored this avenue with *Liquid Dark Side*, in turn derived from the 'The Dark Side Of The Moon with Fruit' experiment, so Peter suggested an Australian emblem, a kookaburra, more in a graphic than figurative shape, to be made as a tray with compartments; into which coloured liquids could be poured and left to interact.

The tray, made of an outer barrier and enclosing convoluted dividers in the shape of the kookaburra, was filled with variously coloured water-based paints, which leaked into each other as hard as we tried to prevent it, one colour contaminating another as magical swirls and psychedelic clouds formed right before our eyes. It was incredible! As a final flourish we added flecks of oil paint, which sat upon the surface creating yet another fantastical dimension.

This quasi-psychedelic, randomly controlled, marbling-type procedure keeps its integrity by maintaining the shape of the kookaburra, until the very end of the contaminations, where one colour bleeding into another eventually produces a muddy mush. Rupert, positioned in the gantry, was taking photographs regularly so that when we came to editing, we simply dumped the last 20% as being too mushy for anyone's taste, since mush is mush and a long way from phantasmagoria!

It was so satisfying that we did it several times, partially for the fun of it, and partially for safety reasons, in case the band changed their mind, which musicians are sometimes known to do...

P.S. As well as this all worked out, the band broke up immediately after the record. They assured me it was prearranged and not as a result of our cover. For a moment I had thought this to be the case and plunged into paranoia. Powderfinger were a number one Australian band, and it was a pleasure to work with them. We wish them well on their separate journeys. As Darren said to me, 'We've been together for twenty years, enough already!' No acrimony - just time to disband. Aussie style.

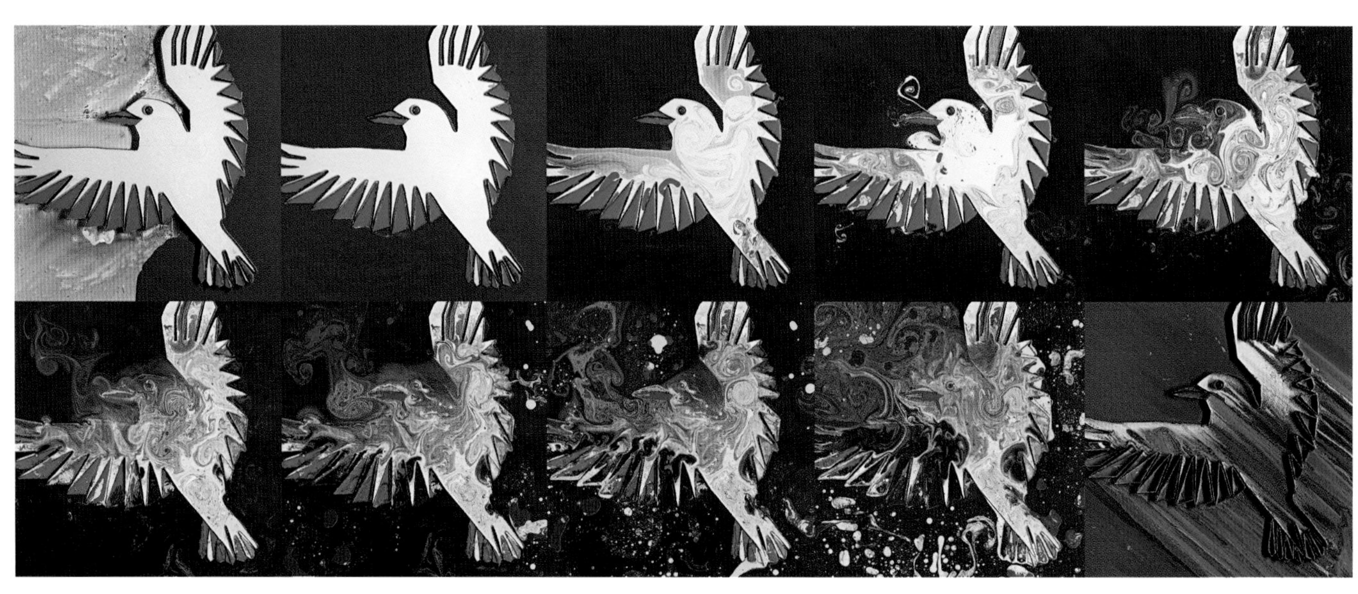

POWDERFINGER
GOLDEN RULE SPERM 2009

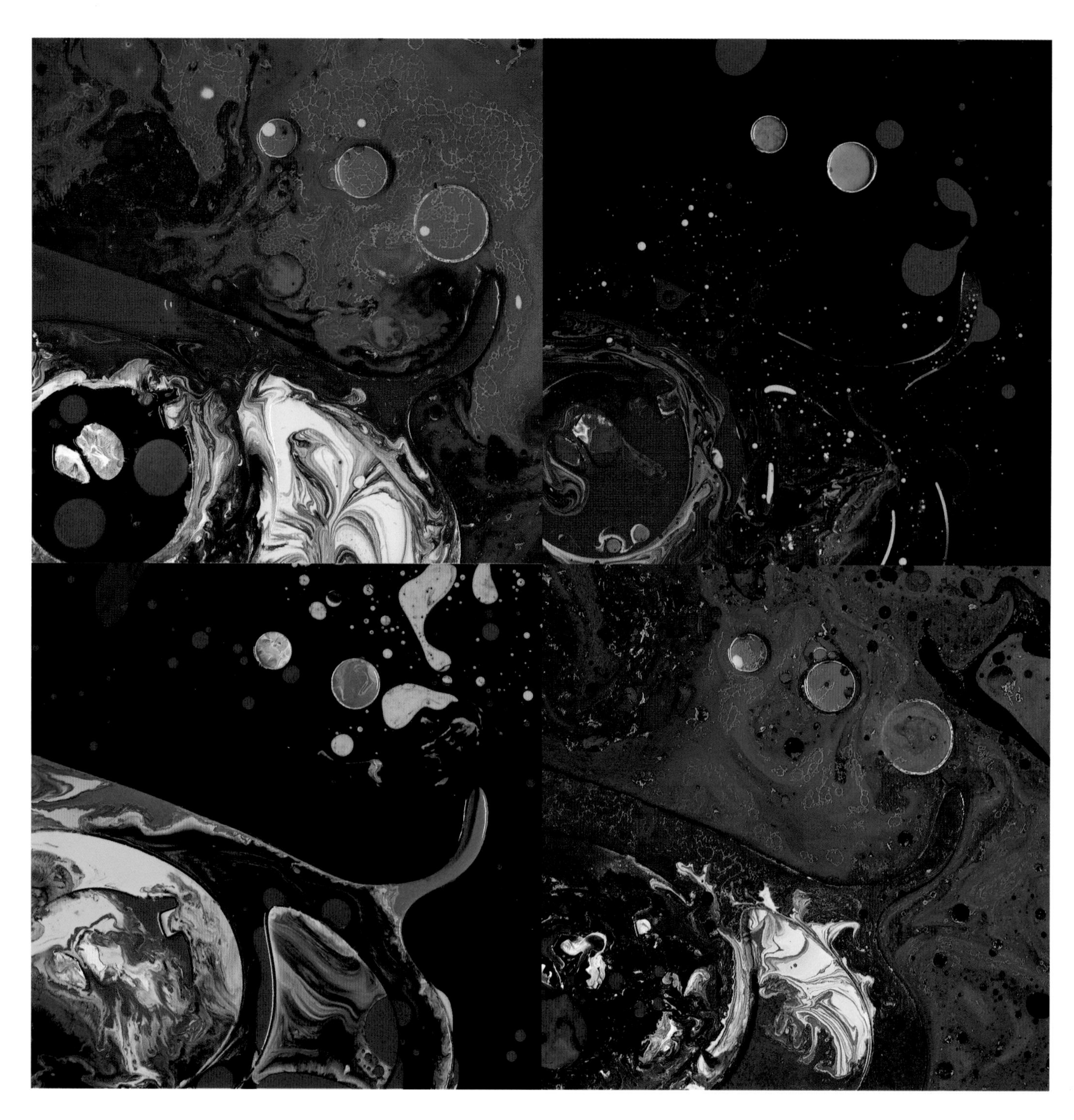

Whilst preparing the Powderfinger shoot we realised that we were putting all our eggs into the proverbial basket which was risky enough, but also years of Rock 'n' Roll dealings had taught me that bands change their minds, when least expected (see Fewsel pg 132) so it behove us to execute a variation.

This variation was known to me as 'spermy' and was a graphic rendition by Peter of the moment of creativity when sperm enters egg and fertilises, which we thought would be up Powderfinger's strasse.

We used the magic tray technique with dividers to contain the liquid paints, which leaked and contaminated neighbouring compartments whatever we did to prevent it, though secretly that's what we wanted all along - cunning ploy huh? We thought it looked fantabulous but the band were not convinced... we were, so here it is - the moment of creation as captured by StormStudios.

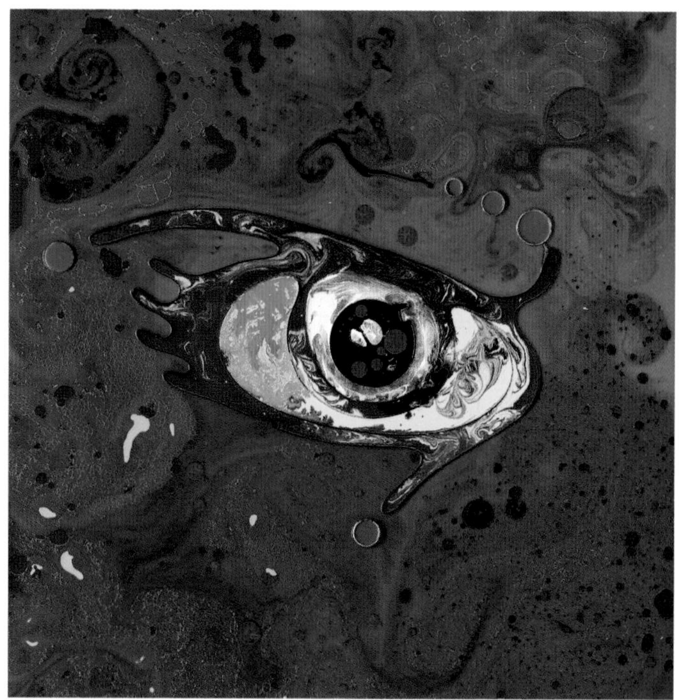

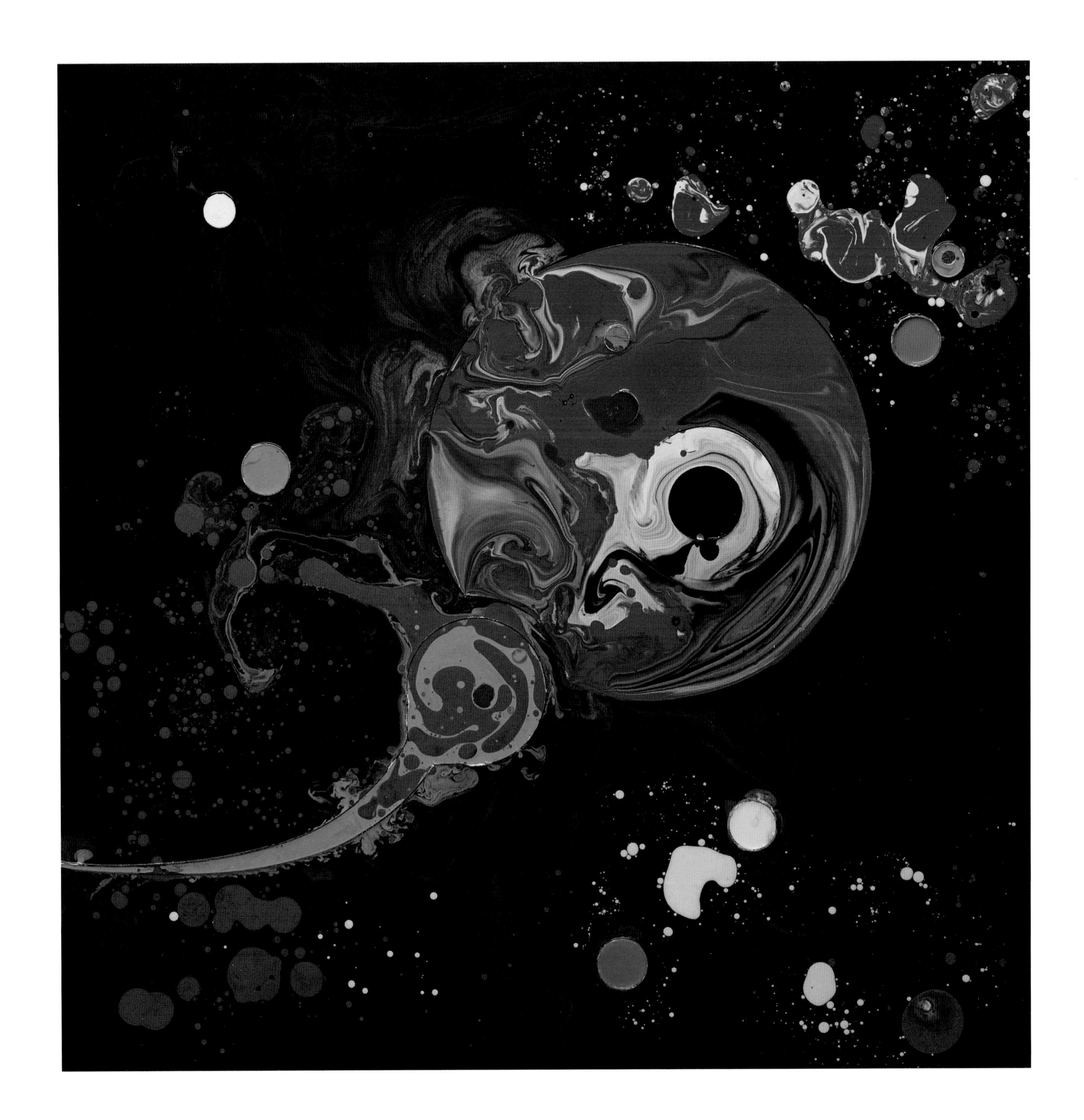

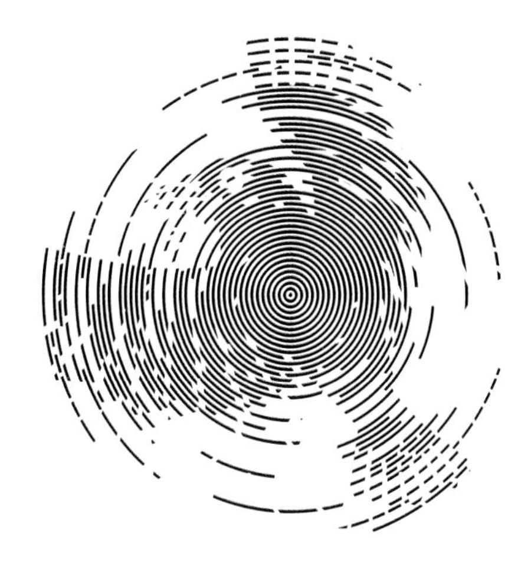

GENESIS
EDITION OF TAKEN BY STORM 2007

Genesis Books publish limited edition books with attachments, extra bits and special covers, presented in boxes or ornate slip cases and the like. They proposed a Genesis version of *Taken By Storm*. Not one to disagree with more stuff about me, we set about devising contents beyond the book, which itself was re-covered in purple imitation leather.

We proposed a monograph on graphics, some coasters, a notebook, some playing cards, a T-shirt and four small fine art prints. Genesis added their pennyworth in the form of a stereo viewer which in fact brought to life sculptures like *The Division Bell* and Anthrax *Stomp 442*, not in bona fide 3D but looking a lot like it. Each book was signed and numbered and the entire enchilada housed in a box which weighed a ton and needed a small van to take it away.

All ingredients apart from the stereo viewer were devised and designed by us and were intended, therefore, as authentic extensions of the book. The graphic monograph contained material not present in the book and was therefore a genuine addition. The fine art prints were clearly not in the book and were also a genuine addition. The coasters were coasters and the T-shirt was emblazoned with a list of words, 1000 of them, naming all the covers and bands in the book and titled *They Say A Picture Is Worth A Thousand Words*. So we did a picture of a thousand words.

The playing cards presented a serious intellectual dilemma: how do you make cards of a design that is yours, whilst maintaining a design that is inherently cardlike? If the design upon the card is too personal, it's hard to play with, and if it's easy to play with it won't have much of your design upon it. It's important to be able to recognise Kings, Queens, Jacks, 6's and 7's quickly in order to play quickly, as opposed to poring over the card to determine what value it is, through the thickets of your own design, as it were. I found this very difficult to deal with and was preoccupied for some days. Our solution can be seen overleaf.

TAKEN BY STORM
MONOGRAPH

MONOGRAPH
GRAPHICS OF STORMSTUDIOS
TO ACCOMPANY
TAKEN BY STORM

NOTEBOOK

TAKEN BY STORM

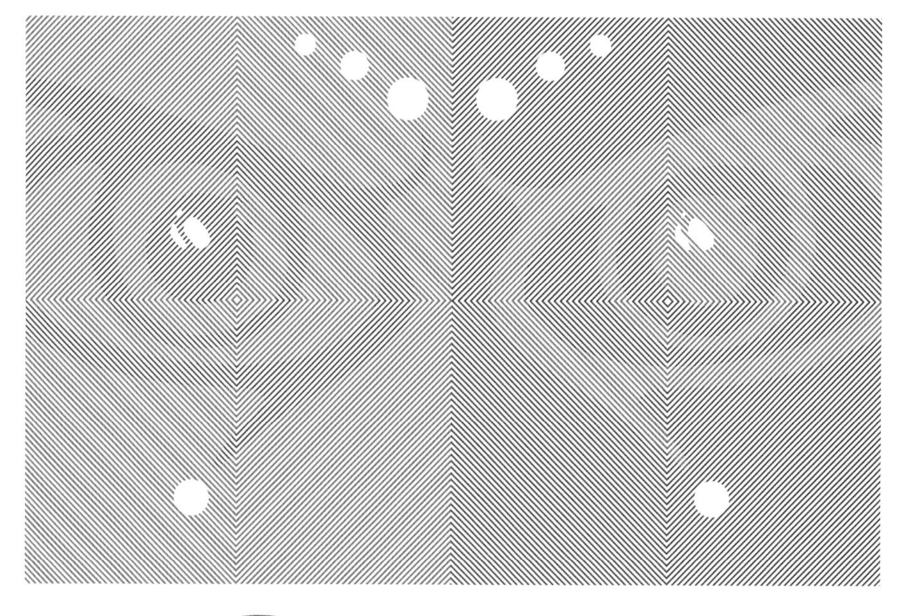

S
T
O
R
M

K

Q

8

Q

J

10

K

J

K

J

A

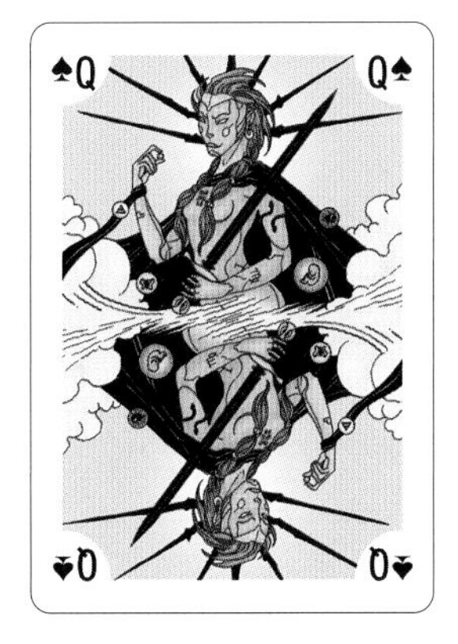
Q

J

7

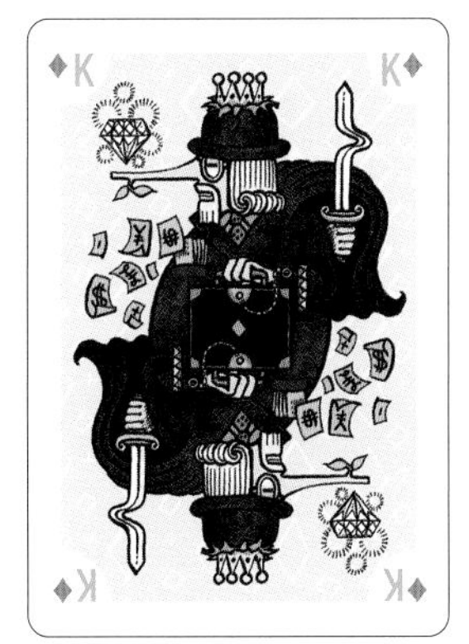
K

Q

This is a funny one. The majority of our work is for musicians and comes via labels, managers or the band themselves. 'Truth movement' is the name of a collection of musicians brought together by, I think, one Cory Feldman, who is better known as an actor, in fact, his film *The Lost Boys* was well received. I met him at lunch with a notorious Rock 'n' Roll manager who shall remain nameless for fear of libel, and for fear of upsetting his wife, who is very nice. Cory Feldman was friendly enough, not that I knew who he was. Sometime later he asked me if I would do an album cover for him. He described his album as in part dealing with a dark future, the downside of computers, the fear that technology could take control of us rather than the other way around... or at least I believe that's what he said.

Some of the music was not at all bad, rather Floyd-like, but better in some ways than one might suspect from a moonlighting film star. We suggested several ideas, two of which you see here, and one rough which I always hoped he would take but didn't - namely the robotic hand inserting a plug into its socket, the idea being the day we should worry is when the computer can plug itself in, and subsequently learn to replicate... you come down one morning from your upstairs bedroom, to find the lower floor rooms crammed with computers, ooer!

He instead preferred the robotic hand proffering an apple, a simple metaphor and a simple prop, as well as the apple core/candlestick illusion. It is our usual custom to do things for real, and build as large a prop or sculpture as we can. But Cory was, as he put it, self-financed, and *The Lost Boys* was sometime past, though I imagine he might have been on the verge of *Lost Boys 2*, such is the way of Hollywood. The apple core represented rottenness and its shape was defined by bites which in turn were profiles of two faces looking at each other, one either sees the core, or the faces. It is more commonly known as the candlestick illusion. Funds would only extend to building a 3-foot, rather than a 30-foot, high prop of an apple core, one green, one red, thus the figure of the man was a little model, but I liked the idea enough to pursue it.

The idea of taking an illusion and building it for real - in the case of *Truth Movement* thanks to Finlay Cowan - is also the basis of *Division Bell* for Pink Floyd, wherein the same illusion was enacted on a much bigger scale, and the Easter Island-type heads were the size of a house, and consequently more imposing. I guess there is a moral here of some kind, some commercial adage about monkeys and nuts, but the more modest enterprise is possibly a compliment to Cory's restraint, untypical of a Hollywood actor, and the result is not so bad (but not so good either).

SHPONGLE
STAIRS OF BUNDHI 2009

Returning to the 2 Simons + 2 Serenas and an Indian ruler aka Shpongle (pg 22), the saga continues... despite the stifling heat of Rajasthan in summer, despite Twisted Records twisted sense of schedules, Rupert and Dan soldiered on to Jaipur and located the old and venerated observatory, one of the first in the world that has fixed entities such as stonewall charts, dishes and stairways to gather astronomical data (see left) including a staircase that seemed to go nowhere, just stopping after ninety odd steps, but why? Beats me. But it looked poetic especially when Serena no. 2 walked down wearing a scarf of infinite length, a heavenly scarf (a scarf that stretched to the heavens). The 'staircase to nowhere' fitted perfectly with the ineffable mysteries (of Shpongleland) or so I thought in my naive way. It was used on the live DVD.

Whilst researching this job I came across these multiform staircases (opposite), more decorative than functional, and was struck by their resemblance to Escher - real live Escher was too hard to resist.

There were a few of these 'monuments' or follies in Rajasthan, but the best was in a place called Bundi... so off the intrepid trio went. They found it easily enough but it was used for rubbish and Dan described the smell as brutal, whereas I was irritated by the vegetation spoiling the Escher-esque quality. I had Lee clean it up assidously and make it presentable, along with blurred figures to affirm its reality - real it may be, but unused it was, and also unseen, 'til now (see opposite).

Being an album of B-sides and outtakes from Biffy Clyro's *Only Revolutions* sessions and only for sale to Biffy fans, it obviously had a much smaller budget, and we had of course even less time in which to complete it (about a week). No surprises there then. So we opted for the really easy route - big horses and their riders, a photographer perched 50ft up in the air in a small metal basket, two naked models, an oversized bed, costumes for the riders and on location, care of a farmer who would let us do all this on their land for the love of it (gawd bless you R and C).

Since this collection of songs came from the same period as *Only Revolutions*, and *Lonely Revolutions* being a very similar title, it seemed appropriate to continue some of the same themes, which is why we have the couple (still) fighting, and the flags, though this time much smaller and held by mysterious horsemen.

The bed came about because 'lonely' revolutions conjure up someone plotting and scheming said revolution in their head, while on their own in bed, probably in a dream state, hence the dark horses, or night mares. Horses also because 'revolution' reminded Peter of an old photo he had seen years earlier of charging horse riders which was taken during the Chinese revolution, and because singer Neil had expressed a fondness for them at that time (see God And Satan pg 31). Horses seemed extremely appropriate.

The circle of flag-bearing riders echoes both the word 'revolution' and the 'satellite' nature of the songs, being smaller or 'minor' offshoots circling their bigger counterparts from the main album. It also added to the slight dreamy quality of the picture.

We encountered a few problems during the shoot, but surprisingly not from the very well-behaved horses. Our usually sweet, mild-mannered model Sadie found it very difficult to act angry or aggressive with her male counterpart, Max. So there were lots of cries of 'hit him harder', or, 'pull his arm back more', 'bust his ribs', all of which Max took very well, almost willingly.

Trying to communicate with our photographer Stuart Nicol, kindly standing in for Rupert, also proved problematic, what with him dangling out of a cherry picker 50ft in the air (which is much higher than you think, dear reader). We tried using walkie talkies via Stuart's assistant, but by the time Stuart got the message the 'moment' would invariably have passed, so we reverted to the basic, yet much more effective, shouting technique.

The biggest difficulty of them all though was the weather. Being a classic mid-July, British, summer's day there wasn't a beam of sunlight to be seen, only grey skies, giving everything a rather flat look. Although in some ways the lack of shadows adds further to the slight oddness of the picture, or so we like to believe.

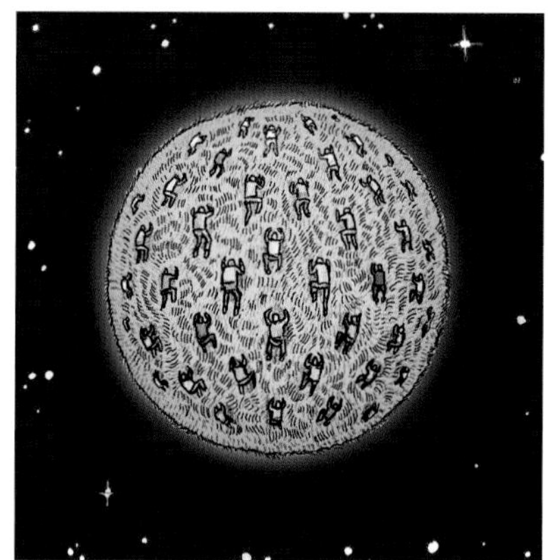

Fewsel are a Geman outfit who requested an EP design for their record *Wrong Side Of The Universe*, and expanded their description by saying the music was about their unrequited wanderlust - always thinking the grass was greener somewhere else. There was this feeling that it wasn't a case of just over the wall or over the fence, but much further i.e. the wrong side of the universe.

Ahhhh such longing.

Our idea was Hopperesque, Edward Hopper being a big favourite with regard to moody lighting and feelings of lonliness. It involved a single soul, a man at the window of a nondescript hotel, reaching out for what he cannot get, what he cannot reach, cannot possibly ever reach.

So we imagined long arms stretching out and upwards as far as one can see... unnaturally long since this image is an attempt at metaphor, trying to present a feeling not an actual thing. Such longing... nicely expressed we thought, but Fewsel didn't, expressing their wanderlust again, thinking the grass was greener, thinking something better lay around the corner.

P.S. In a vastly different mode, Rupert, our beloved photographer, brought along a duckling, A DUCKLING? which he'd rescued for his kids. 'What's breakfast doing here?' we joked. 'Where's your camera?' - 'CAMERA? Isn't the duckling enough?' replied Rupert indignantly.

YOUNGER BROTHER
TRAFFIC COP UNUSED 2011

Where does inspiration come from? The brain? The heart? From one's upbringing or culture? Or, as often seems to be the case, from Kettering, a small town in the Midlands? How does one *get ideas?*

Mostly from working at it, is the boring but true answer - 'perseverance furthers' as the I Ching says (rather too often for my taste). I guess one needs to start thinking about it, turning it over in one's mind and sketching it, discussing it with one's colleagues. Then doing it all over again, and then again if necessary.

Alternatively, one could explore the other hemisphere via un-deliberated procedures, like jokes or aphorisms, subversions, inversions and reversals, all diced with theft and plagiarism. We are amoral when it comes to design - it can come from anywhere so long as it feels a bit custom, relatively original, and we like it. Deadlines then push at us to envisage, to realise, to put something on paper for clients to behold (not too complex visually, of course... we're talking musos here).

In music design, inspiration is derived mainly from the music but also from the lyrics, a title, any words of wisdom from the musicians concerned, or any crisscross combination thereof.

So... Younger Brother were telling me about their music and how words came second, not in the manner of Dylan but, as Benji said, with the music always coming before the words. And there it was - the basis of an idea, a visual portrayal of words coming before music as if being directed like traffic, one line of cars before another - 'words' being held up, say, at a junction whilst music, represented by birds, can pass freely in front of them, like traffic control Italian style.

And it came to pass: we emerged with an Italian traffic cop literally holding up the flow of words with one hand whilst ushering through the music or a line of birds, as if at an intersection, with the other. Beats me why it's Italian, though their uniforms are better if not more colourful.

The words being 'held up' were carved in 3D from polystyrene and they cast a shadow upon the ground, imbuing the the idea with a 30's feel like the text from a Dubonnet ad of the same era. I was excited by this design, which followed hard upon words from the horse's mouth and was both graphic in a slightly dated way and had a narrative: simple, particular and quaint,what could be more appropriate?

The full irony of all this is that Benji, the musician in question from Younger Brother, didn't care for it one jot and unceremoniously blew it away, vexing me greatly.
Now I have an opportunity to display it...

'Vaffanculo Benji' as they say in Milan, Italian style.

WORDSWORDSWORDSWORDS
WORDSWORDSWORDSWORDS

THE PLEA
GUITARS ON TREES 2011

The Belgian manager of Plea, one Renaat, is refreshingly direct, and said 'I so much like a design of yours Storm, called 'Guitars On Trees', can you do that for us too ? As a companion to the 'tunnel' (pg 27). We can use it as the inner spread of a gatefold vinyl', he added enthusiastically, and here it is.

Seen by me at least as a homage, a ritualistic, slightly Japanese offering, despite the band being Irish, the manager Belgian, me being Norwegian and the typist being South African. The idea goes like this... as Rock 'n' Roll guitars are invariably made of wood, theirs are being returned to their source, tied neatly with rope as if an offering of libation, and what you see is what you get. This little pine wood near Cape Town is a favourite spot for picnics. At the time of the shoot, there were 2 cars in the background, which our scout Brendon went over to move. There was a beaten up Ford and a rather new BMW. Brendan discovered a couple copulating and the woman was most embarrassed... they disengaged and drove off in their separate vehicles. Brendon said that he was surprised they were screwing in the old Ford and not in the BMW - there must be some economic reason for this that escapes me, and this of course has nothing to do with 'Guitars On Trees', except that many a wag would claim vigorously that the substrate of Rock 'n' Roll was sex; so, Brendan, no surprises there, all in a day's work, my friend.

10CC

CLEVER CLOGS (DVD COVER) 2008

10cc

It seems sometimes that the spirit of a band is sustained by a single individual, touring and playing the band's past material, much as Paul McCartney does with Beatles songs (and quite successfully at that). The spirit of 10cc is maintained by Graham Gouldman, who has always played bass, sung backing vocals and helped compose much of their best material.

At Hipgnosis we had a long and fruitful relationship with 10cc in their heyday in the middle to late 70's. Their single I'm Not In Love' is one of the great singles of all time, in my humble opinion. When Graham toured the band in 2008/9, he decided to make a DVD of the shows, including many of their best songs. Although many people regarded 10cc as either humorous, conceptual, wordy, clever or catchy, Graham felt that many of their songs were in fact quite up-tempo and rocky, which would explain why there was quite a lot of dancing at their gigs.

My view of 10cc is that they are quirky, musically adept and very inventive, as well as clever with words and descriptions. They were always musical and danceable so for our commission we were going to need quirky dancers who would wear quirky dancing shoes, namely clogs, inscribed with complex equations which would effectively make them clever. There's nothing, we felt, like a joke or a touch of self deprecation (10cc being the average volume of a male ejaculation). In addition, 10cc were not averse to homage and reference, so our picture of clogs inscribed with equations suggested by my son (Distinction in Maths), and written in the graphic hand of Peter Curzon, sees the clogs placed on a chair like a Van Gogh, who was Dutch, as were our clogs. Clever, huh? Clever clogs, clever Dick not clever Dirk.

Machineri from Capetown played mean rock blues and comprised 2 blokes on guitar and drums fronted by a female singer on vocals and guitar. I remembered a Japanese photograph of a female nude sitting crouched, imitating a boulder by leaning forward thus hiding her head from easy view. I also remembered Boulders Beach in Cape Town which has huge rounded boulders, and is home to a colony of penguins. Both were both beautiful and imposing. I put these two together, added some body painting of machinery to compliment the name of the band and their lead singer Sannie Fox who was female but played dirty blues as she called it - a genre more often inhabited by men. Both the cogs of the body painting and the rugged scenery contrast with the the soft curves of the nude female model - male and female elements to reflect the same elements in the band.

This shoot took place in Yorkshire, would you believe? It was the most gorgeous light possible, usually unimaginable in this part of England. Nude + body painting + light + scenery + good photographer (without duckling) = much pleasure. At least for me and I hope the band, back there in sunny Capetown. A truly beautiful place.

SYD BARRETT
AN INTRODUCTION TO... 2010

A motley collection of Syd Barrett material - some solo, some with the Floyd - was proposed and aimed, we guess, at those who didn't know that the songs which propelled Pink Floyd from obscurity to chart recognition were penned and sung by Syd. 'An introduction' was a fitting title for the legion of fans who already possessed the original albums... but such is the record business... especially in these days of parsimony.

Syd's creativity was very spontaneous and was, we felt, partly fuelled by a distrust of authority, particularly in education, hence the swan escaping from a school desk - these were the early days. Fast forward to the later years sees a dysfunctional Syd walking alone beneath feather trees of sadness - an image of melancholy to reflect both Syd's reclusiveness and our own sadness at the premature loss of a friend and of a free flying creative spirit who was like a comet briefly but beautifully illuminating the night sky. The middle years of flowering when Syd wrote most of his songs and fronted the Floyd, and his subsequent decline when he was derailed and 'left' the band is represented by the mirror illusion, as Peter describes below:

'On reading his lyrics and hearing the many tales about him it always seemed to me that Syd occupied two worlds - the one we all inhabit and the one inside his head - where his creativity, or drugs, would take him. His body may have been here but at times he could have been in another far away fantasy world. This 'here but not here' aspect implied a blurred boundary - so we have here a mirror (nod to Lewis Carroll), or frame that appears to both reflect and be see-through. The figure (Syd?) and other objects are reflected, but the tree and background most definitely are not - so is he reflected or are there two figures? Confused? We were, so much so that we were going to paint a green and red pattern on the mask, but for one reason or another it didn't get done. But on reflection (apologies), it works better this way, allowing the viewer to attach their own meaning or images.

Added to the mix and to the Primrose Hill location (a park in North London), were objects and people to represent different songs, vivid colors to match the colourful netherworlds of Syd, replete with charming characters and whimsical situations. And the red suit because Storm remembered Syd often wearing just such a velvet suit.'

An introduction and we fear a farewell. See you Syd on the other side.

RIVAL SONS
PRESSURE & TIME 2011

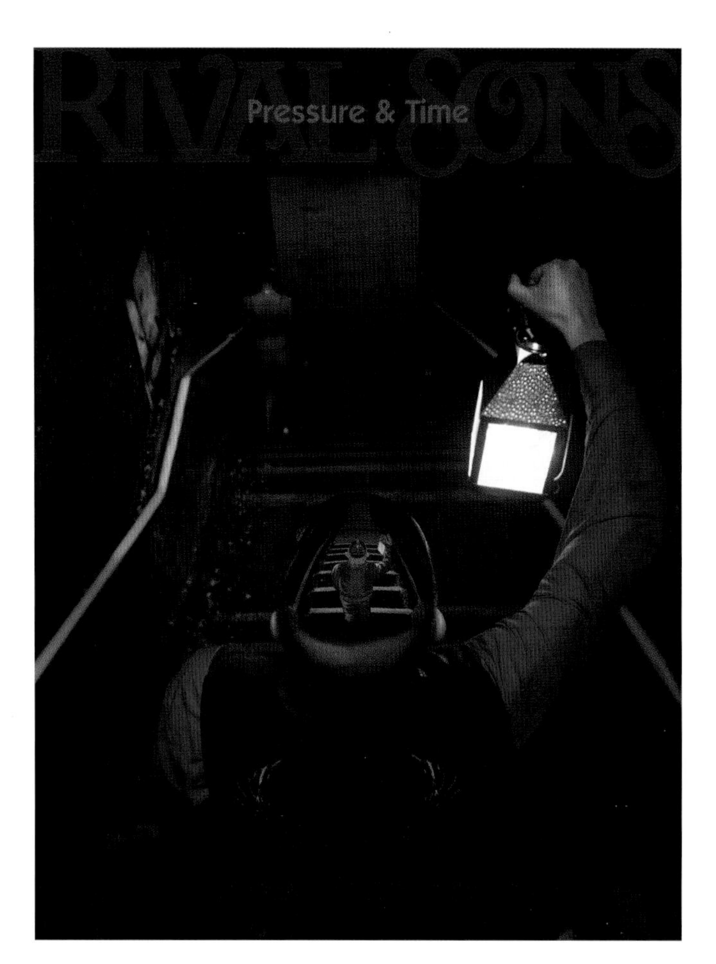

All the designs we do are music-related. They emerge as a result of listening to the music, talking amongst ourselves about it, reading the lyrics of the songs and questioning the musicians themselves. We may believe we know what is appropriate, we may even think that a design created for band X is only, or likely to be only, suitable for band X. Common sense you'd think - but we are wrong.

Under certain circumstances, like being in a hurry because of release schedules, or being temporarily short of inspiration, or being greedy and having too much on our plate, we sometimes suggest old ideas. I feel a bit uncomfortable about this, that is to say guilty, but only a bit, since old ideas could still be good ones that haven't seen the light of day. If a band accepts or rejects them who am I to disagree? Presumably a band isn't stupid or masochistic enough to have an album cover they don't like. Presumably. Rival Sons, a rock band from LA, not only wanted a cover in a hurry but also had modest funds. However, we liked their music, their energy and their enthusiasm about working with us. A flurry of emails followed and out of a range of designs they chose - after to a little persuasion and another flurry of emails - an old idea, a design about the imminent future, a kind of mini déja vu in reverse.

We see from above a man going downstairs with a picture in his mind of where he's going, represented as an actual painting on his (bald) head. In this painting is a further painting, within the 'painted'head. We also see where he is actually going as well as where he thinks he's going and the two are not quite the same. Perhaps we are seeing his imagining, his fear of what's to come. Maybe we are seeing directly through his eyes or perhaps it's just an infinite regression, a thing within a thing within a thing - a theme we have visited before. It may be that what lurks ahead is actually unwelcome.

I like the sense of foreboding, and the suggestion that what lies ahead contains an element of danger which is implied but not explained. You may draw your own conclusions and ask, if inclined, why he is going downstairs, bearing in mind that a little bit of danger and a little bit of sex are intrinsic to Rock 'n' Roll.

I couldn't decide between grand or seedy surroundings for the image so we photographed it twice, which was not so simple since the painting had, of course, to be re-done to echo the setting. Rival Sons surprised me a tad by preferring the grand staircase to the scuzzy one. They couldn't use both, but we can, so ya boo to you Rock 'n' Rollers, in the nicest possible way.

PENDULUM
WATERCOLOUR / THE ISLAND 2010

Pendulum chose two other designs for their next singles. 'Watercolour' consisted of inert black boxes floating down the river in mysterious profusion. It was staged in the River Etive on Rannoch Moor in Scotland, a very natural place, with an un-nature-like addition that would reflect, in miniature versions, both the mechanical aspects of drum & bass and my own black box obsession (pg 20). Rob Swire again wanted to change it but I protested. He simply wanted to make the boxes

a little darker , reported Jennifer. Somewhat hysterically and with ill-concealed sarcasm I asked 'What, no whales?' and she said 'No, no, don't be stupid, what would a whale be doing in Scotland?' and I replied meekly, 'Yeah. You're right. Okay,' clearly currying yet more favour.

When it came to 'Island', the second single, Rob, much to my surprise, selected another of our designs, I had the gumption to say, 'NO - no changes allowed. Out of the question.' They agreed, so what we call the Airfix Bird is as intended, it's exactly what we wanted, down to the last feather. I had had an idea that Rob Swire aspired to more melody than in his earlier work. I have no idea if it was true, but it was something I felt, so we thought of the bird as a symbol of melody - birdsong - and our bird is preparing to take flight. It may, in fact. have just been built and its maiden voyage is being witnessed by dignitaries. I thought both Dan's design of the bird and the modelmaking by Hothouse, aka Jez Clarke, were both superb. It was a bird, not a real bird, but a musical bird, an art bird, and a beautiful thang to boot.

THE PINEAPPLE THIEF
SOMEONE HERE IS MISSING 2010

As best we remember Bruce Soord, the Pineapple Thief himself, was somewhat preoccupied with the uneasy balance of personal relationships and life as a struggling musician, between the pull of his family, and the pull of his desire to play music. Perhaps "real life" was bound to suffer if one insisted on slavishly following the call of one's muse. Put simply playing gigs meant he wasn't home, commitment to recording vied uneasily with commitment to the home fires.

Bruce sometimes envisaged music as a barrier between the inner world and the outer world, seeing Art as a hindrance rather than a fulfilment - music got in the way and prevented doing other things, concealing from view... in effect restricting vision. So we imagined a poetic figure covered in a bandage like material, concealed from our view - we decided in effect to mummify with music. We covered Bruce from head to toe with his own music, little paper notes with scraps of his lyrics from the album. A whimsical sad figure at the window but unable to see out, blinded by the music which he loved to play.

After a couple of hours of this Chinese paper torture, it was clear that Bruce was suffering for his art, tarred and feathered by his own words, unable to move, occasionally uttering a muffled groan. Ham strung by his own creativity and forgetfulness, blinded by his own words, attached by Post-It notes as if to remind him of something that he can't quite recall, hampered by his own creativity, hoisted by his own petard, a melancholic figure, standing by a window, thinking about what might have been, engulfed rather than liberated by his art... sad and poignant.

On the day of the shoot, Bruce announced that the album was to be called *Someone Here Is Missing*. How apt, for the star of the show appears on his own cover and then again, he doesn't.

A bit of pontificating at the end if you can bear it - time to get serious for a moment, well semi serious. Let us put aside temporarily the frivolities of Rock 'n' Roll...

In most instances we refrain from trying to represent sounds/music directly. since we are unconvinced that it is even possible - a straight one for one transliteration of an audio event into a visual one strikes us as unlikely to work let alone exist at all - they are different animals. Seeing is not Hearing and vice versa, except for synesthetes who claim to hear colours, but this is in their head not easily available to the general public, or so it seems. The masses viz. you and I dear reader, are not necessarily privy to this occurrence either standing in front of a gaudy flower or studying a picture of one.

Different organs do the receiving, eyes and ears, different parts of the brain do the interpreting (audio cortex/visual cortex) ear drum vibrations are very different mechanically from chemical changes in the rods and cones of the retina, thus one should not perhaps expect too much concurrency, not forgetting that the visual cortex is eight times larger than the audio cortex. Seeing and healing are not the same. However we invariably 'see' pictures in our minds when listening to music, or certainly have the ability to do so if called upon, likewise thoughts and feelings, which are different again.

We suspect it is the brain doing much of the work- re-interpreting one medium into another, not a faculty of the stimulus itself, image or music. It is our minds that do the correlating; thus we attempt to devise a design which engenders thoughts, feelings and visualisations occurring in the head akin to those instigated by the music. We try to visually imitate the same ideas or preoccupations which lie behind the music - the undercurrent informing the music is then the same undercurrent which informs the design, not a direct sound and visual connexion.

Well thats the general thesis/theoretical bullshit, but what of it? Is it relevant? Does one give a monkeys? Clearly not the 'man eating mirror' herewith which is trying to do what I just said was impossible i.e. be a sound... the crunch of teeth on glass. The snap of broken mirror seemed almost audible as it evoked the actual sounds or so I imagined. One might cringe at the sight (or thought) of it. Wrestling with this whole issue gave rise to the image at least - the image of a bizarre masochistic act,that of a narcissistic madman consuming his own likeness, eating bits of mirror and leaving a trail of half eaten pieces (sky holes in the ground)... reminiscent of the sound of chalk on blackboard or knife on plate edge, viscerally uncomfortable, it hurts a bit to witness. As it does to witness too much pontifying (sic).

Time to go.

15

First published in 2019 by Motorbooks, an imprint of The Quarto Group, 100 Cummings Center Suite, 265D, Beverly, MA 01915 USA.

10 9 8 7 6 5 4

ISBN: 978-0-7603-6221-1

Library of Congress Cataloging-in-Publication Data is available.

Acquiring Editor: Zack Miller and Jassi Schatz
Project Manager: Alyssa Bluhm
Art Director: Laura Drew
Cover Designer: Faceout
Layout: James Kegley

On the front cover: American Dan Gurney wins the 1967 Belgian Grand Prix in a car of his own construction.
On the back cover: Arturo Merzario in the Williams FW05 at the 1976 United States Grand Prix, Watkins Glen.
On the frontis: Generations of Grand Prix greats. From left to right: Sir Stirling Moss, Juan Manuel Fangio, Innes Ireland, Richie Ginther, René Dreyfus, Dan Gurney, Phil Hill, and Maurice Trintignant at the first Long Beach Grand Prix of the United States, 1976.
On the title page: Englishman John Surtees scores a comeback victory at Spa in Mauro Forghieri's exquisite Ferrari 312.

Printed in China

F1 MAVERICKS

THE MEN AND MACHINES THAT REVOLUTIONIZED FORMULA 1 RACING

PETE BIRO AND GEORGE LEVY

Foreword by Mario Andretti | Afterword by Niki Lauda

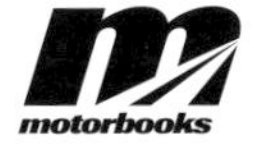

6

TABLE OF CONTENTS

INTRODUCTION

How did we get here?

When you look back across the 120-year history of Grand Prix racing, that's the question you ask yourself. How did we get here? How did we go from the lumbering *tanks* that were the first Grand Prix cars to the rocket-sleds we have today? How did the species evolve from mastodons to cheetahs in just over a century?

It would be reasonable to presume that it happened in a neat, drip-drip-drip, leaky-faucet progression. And sure, most of the time it was like that. Gradual improvements happened year over year. But look closer and you'll see something else: a concentrated period when the spigot was turned on full. In the twenty-five-year span including the 1958 through 1982 seasons, the stream of innovations in Formula One quickly became a torrent. From front engines to rear engines. From carburetors to turbos. From flexible-flyer space frames to carbon-fiber monocoques. From cars that went around corners on tiptoes to ones that generated so much downforce they could literally drive on the ceiling. And then, just as suddenly, the gush reverted to a drip-drip-drip.

That twenty-five-year period—and the people responsible for it—are what *F1 Mavericks* is all about. Arguably the most glamorous era in the sport's history. Certainly the most dangerous. And the one that produced the greatest advances in speed and technology the sport has ever known.

Did it happen because the people who designed and built the cars simply were more clever and motivated than their predecessors and successors? It can't be rejected out of hand. This was, after all, the era of Chapman, Cooper, Forghieri, Murray, Barnard, and Sir Patrick Head. Mavericks all. Geniuses in many cases. But the times were different too. Different rules, different culture, different technologies. And very, very different levels of funding, as F1 mastermind Bernie Ecclestone will attest later in the book. Formula One, meet the Fortune 500.

All of these things together created a perfect hothouse for new ideas.

Illustrating our journey through those very good years will be the photography of the great motorsports photographer Pete Biro, on hand to shoot F1 from the 1960 United States Grand Prix at Riverside to the 1982 United States Grand Prix events at Las Vegas and Long Beach, nearly the entire period in question. Supplementing Pete's archive with images from the 1958 season and other key moments during the Maverick Era are some treasures from father-and-son Formula One photographic legends Bernard and Paul-Henri Cahier. We are very grateful for their help. For sure there are other books that serve as better references for every car at every race, if that's your goal, but if you're looking for great shots from several masters during a golden time, you've come to the right place.

You'll find in each chapter, too, a portrait of a different maverick who was particularly relevant to that stage in our chronology. Be forewarned that the dozen or so we highlight aren't the *only* F1 mavericks or even necessarily the most significant. It was a time of mavericks; this is merely a sampling.

Finally, heed the wisdom of the legendary motorsports author and pioneer Denise McCluggage, who, when asked to try and explain the Formula One she was part of in the 1950s and early 1960s—palling around with friends Phil, Stirling, Peter, Louise, and Taffy—would begin with the opening line of the 1953 L. P. Hartley novel *The Go-Between*: "The past is a foreign country; they do things differently there."

The Formula One of the period that is the subject of this book *is* a foreign country. They did almost *everything* differently there from the way it'd been done previously and the way it's been done since.

So grab your passport and let *F1 Mavericks* serve as your guidebook to a distant and exotic place that, like Atlantis, shone brightly once upon a time and lives on today in the memories of those who were fortunate enough to witness racing's most glamorous, glorious, and star-studded stage.

Welcome to the Maverick Era of Formula One.

STP
Mario Andretti

FOREWORD

MARIO ANDRETTI

Mario Andretti saw his first Grand Prix at Monza in 1954. He made his first attempt to qualify for an F1 race at the same track fourteen years later, won the Italian Grand Prix in 1977, and clinched his World Championship at the famed Autodromo the following year. Few are as qualified to speak of the development of F1 from the 1950s to the 1980s as the only man in history to win an Indy 500, Daytona 500, and Formula One World Driving Championship. Andretti raced almost forty years. When people ask how he stayed motivated for that long, he always says that his passion came from the challenge. And it was the many changes and continuous startling developments that kept him stimulated. Although F1 Mavericks focuses on the innovations, technological and otherwise, that so shaped the sport during the Maverick Era, we asked Formula One World Champions Mario Andretti and Niki Lauda to bookend the narrative with two drivers' perspectives on what it was like to compete during that period.

When did your love of Formula One begin?

My love of Formula One began when I was a child growing up in Italy. In those days, motor racing was more popular than any other sport in Italy. That was especially true in the 1950s, when Ferrari, Maserati, and Alfa Romeo were the top players. And the World Champion at that time was Alberto Ascari—my idol. In 1954, I went to the Italian Grand Prix at Monza. I was fourteen years old, and it was my first time seeing Grand Prix cars. I rode every lap with Ascari that day as he battled it out with Fangio. It was a day I would never forget. And the die was truly cast. I decided that day that I wanted to be a racer.

When I was fifteen, my family moved to America. I thought for sure my dream of racing in Formula One was over. But even when I was driving stock cars, Formula One was always my ultimate goal.

How did you keep your F1 dream alive?

While my objective was always F1, it didn't happen overnight. Especially living in America. I had to establish myself and get personally exposed enough to earn a ride in stock cars. After that, midgets. Then sprint cars. Then Indy cars.

In my rookie season at Indianapolis in 1965, Lotus founder Colin Chapman was there with Jim Clark, and I made every effort

Overjoyed STP boss Andy Granatelli planting one on Mario in victory lane at the 1969 Indianapolis 500.

to get to know them and rub elbows with them. As my luck would have it, they took notice because I did quite well. *[Clark won the race and Andretti was named Rookie of the Year—Ed.]* After the postrace banquet, I saw Colin and said to him, "Colin, someday I'd like to do Formula One." He replied, "Mario, when you think you're ready, call me."

In 1968, I felt I was ready. I called Colin and, true to his word, without hesitating for a second, he agreed to give me a ride that same year. In my first official race, which was Watkins Glen, I was on pole. That was pure satisfaction for me.

Comment on the safety movement that began in the 1960s.

Fatalities are truly the dark side of the sport. I was among the many drivers who welcomed the safety movement, and it was something that had to be spearheaded by drivers. There was no way an engineer was going to volunteer any safety features, because every safety feature in a race car is a performance penalty, whether it's in weight or aerodynamics or anything else.

To get safety elements mandated was a daunting job. But every year in the 1960s and 1970s we were making so much progress in performance, there was no reason why some of that knowledge couldn't be used to make the cars safer. We all wanted to live to race another day. And we realized it was the drivers who could make a difference, guys that the press would listen to. That's how the movement gained traction. Jackie Stewart was behind it . . . and Niki Lauda and James Hunt and myself. The entire contingent. And little by little the sanctioning bodies started paying attention to us and began to legislate some of the safety features in the cars.

What do you feel is the biggest change during the Maverick Era?

The aerodynamic aspect took on a whole new life in that period. It was the beginning of exploiting aerodynamics to its fullest efficiency. Mainly ground effect. I recall at the end of the 1976 season, we were having a Lotus team meeting in England. The engineers and aerodynamicists asked what more I wanted out of the race car. Well, I could think of one thing, but it really seemed irrational. At that point in time, when you adjusted more downforce into the race car, you would pay dearly in drag penalty. Off the cuff, I said, "I want downforce without any drag." And I laughed because I knew I was asking for something unattainable. But the engineers on the team were not laughing. By the next season, they had discovered ground effect. This team was motivated by pure curiosity.

Do technology changes affect the relative performance of drivers?

Definitely, yes. Any development is something new. And whoever adapts quicker does better. Some drivers stay with their certain style, and others change accordingly. It's all about adapting to change. If you resist it, you fall behind.

Your thoughts on sharing knowledge with teammates?

Back when we didn't have sophisticated data, when we couldn't sit and compare computer screen data with our teammates and engineers . . . we tried to talk openly and hoped that our teammate would be forthcoming. Well, hope is not reliable. If I was asked about something, I wasn't always open and informative. Why should I? *[Andretti says this with a wink—Ed.]* I'm trying to help myself win, not help someone else win. But today, you can't hide information, because it's on the computer screen, and everyone can see it.

The dream comes true: 1978 Formula One World Champion.

Does today's data narrow the gap between talent on the grid?

Data definitely narrows the gap between the greater and lesser talents on the grid. And not just drivers, but teams. Some of the lesser-budget teams are able to come within striking distance of top teams because of knowledge. The lesser teams are accustomed to doing more with less. A team with one-third the budget, but with a top engineer who knows how to interpret information, can produce victories for a team not regarded to be amongst the top-level teams.

The F1 car you would like to drive again?

I would love to have more time with the Ferrari I drove in 1982 at Monza. The Lotus 78 and 79 in which I won most of my races were memorable cars. But the reason I like the Ferrari from 1982 is because of the power. All of a sudden, we were teetering around in 900 to 950 horsepower. In qualifying, they were telling me probably around 1,000 horsepower. And there's nothing that a driver relishes more than horsepower.

Has the sport improved as it has evolved?

In most cases yes, but not always. One example: listen to the 18,000 rpm normally aspirated engines of the past versus the sound of the hybrid engines of today. For the technical mind, a hybrid engine with Energy Recovery System (ERS) is a marvel. For me, it isn't. For me, motor racing is still ultimately a spectacle, so you can't overlook the value of the sound. Listen to the audio of a race from three or four years ago and compare it to a race today; only one will make the hairs on the back of your neck stand up. So, you've got to look at both sides, the spectacle value and the technical value, and try to satisfy both.

What makes F1 F1, both then and now?

First, Formula One is the only discipline in motorsport that is truly international. It's like an Olympic event—every year. Two, F1 maintains the criteria of being at the top of technology by having each team be its own manufacturer. It sets the technology bar impressively high. And third, while the cars look different from one another, on the racetrack their performance is within a tenth of a second. All these things are part of the integrity that's been maintained in Formula One and what sets it apart from the rest of motorsport.

My love for Formula One isn't just for my era. It's not just about my personal experience. I have had a lifelong passion for F1, and my mind is full of grand memories, good and bad, happiness and grief. It's part of living that life. It has now been almost sixty-five years since I watched Ascari, Fangio, and Moss at the 1954 Italian Grand Prix. And I still watch every race. My passion is the same.

FORD
58
GENERA
TIRE
10
4

CHAPTER 1: 1958–1961

PUTTING THE CART BEFORE THE HORSE

The tsunami of F1 innovation was triggered by a little-noticed seismic event the better part of ten years earlier. The men responsible were two of motor racing's greatest mavericks, father and son Charles and John Cooper.

It's not that putting the engine behind the driver hadn't occurred to anyone before. In the run-up to World War II, Auto Union had demonstrated it to be a perfectly viable alternative to the traditional front-engine configuration, if not yet a clear advantage. And in fairness, it took some time before even the Coopers seemed to grasp the full magnitude of the opportunity. The great British motorsports historian Doug Nye:

At Monaco in 1950 a rear-engined Cooper ran in the Grand Prix, driven by a Franco-American, Harry Schell. Didn't do any good, but never mind. It was a 1000cc car with the engine in the back, and chain drive to the back axle.

Then we jump forward to 1957, when Roy Salvadori suggested to (Johnnie Walker heir and F1 entrant) Rob Walker that the little Formula Two Cooper with a slightly enlarged engine—1.9 liters instead of only 1.5—for Formula One would be a jolly good runner around the houses in Monte Carlo. Rob immediately jumped at the idea and said, "Well, I'd fund that." He paid for an engine to be built and fitted into a car, which was driven for him by Jack Brabham, and Jack was running third until very close to the finish, when the car broke under him in the tunnel, and he pushed it all the way to the finish, and placed sixth.

People thought, "Oh, these little Coopers, they're interesting things." More rear-engined Coopers ran in Formula One through

Tony Brooks's four-cylinder Vanwall VW5 (4) about to lap American Harry Schell's BRM (10). Schell had driven a rear-engine 1000cc Cooper in the 1950 Monaco Grand Prix, an augury. The Vanwall was designed by Colin Chapman, with aerodynamic help from Mike Costin, two who would soon make noise as heads of their own firms. *Bernard Cahier/The Cahier Archive*

1957 into 1958. In 1958 they were using 2.2-liter engines, with the exception of the Rob Walker car right at the start of the year, which still had only a 1.96-liter. Stirling Moss drove it in the late-announced Argentine Grand Prix, which opened that year's World Championship series, at short notice.

Stirling went there with just himself and his first wife and two mechanics. Rob didn't go. But Stirling won the race, beat Ferrari, and absolutely staggered everybody with his little car, despite its tires being worn through to the canvas, because Stirling didn't stop to change the wheels. Ferrari had just sat there, fat and happy, thinking, well, he's got to stop, he's got to stop, and he never did. Then the very next race in the World Championship was at Monaco, and Rob Walker's other driver, Maurice Trintignant, won that one with a 2.1-liter Climax engine in another of Rob's Cooper chassis.

So the first two races in 1958 had actually been won by rear-engined cars.

The Coopers' rear-engine insurgency might have been even more preemptive had they had more powerful engines. Note the size of their Climax units at a time when the upper capacity limit was 2.5 liters. This was the way Formula One was in 1958. If you didn't make your own engines, like Ferrari and British Racing Motors (BRM), you had to scrounge the most adaptable off-the-shelf units you could beg, borrow, or steal.

The year 1958 was a turning point for other reasons as well. It was the end of the line for the man who had come to define Formula One's first decade,[1] five-time Formula One Champion Juan Manuel Fangio. And it was the year that Formula One suffered its inevitable loss of innocence. Amazingly, no *piloti* had yet perished at a Formula One event. Then, just like that, three were gone. Luigi Musso at Reims, Peter Collins at the Nürburgring, and Stuart Lewis-Evans at the last race of the year in Morocco, where Mike Hawthorn clinched his World Championship.

Hawthorn announced his retirement immediately thereafter, citing in part the death of Collins, his *mon ami* mate. Six months later, the first English World Champion himself perished in a road accident.

The F1 community carried on. That's what one did then. You couldn't afford to brood.

Three years earlier Hawthorn had triggered the 1955 Le Mans disaster when he made an abrupt but legal dive into his pit box. The accident unfolded in front of teammate and longtime Jaguar test driver Norman Dewis, who saw Pierre Levegh's Mercedes ramp the back of Lance Macklin's Austin-Healey 100S and lawnmower through the crowd. Levegh and eighty-three spectators were killed. Someone asked Dewis later if he was horrified by what he'd witnessed. No.

"I'd seen bad things in the war," he explained, "and there was a job to do."

As the 1959 season began, fortune was about to smile even more brightly on the racing Coopers. Nye again:

In 1959 Coventry Climax built a full 2.5-liter Formula One engine for the first time, because it was a 2.5-liter class. That was the year when Jack Brabham won the Monaco Grand Prix, and the British Grand Prix, and (nearly) the United States Grand Prix, and took the Drivers' Championship title for himself and the Constructors' Championship for Cooper-Climax.

It was that year, 1959, that convinced all the people who were running front-engined designs that their cars were no longer competitive with these agile little rear-engined cars, which could be lighter, and were smaller and quicker.

---

1 "Don't believe any of this bullshit about Formula One coincides with the World Championship, starting in 1950, because it doesn't," says Nye. He's right. The Federation Internationale de l'Automobile (FIA) sanctioning body decided the rules in 1946, with the first F1 event later that year in Turin.

Well, almost everyone. Enzo Ferrari was at the forefront of the resistance, famously proclaiming, "The horses should pull the carriages, not push them." Which probably explains why the Coopers were even *more* dominant in 1960. They won every race but the Indianapolis 500 (which was quaintly included in the Formula One schedule from 1950 to 1960 despite the fact almost none of the F1 teams took part), Monaco and the United States Grand Prix at Riverside (won by Moss), and Italy, where Phil Hill defended Ferrari's honor with the first Grand Prix victory by an American since Jimmy Murphy in 1921—and the last-ever Formula One triumph by a front-engined car.

At this juncture, even Enzo had seen enough. When the FIA introduced a new 1.5-liter formula in 1961 to help combat rising speeds, only Ferrari came to the table with a new engine and put it into a completely new rear-engine chassis. The 120-degree Ferrari DOHC V-6 featured just two valves per cylinder, but connected to a Type 543/C 5-speed transaxle and placed in Carlo Chiti's elegant 156, it was comprehensively the fastest car of the season. Ferrari drivers Count Wolfgang von Trips and American Phil Hill slugged it out for the championship, with Hill clinching the title in the penultimate race at Monza when von Trips crashed to his death on lap two.

The prevailing opinion even today is that von Trips "deserved" the championship. After all, he'd held a four-point lead heading into Monza, with a maximum eighteen points still to be earned. (Back then, F1 used a 9-6-4-3-2-1 points system, with only the best five finishes counting toward your total.)

But the opinion is both spectacularly unfair to Hill and greatly at odds with the facts. First, as good as both were, Hill had been faster at every prior race that year. The American came into the event having won five straight poles. Yes, at Monza von Trips was fastest qualifier by almost a second over Phil, but the issue was a faulty engine in Hill's car. He insisted the team install a new V-6 the night before the race, and this act alone probably decided the championship. When the green flag flew the following morning, so did the American.

At the time of the accident, not only was Hill in the lead but von Trips had already lost the crucial slipstream of the leading pack. Hill left Monza with his second straight Italian Grand Prix victory and maximum championship points.

A bigger ramification of von Trips's accident was its influence on the perception of the sport. Fifteen spectators perished with him. Coming so soon after the tragedy at Le Mans, there were once again calls from around the world to ban racing entirely. Shortly before the season finale at Watkins Glen, the American *Hartford Courant* ran an editorial that read in part:

> **Grand Prix racing has its vehement aficionados, to whom, like bullfighting, it is almost a mystique. They have claimed auto racing to be the purest form of the arts, the noblest of sports, the heroic way of life. But even among sports devotees there are vehement critics of the Grand Prix. Because of the many deaths that have occurred in connection with these competitions, they have been called senseless purges by the opposition, and the courses themselves termed abattoirs.**

Imagine if football stadiums or tennis courts were considered abattoirs. If Diego Maradona or Rafael Nadal lay mortally wounded on their respective fields of battle. The public wouldn't stand for it.

Engine location aside, as 1961 came to a close, it was a fair question whether Formula One could ever ascend to the level of other major sports so long as it continued to tolerate the slaughter of fans and protagonists alike.

BELGIAN GRAND PRIX

June 15, 1958

Spa-Francorchamps

14.12 km (8.774 mi)

Pole Position: Mike Hawthorn (3:57.1)

Fastest Lap: Mike Hawthorn (3:58.3)

Winner: Tony Brooks (+20.7)

The start of the Maverick Era. Front-engine cars with drivers sitting upright, sawing at giant ship's wheels, rule the roost, as they had since the sport's earliest days. *Bernard Cahier/The Cahier Archive*

The state of the Grand Prix car is defined by Hawthorn's championship-winning Ferrari Dino 246 (16), designed by Vittorio Jano and Carlo Chiti, but the future belongs to Charlie Cooper's rear-engined Cooper T45-Climax. After 1958, a front-engine car will never win another championship.
Bernard Cahier/The Cahier Archive

4

Left: "It was a Monday evening when I first met the English racing driver Peter Collins," American actress Louise King told the *Guardian*, "and a week later we were married. I knew he wasn't indestructible, but he knew how to manage the risks. He was a great driver: when he won the British Grand Prix in July 1958, they even said he might become the best. He was twenty-six. He died three weeks later." *Bernard Cahier/The Cahier Archive*

Opposite: Brooks's win over Hawthorn and Stuart Lewis-Evans's third helped propel Vanwall to the first-ever World Constructors' Championship, but the latter driver's death in the season finale at Morocco affected team owner and Thinwall bearing magnate Tony Vandervell so deeply that he withdrew from the sport. *Bernard Cahier/The Cahier Archive*

Right: Hawthorn (left) and Collins were "*mon ami* mates." Hawthorn was directly behind Collins when Collins crashed to his death at the Nürburgring. For the rest of her life, journalist Denise McCluggage would remember the look on Hawthorn's face as he entered the room at the Sporthotel where the F1 "family" was gathered, Collins's shattered helmet in his hand. That's when they knew F1's age of innocence was over. *Bernard Cahier/The Cahier Archive*

UNITED STATES GRAND PRIX

November 20, 1960

Riverside International Raceway

5.271 km (3.275 mi)

Pole Position: Stirling Moss (1:54.4)

Fastest Lap: Jack Brabham (1:56.3)

Winner: Stirling Moss (+38.0)

Sir Stirling Moss (5) was considered the heir apparent to retired five-time champion Juan Manuel Fangio, but his reign was cut short by a still-unexplained accident at Goodwood in 1962. Almost always driving for privateers and underdogs, the brilliant Moss never won a title. Here he captured pole and race in Rob Walker's Lotus.

1959 Le Mans winner Roy Salvadori (14) was eighth in an older Cooper. Bruce McLaren (3) was a surprise third for John Cooper after team leader Jack Brabham had to pit twice for engine fires while battling Moss, who quipped afterward, "What happened to Brabham when I flipped that match at him?" The Cooper and Lotus attracted a new generation of fans to F1. Future Formula One race reporter Pete Lyons remembers, "I was a teenager when those two cars came along. It was a revelation seeing how small and tiny they were. You put the same horsepower in the back of a Cooper or Lotus as you had in the front of a BRM or a Ferrari, and it was physically smaller, lighter, better balanced, nimbler. It had much better acceleration. It was like, 'Wow. This is a whole new generation of car.'"

Moss (5) had won Monaco earlier in the year, in so doing giving Lotus its first two F1 victories. Maurice Trintignant (18) had also won Monaco for Rob Walker, in a Cooper, but could manage only fifteenth. Innes Ireland (10, not pictured) came second, giving Lotus the first two places. Trintignant's Scuderia Centro Sud teammate Ian Burgess (19) retired when his Cooper-Maserati suffered ignition failure. Note the pencil-thin tires and complete absence of roll bars and safety belts.

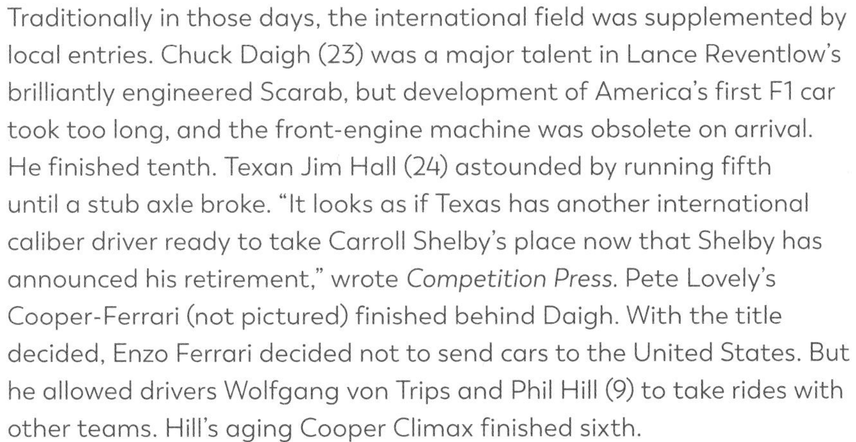

Traditionally in those days, the international field was supplemented by local entries. Chuck Daigh (23) was a major talent in Lance Reventlow's brilliantly engineered Scarab, but development of America's first F1 car took too long, and the front-engine machine was obsolete on arrival. He finished tenth. Texan Jim Hall (24) astounded by running fifth until a stub axle broke. "It looks as if Texas has another international caliber driver ready to take Carroll Shelby's place now that Shelby has announced his retirement," wrote *Competition Press*. Pete Lovely's Cooper-Ferrari (not pictured) finished behind Daigh. With the title decided, Enzo Ferrari decided not to send cars to the United States. But he allowed drivers Wolfgang von Trips and Phil Hill (9) to take rides with other teams. Hill's aging Cooper Climax finished sixth.

F1 MAVERICK

Charles and John Cooper

Many are the major innovations that were not invented by the people who made them famous. Charles Cooper was not the first to build a rear-engine Formula One car. Auto Union had done it successfully prior to World War II. But it was the Coopers, father and son, who foresaw the modern F1 car and said the cart should come before the horse.

As with many innovations, you instantly wondered why more people hadn't tried it previously, and why everyone else didn't copy it sooner.

Even Cooper himself downplayed the thinking that led to the first rear-engine Cooper. It was a small 500cc single-seater powered by a chain-driven motorcycle engine, and he said it was simply more practical to locate the engine near the driven wheels.

But a rear-engine layout allowed for lower weight (no driveshafts or separate differentials), lower center of gravity, better weight distribution, and generally superior aerodynamics and vehicle dynamics.

Coopers walked the World Championship in 1959 and 1960 before the adoption of 1961's controversial 1.5-liter engine formula. In 1959, titlist Jack Brabham, Bruce McLaren, and Stirling Moss won five of the eight pure F1 rounds. The following year, the team took six of nine rounds—again, excluding the 500.

Cooper still had arguably the best car in 1961, but Ferrari were first with a great engine built for the formula which they duly put in their first rear-engine F1 car. At a serious horsepower deficit, Cooper won no races and finished fourth in the Constructors' Championship.

It was a milestone season nevertheless for another reason. Rodger Ward convinced the Coopers to bring one of their cars to Indianapolis, where Jack Brabham finished ninth in the 1961 event, precipitating the rear-engine revolution in Indy car racing as well.

Thereafter, Cooper's F1 fortunes steadily eroded. It won only three more races after 1960 and never seriously threatened for another championship. Charles died in 1964, and John sold the team the following year. Cooper left the sport after the 1969 season, but the Coopers' place among F1's immortals had long been secured.

Charles Cooper, arms folded, shares a moment with drivers Jo Siffert, left, and Jochen Rindt, right.

CHAPTER 2: 1962–1964

SIMPLIFY, THEN ADD LIGHTNESS

What the Coopers started, Chapman improved upon.

As 1962 began, and armed at last with competitive engines—that hot new Climax V-8—the British teams not only caught but passed Ferrari. Graham Hill and BRM collected the championship, but it was Colin Chapman and Team Lotus who showed the way forward.

Chapman's philosophy was, he said, to "simplify, then add lightness." For the rest of his career, his cars would generally be lower and lighter than anything else out there. No model better exemplified this than his Lotus 25, the first F1 car with a fully stressed monocoque. Monocoque construction had been used for years in aviation, where light, strong structures are essential. It had been tried previously in the racing world as well, but it was Chapman who made it stick.

In simple terms, you want a racing chassis to be as rigid as possible and as light as possible. If the chassis flexes, it's impossible to tune it effectively to maximize performance for a given track. Previously, most F1 cars had space frame chassis that carried all the loads, to which were added body panels, fuel tanks, engines, and everything else. With the Lotus 25, Chapman asked, what if you integrated those elements as much as possible? What if the fuel tanks and body, for example, were part of the structure instead of added to it; wouldn't that result in a lighter, stiffer car?

It would. The results were instantaneous. During the 1962 season, Jim Clark's Lotus 25 took pole in six of the nine races and registered fastest lap in five. Only the unreliability of the new car kept it from capturing the championship. Champion Hill's BRM scored points in all nine rounds. Clark failed to finish four times.

Perhaps there was no greater evidence of the Lotus's superiority than the season-ending, nonchampionship Mexican Grand Prix. Clark took over teammate Trevor Taylor's car after his own had

The Lotus 25 transformed the sport as the rear-engine Cooper had before it. The first fully stressed monocoque, it nearly swept the board during the 1963 season. Clark (9) scored seven poles, set six fastest laps, and captured seven wins of the season's 10 races on his way to his first Drivers' Championship. *Bernard Cahier/The Cahier Archive*

been disqualified twenty minutes into the race for an illegal push start. Clark left the pits sixty-eight seconds behind the leader. Over the remaining fifty laps, he proceeded not only to reel in two-time champion Jack Brabham, but to win by over a minute. Wrote Robert Cumberford in *Car and Driver*, "He demonstrated an ease at the wheel which has been seen only a few times in years past, when Ascari or Fangio or Moss have been at the top of their form. If Clark does become World Champion, it will be no surprise to anyone who was in Mexico on last November 4."

As they had done when the Coopers demonstrated the superiority of a rear-engine layout, all of the other teams began to copy Chapman's monocoque, although not necessarily immediately. Brabham would persevere with space frames through the end of the decade in part because it was one of the increasingly small number of teams that sold customer versions of its cars. Racing cars frequently get bent or pranged over the course of a race weekend. It was more difficult to repair a bent monocoque in the field than a simple welded conventional frame, especially for the privateers who comprised Brabham's customer base. It's a tribute to the cleverness of Brabham and partner Ron Tauranac that their nonmonocoque cars remained competitive into 1970, winning two championships over that span.

Having ironed out the new car's glitches during the 1962 season, the Lotus blitzed 1963. The F1 calendar was expanded to ten races, and Clark won seven of them. Seven times he put the Lotus on pole. Six times he set fastest lap. He collected at least one of the three milestones—victory, pole, fastest lap—at every venue. How dominant were the Scot and the 25? Clark's record seven wins in a season would not be equaled until 1984 (Alain Prost) or exceeded until 1988 (Ayrton Senna), at a time when the F1 calendar had been expanded to sixteen races.

It was in the midst of this period that F1 began to lose the nationalism that had defined Grand Prix racing from the beginning. It had been conceived at the outset as a contest in part between nations and their national automotive industries. Starting as early as 1900, cars competing in international events appeared in national colors. The Italian cars wore red. The Germans, silver. The British cars were British racing green. Ever wonder why Dan Gurney's Eagles were blue and white? These were the American racing colors. At the end of each race, they played the national anthems of the top three finishers.

This flag waving was more than skin deep. The makeup of the teams reflected their countries of origin. Ferrari was comprised almost entirely of Italian designers and mechanics and, just as importantly, Italian ideas. Hence Enzo's hesitation to appropriate the British innovations of rear engines and disc brakes. The Germans had their way of doing things. So did the British. The cars reflected those differences. Dissimilar cultures and mindsets were so characteristic of the sport that in 1960, Academy Award–winning British actor, humorist, and Formula One fan Peter Ustinov released a popular comedy album lampooning them. In *The Grand Prix of Gibraltar*, the multilingual Ustinov did all the voices, from the very properly British Foss (Moss) to the Argentinean Fandango (Fangio), and the rigidly Teutonic Wolfram Von Grips (von Trips) and Albauer (Mercedes-Benz team manager Alfred Neubauer). At one point, Albauer explains to the interviewer that after great study, the Germans have determined that it is essential for their drivers to blow their nose exactly seven and one-half minutes before the start of the race because the extra weight of a handkerchief kept in the right or left breast pocket "would completely destroy the balance" of the car.

The purity of each nation's heritage began to ebb when John Surtees joined Ferrari for the 1963 season. The Englishman had driven Lotuses and Lolas previously and saw how both the British and Italian cars could be improved by adopting the best practices of the other. The British teams were using fiberglass body panels, which were lighter and therefore helped the car go faster. Surtees convinced Ferrari to follow suit and to start looking beyond Italy's borders for other good ideas. The same epiphany was occurring at the other teams. Gradually, F1 became a little more global and a little less provincial. The cars got faster, but also more homogenized. A little of the charm and ambience were gone.

If 1963 had been a rout, the 1964 season would prove one of the most competitive on record. Once again, Clark's Lotus was the fastest car; once again, it was let down by reliability issues. Clark won pole for fully half of the ten races, but retired four times. Graham Hill's more reliable BRM seemed in control of the championship heading into the final race in Mexico, but a controversial collision with Surtees's Ferrari teammate Lorenzo Bandini put Clark in position to snatch the title. Which he had firmly in his grasp until the final lap, when an oil leak dropped him from the lead. Whereupon the Ferrari team hastily signaled Bandini to let Surtees through to finish second behind American Dan Gurney and in so doing accumulate enough points to take the title by one over Hill. Surtees's pace throughout the year was abetted by the superb semimonocoque Ferrari 158 chassis designed by newcomer Mauro Forghieri, who would prove himself to be one of the greatest technical directors in Scuderia Ferrari's history.

Speaking of nationalism, a new entrant was the all-Japanese Honda team, and just so no one would be confused, its RA271, fitted with an earsplitting V-12, was painted to resemble a giant Japanese flag.

As had been the case going back to the late 1950s, all the teams were using Dunlop rubber. It's hard to imagine today just how primitive F1 tire technology was then. Cedric Selzer, one of the mechanics on Clark's 1963 championship-winning team, remembers going three or four races between tire changes.

"They were a pretty hard compound," Selzer says. "Normal road tires of today were probably ten or twenty times better than the racing cars' tires of that period. Things move on."

They were about to move on in a big way.

MEXICAN GRAND PRIX

October 25, 1964

Mexico City

5.000 km (3.107 mi)

Pole Position: Jim Clark (1:57.24)

Fastest Lap: Jim Clark (1:58.37)

Winner: Dan Gurney (+1:08.94)

American Dan Gurney gave Jack Brabham's team its first and second F1 wins, in France and here in the season finale in Mexico.

Above: Two of the greats of the Maverick Era, Ferrari's Mauro Forghieri (left) and John Surtees. By weekend's end they would clinch Ferrari's second and final World Constructors' Championship of the 1960s.

Right: Team Lotus waits out qualifying. Colin Chapman (seated) and nail-biting Jim Clark will be relieved to learn Clark's 1:57.24 will take pole by almost a second from Gurney. The Scot will have the title in hand until his engine seizes on the final lap.

F1 MAVERICK

Colin Chapman

No one better epitomizes the Maverick Era than the man whose career neatly bookends it. Anthony Colin Bruce Chapman's Team Lotus made its initial foray into Formula One at the 1958 Monaco Grand Prix, and he was still at the helm when he died of a heart attack at fifty-four in 1982. During those twenty-five seasons, Chapman led Team Lotus to seven Constructors' Championships and six Drivers' titles.

But beyond the trophies was the way he led and shaped the sport in technical innovation. Some people succeed by doing the same things everyone else is doing, only smarter and better. Others succeed by ignoring what everyone else is doing and blazing their own trail—which the rest end up following.

Chapman belonged squarely in the second category. When he introduced the first fully stressed monocoque, the other teams followed. When he introduced inboard front brakes and side-mounted radiators, the other teams followed. When he introduced ground effect in 1977, the entire sport followed. "Downforce without any drag," as Mario Andretti put it. Chapman had changed racing forever.

"He was just very innovative and a very futuristic thinker," says Eamon "Chalkie" Fullalove, a mechanic for Lotus from 1965 through 1969 save for 1968, when he went to Brabham. "He was an aircraft designer, so he understood what needed to happen in a Formula One car. He wasn't afraid to tackle anything. Not a thing. His mind was so fucking flexible it was unbelievable. Once he had one car done, that was it. All he thought about was the next one, even before it had been on the racetrack."

Chapman was obsessed with simplicity and weight reduction. "Adding power makes you faster on the straights," he'd say. "Subtracting weight makes you faster everywhere." In the early days, before the advent of superlightweight materials, it made a big difference. Lotuses were often the lightest—and lowest—things out there.

Some felt the obsession went too far. The list of drivers who perished or suffered career-ending injuries in Chapman's cars following suspected mechanical failure is long: Jim Clark, Stirling Moss, Bobby Marshman, Ricardo Rodriguez, and Jochen Rindt among them.

More than one driver refused to drive for Chapman. American Parnelli Jones passed on an offer to pilot the Lotus 56 STP turbine the year after he'd nearly won the 1967 Indianapolis 500 in the previous STP turbine *Silent Sam*, because he was skeptical of the former's engineering. The front wishbones, he said, didn't look any stouter on the 56 than on any other Lotus—and this one had four-wheel drive.

Chapman invited Jackie Stewart to join his team twice.

"I refused both times," Stewart told *Motor Trend* in 1970, months before Rindt died. "I like to race for people like Ken Tyrrell. Not just because he was the one who gave me my first true chance. But because he is the most serious of all present team managers. He is a man who knows how to figure out every risk. He would rather lose a race than lose a driver."

But longer is the list of drivers who would give anything to drive a Chapman-designed car—and who enjoyed their greatest career success in his designs. Chapman supplied the car that made Emerson Fittipaldi, at twenty-five, the youngest-ever World Champion, a record that stood for more than three decades.

"I always say Colin was a genius. I never worked with anybody who had so much intuition about how a race car is working," 1972 titlist Fittipaldi told *Motor Sport*. "He was the best school a driver could have.

"Sometimes if my car wasn't working right, we went for dinner, I told Colin exactly what it was doing, he'd go back to the garage to think about it, and the next day it was better. His solutions to problems always came so quick. And he always wanted to win. He was absolutely committed to winning."

Like any successful team leader, he had help. Not just a terrific group of mechanics like Bob Dance, Chalkie Fullalove, Cedric Selzer, David "Beaky" Sims, and too many more to list, but first-rate designers and engineers like Len Terry, Maurice Philippe, Tony Rudd, Tony Southgate, and Peter Wright.

But it was Chapman who had the vision, set the direction, ran the show.

"Despite his interest almost only in new ideas, Colin Chapman has to be considered the greatest innovator of the [Maverick Era]," says former technical director of Williams Grand Prix Engineering Sir Patrick Head, "whether it be the Lotus 25 with its monocoque chassis, or the Indy cars including the turbine 4WD cars. Although the 4WD F1 cars were unsuccessful, the Lotus 63 was probably the best.

"[In later years] Chapman started taking on many challenges, in boats and road cars, including the DeLorean project, and this took his attention away from his racing team and car designs, but 'ground effect' awakened his interest. No doubt in my mind that Colin Chapman had the most influence in this period."

5

CHAPTER 3: 1965

IT WAS A VERY GOODYEAR

Technically, the modern tire wars in F1 began in 1964, when Portuguese driver Mário Veloso de Araújo Cabral participated in the Italian Grand Prix in a Derrington-Francis ATS shod with Goodyear tires. Everyone else was on Dunlops. But the proper start came in 1965, when Goodyear enlisted Honda and Brabham.

The battle would intensify the following year when fellow American tire giant Firestone joined the fray. The open warfare between tire makers introduced two fundamental changes to the sport. One, the way it was funded. Suddenly, teams were being offered large amounts of money to align with one of the three firms. Two, the role of testing. The tire companies would invite their teams to frequent development sessions, during which they also developed their cars. It helped everyone improve.

It was a fairly moot point through most of 1965. Lotus introduced the successor to the 25, the 33, and with it, Clark won six of the first seven races and his second title. The exception was Monaco, which he skipped to win the Indianapolis 500. Hill was runner-up for BRM, followed by teammate and rookie sensation Jackie Stewart.

"Three times in that first year, I finished second to Jim Clark," Stewart says. "That was an enormous achievement for me, for the two Scotsmen to be on the podium, and there was all the jokes going around that it was Batman and Robin—and there was no doubt as to who was Batman and who was Robin!"

Goodyear faced a steep learning curve, as did its teams, but it began to come good in the second half of 1965. Gurney was on the podium at each of the last five races, showcasing Brabham's potential, and Richie Ginther broke through at the Mexican season finale to score his, Goodyear's, and Honda's first Grand Prix victory.

Ginther would never win another F1 race. Goodyear was just getting started.

In a season in which only a driver's six best finishes counted, Clark (5) came to Mexico having won six times and long since clinched the title.

MEXICAN GRAND PRIX

October 24, 1965

Mexico City

5.000 km (3.107 mi)

Pole Position: Jim Clark (1:56.17)

Fastest Lap: Dan Gurney (1:55.84)

Winner: Richie Ginther (+2.89)

A year dominated by Lotus and BRM—up until Mexico, only champion Jim Clark and BRM twins Graham Hill and Jackie Stewart had won races—ends with a triple breakthrough victory for Honda, Richie Ginther, and Goodyear.

Above: Mexican hero Pedro Rodriguez (24) makes another North American start for Luigi Chinetti's North American Racing Team, the Ferrari importer for whom both Rodriguez brothers shined in major sports car races. He'll finish seventh.

Left: The Honda team is almost all Japanese outside the cockpit. Formula One teams represented their countries of origin in the early days of the Maverick Era.

Mexico is also the last race of the 1.5-liter formula. All of these engines, including this gorgeous Ferrari V-12 with its "bundle of snakes" exhaust, Colin Chapman tells *Road & Track*, are "fit now only for giving away with corn flakes."

Above: During the early days of the Maverick Era, mechanics' coveralls still got dirty, and even the drivers—in this case, Lorenzo Bandini—pitched in.

Right: Or sometimes they just wondered how they might fare in the race ahead. American Ronnie Bucknum will finish a best-ever fifth, his sole points finish in eleven career starts.

F1 MAVERICK

Jack Brabham

All the time Jack Brabham was at Coopers, he wasn't just driving. He was watching and learning. At a certain point he decided, "I can do this better myself."

Leave it to Jack to show that he could. In 1966, he became the first (and is still the only) World Champion in a car of his own construction and name. Said Dan Gurney, the driver who gave *Brabham* its first Formula One victory in the 1964 French Grand Prix, upon the Australian's passing in 2014:

> **A motor racing giant has left our planet whose combined achievements of F1 World Championship driver and car constructor in all likelihood will never be equaled. Dark-haired "Black Jack" was a fierce competitor, an outstanding engineer, a tiger of a driver, an excellent politician, and a hands-on creator and visionary; he opened the rear-engine door at Indianapolis and raced there. He was a doer, a true Aussie pioneer!**

The son of a grocery store owner, Brabham had become a capable mechanic while serving in the Australian Air Force in World War II. It was in Australia that he met fellow racing fan Ron Tauranac and they quickly found that their talents for mechanical engineering complemented each other. Soon Brabham progressed from the rough-and-tumble of Australian circle-track racing—where he got his trademark tail-out style—to international road racing. He made his Formula One debut in 1955 in a Cooper he'd, appropriately enough, built himself. He began driving full-time for the factory in 1958 and contributed mightily not only as a driver but in the engineering of the cars. A year later he won the first of two championships.

He started his own team then with Tauranac, and they entered their first Grand Prix in 1962. Tauranac would handle the designs; Brabham would do the testing and manage the team. He sold Brabham to Tauranac in 1970 after fulfilling a promise to his wife to retire from Grand Prix racing at the end of the year. When he left, he had "plenty of gas left in my tank," as he put it, even at age forty-four. He won the opening South African round in that farewell season, looked a likely winner in Spain until engine woes, and lost the Monaco and British GPs on the final lap.

Said former McLaren executive chairman Ron Dennis to the *Independent* upon Brabham's passing:

> **When I started out in Formula One in the late 1960s, I worked first for Cooper and then for Brabham. Even as a callow youth, I could recognize greatness when I saw it, and I'll always regard it as an honor and a privilege to have worked for Sir Jack.**

His influence went far beyond Formula One and Indy. In the 1960s, Brabham was said to be the largest producer of customer open-wheel racing cars, and he found outstanding success in Formula Two and Three. And Jack himself mentored and inspired other driver-constructors, most notably Gurney and his Cooper teammate Bruce McLaren.

As the sport has grown, and teams now are composed of hundreds of specialists, it seems unlikely we'll ever again see someone so thoroughly immersed in and adept at every aspect of the undertaking. Former Lotus driver Jackie Oliver, who would later form the Arrows team, remembers Jack Brabham from his childhood:

> **My father took me to Brands Hatch when there were some Formula One cars testing there. And Jack Brabham was pretty famous then, before I even started to be a professional driver. And the thing that really struck me was, he was sitting in the car with a spanner to do something up in the car, and then he threw the spanner onto the ground outside, started the car up, and drove out for practice. And as a young person then, I thought, why didn't he have someone else to do that job?**

As Brabham explained shortly before he died, "I had just as much enjoyment out of being a mechanic and looking after and getting the cars to the line as I did out of driving. The driving part was just relaxation after it had all happened."

Few have ever done so much so well.

5

CHAPTER 4: 1966

ALL HAIL THE DRIVER-CONSTRUCTOR

If you thought that the lords and masters of Formula One, having been caught out once by a change in engine displacement five years earlier, would have been better prepared this time, you'd be greatly mistaken. The year 1966 saw the doubling of engine capacities to 3.0 liters. Near chaos ensued.

Lotus, Cooper, and Brabham found their best-laid plans scrambled when Climax abruptly decided to abandon the F1 business. There were still plenty of the smaller Climax engines around, but no new 3.0-liter. That should have left Ferrari once again in the catbird seat, but neither its 2.4- nor 3.0-liter engines proved as competitive as Ferrari had hoped. The team blamed the drivers.

The advantage should have gone to the other organization building its own engines; BRM stood for British Racing Motors, after all. But in perhaps the most crucial decision in its history, BRM forsook both V-8 and V-12 options and put all its chips instead on an H16 configuration, in essence a doubling of one of its 1.5s: four banks of four, arranged in essence like two flat eights. A neat but overly complicated solution further sabotaged by engine castings that came in much heavier than planned. (The sports car–based Ferrari V-12 was also heavier than it needed to be, ballast that Mauro Forghieri's tidy 312 chassis could ill afford.) The H16 would never come right, dashing title prospects at both BRM and Lotus—Lotus had come hat in hand to the Bourne, England–based firm, once it sussed that Climax engines puffed out to 2.0-liters weren't going to make the grade. That quickly, both of 1965's top entrants were relegated to also-rans. The H16 would win only one race that counted, the United States Grand Prix late in the season, long after the title was out of reach.

The upstart McLaren team thought it had the solution in the Ford Indy engine, which had captured the 500 in both 1965 and 1966. Ford looked fondly upon McLaren. Bruce had done much of

Brabham became the first man in history to win a Formula One title in his own car.

the development work on the Ford GT and during the course of 1966 would win, with fellow Kiwi Chris Amon, the prize company chairman Henry Ford II lusted after most, the 24 Hours of Le Mans. Take that, Enzo. But the Indy engine, destroked from 4.2 liters to 3.0 and converted to run on gasoline, was a disaster.

In the end, the two entrants best positioned to capitalize on the new engine rules were the two that improvised the most cleverly, Cooper and Brabham. Cooper arranged with Maserati to take its ten-year-old V-12 out of mothballs and update it for service in the new F1. No, seriously. And it mostly worked. For its part, Brabham took a hard look at its 2.5-liter Oldsmobile-based aluminum V-8 Tasman Series motor and asked engine-building partner Repco, the Australian aftermarket parts maker, whether it could be expanded to 3.0. It could.

Brabham and Cooper took the first four places in the championship.

Beyond the change in engine formula, 1966 was also the year of the driver-constructor, a new phenomenon in F1. Brabham's outfit had been in operation for several seasons now, but over the course of 1966, Black Jack became both the first man to win a Formula One race in his own car and the first (and still the only) to win a championship. He was soon joined by Bruce McLaren and Dan Gurney in the pursuit. Each of the three had his own motivations for building his own cars, but part of it had to do with the recognition of a fundamental shift in the balance between driver and machine. In the 1950s, car and driver were felt to be roughly equal contributors to a team's success. A good driver could overcome a lesser car. Fangio and Moss proved that time and time again.

This was no longer the case.

"There isn't as much difference between the drivers as there is between the cars," McLaren told Peter Manso in 1969 in Manso's landmark book of F1 interviews, *VROOOM!!* "You can see it, just study lap times carefully—once you get a bunch of fairly good drivers, you've got the same lap times. If you take the best driver in the world, put him in a car of two years ago, he's going to be last. That's the reason for Gurney, Surtees,[1] Brabham, and my own relationship with [building] the car. The car, the quality of its engineering is 75 percent of one's success."

A turning point in the season came in the second race, in Belgium. Rain was common at Spa. Partly because it was Belgium, partly because the track then ran 8.77 miles, a large enough expanse that it could be raining on one part of the circuit and sunny on another. The weather this year was particularly bad. So much so that on the opening lap, half the starting field retired from the race, cars aquaplaning everywhere. Jackie Stewart ended up in a ditch by the Masta Kink, soaked in gasoline, trapped by the steering wheel in his twisted BRM with no means to cut the electrics. Not a marshal in sight. Only the brave intervention of Bob Bondurant and Graham Hill, both of whom had crashed nearby, and a wrench borrowed from a spectator to remove the wheel, kept the incident from turning into a disaster. Stewart would keep a wrench taped to the inside of his cockpit for the rest of his career.

It was a watershed moment for Stewart and an even bigger one for Formula One. The safety movement had begun.

Another turning point, one that would alter the trajectory of the Ferrari team, came at the end of the race. Belgium was the first championship F1 race for John Surtees since a horrific crash at Mosport the previous September had left him so grievously injured that there was longstanding doubt he would race again.

"Flat-out past the pits a front upright broke. The car went off, and over and over," he told *Motor Sport*.

---

1 Surtees would begin fielding his own eponymous entries in 1969, the same year McLaren spoke to Manso.

His legs were so badly damaged that even after several operations by the same doctor who had put Moss back together a few years earlier, they would never be the same length again. Ferrari graciously promised Surtees that there would be a car for him whenever he came back, even if it meant it had to be outfitted with an automatic transmission.

Fortunately, it didn't come to that, although the recovery came in painful stages: the first time he drove an F1 car after the accident, the mechanics had to use an engine hoist to lift him in and out. At Belgium, Surtees shocked perhaps everyone but himself when he put his Ferrari on pole. He followed this up on race day with a masterful victory over Rindt's Cooper.

Then the trouble started. Instead of congratulating Surtees's dramatic return to form, Ferrari team manager Eugenio Dragoni reported back to Maranello that Surtees had disgraced the team by running second for most of the twenty-eight laps to a Maserati-powered car. *How dare he.* Dragoni had either missed or ignored the fact that this was the strategy that had won Surtees the race. One of the dangers at Spa in those conditions was the streams of water that ran across the track, instantly inducing an aquaplane condition that could be impossible to recover from. Surtees had cannily tucked in behind Rindt, whose Cooper was on superior Dunlop rain tires, so that he could drive in his tracks until conditions improved.

The insult was compounded almost immediately.

"A few days later we were at Le Mans," Surtees told *Motor Sport*. "I said to Dragoni: 'The Fords are being driven by real racers—Gurney, Andretti, Amon, McLaren—and the only way we'll beat them is if I go flat out from the fall of the flag and try to break them.' But when Dragoni heard that Gianni Agnelli, the head of Fiat,[2] was coming to watch the race, he decided that my codriver Scarfiotti—who was not only Italian but was actually related to Agnelli—would drive from the start."

Ludovico Scarfiotti, a hillclimb specialist, had been proclaimed Italy's best driver in 1962 and 1965 and won Le Mans in 1963. But no one, including Ferrari, had ever considered him at Surtees's level.

The man the Italians called *Il Grande John* had had enough. He left the team and joined Cooper, where he might have challenged for the championship had Cooper enjoyed any reliability at all. It didn't. Surtees never finished lower than third in the remaining seven races, including winning the season finale in Mexico with that ten-year-old Maserati engine strapped to his back, but he dropped out of four of them. He came second to Brabham in the final standings.

Finally, 1966 was the year of John Frankenheimer's landmark film *Grand Prix*, which became one of the top ten grossing movies of the year and propelled F1 to a new degree of consciousness and prestige throughout the world.

Many felt the plot was pure hokum, but the racing scenes were spectacular. The most memorable lines were lifted straight from Robert Daley's bestseller *The Cruel Sport*, including when Yves Montand as Jean-Pierre Sarti says, "[When I was younger] I'd see an accident like that and be so weak inside that I wanted to quit—stop the car and walk away. I could hardly make myself go past it. But I'm older now. When I see something really horrible, I put my foot down. Hard! Because I know that everyone else is lifting his."

It was something Phil Hill had told Daley years earlier.

2 After negotiations with Ford fell through a few years prior, Ferrari increasingly looked to Fiat for its salvation. In fact, Fiat would go on to acquire a major stake in Ferrari three years later.

BELGIAN GRAND PRIX

June 12, 1966

Spa-Francorchamps

14.12 km (8.770 mi)

Pole Position: John Surtees (3:38.0)

Fastest Lap: John Surtees (4:18.7)

Winner: John Surtees (+42.1)

"I made the decision to follow Jochen Rindt in his Cooper-Maserati, which had Dunlop all-weather tires," John Surtees said in his autobiography, "and sat behind him for some laps before passing and going on to a comfortable win. Only five cars survived the soaking conditions. Team manager Dragoni's response was to criticize me for having allowed a Maserati-engined car to lead!"

Start of the race. Third-fastest qualifier Jackie Stewart (15) in the Dunlop-shod BRM P261 waits for Jochen Rindt (19) in the Maserati-powered Cooper T81 and pole sitter John Surtees (6) in the Firestone-shod Ferrari 312. One of the mechanics has discreetly placed a sandbag under the BRM's front tire to keep the car from rolling forward on the slightly downhill starting line.

GOODYEAR

Opposite: During the weekend, filming continued on John Frankenheimer's epic *Grand Prix*. Here, Eva Marie Saint and Yves Montand, who played the Jean-Pierre Sarti character, face the camera. French singer-heartthrob Françoise Hardy leans against the pitbox wall. 1961 World Champion Phil Hill was allowed on the track in a Ford GT camera car to film the opening lap. Imagine that happening today.

Top right: *Grand Prix* star James Garner (right) with All-American Racers cofounder Carroll Shelby. "At the end of three hours, you felt as though you'd been in the races, not at the races," Garner said years later. "I think it's still the greatest auto racing picture ever made."

Bottom right: Frankenheimer (left) insisted on shooting much of the movie at the actual races. "When I look back, I don't know how the hell we ever did that film," he told *Motor Sport*. "We were always shooting, usually where we weren't wanted, and usually with everything out of our control. But we just *had* to get those crowds."

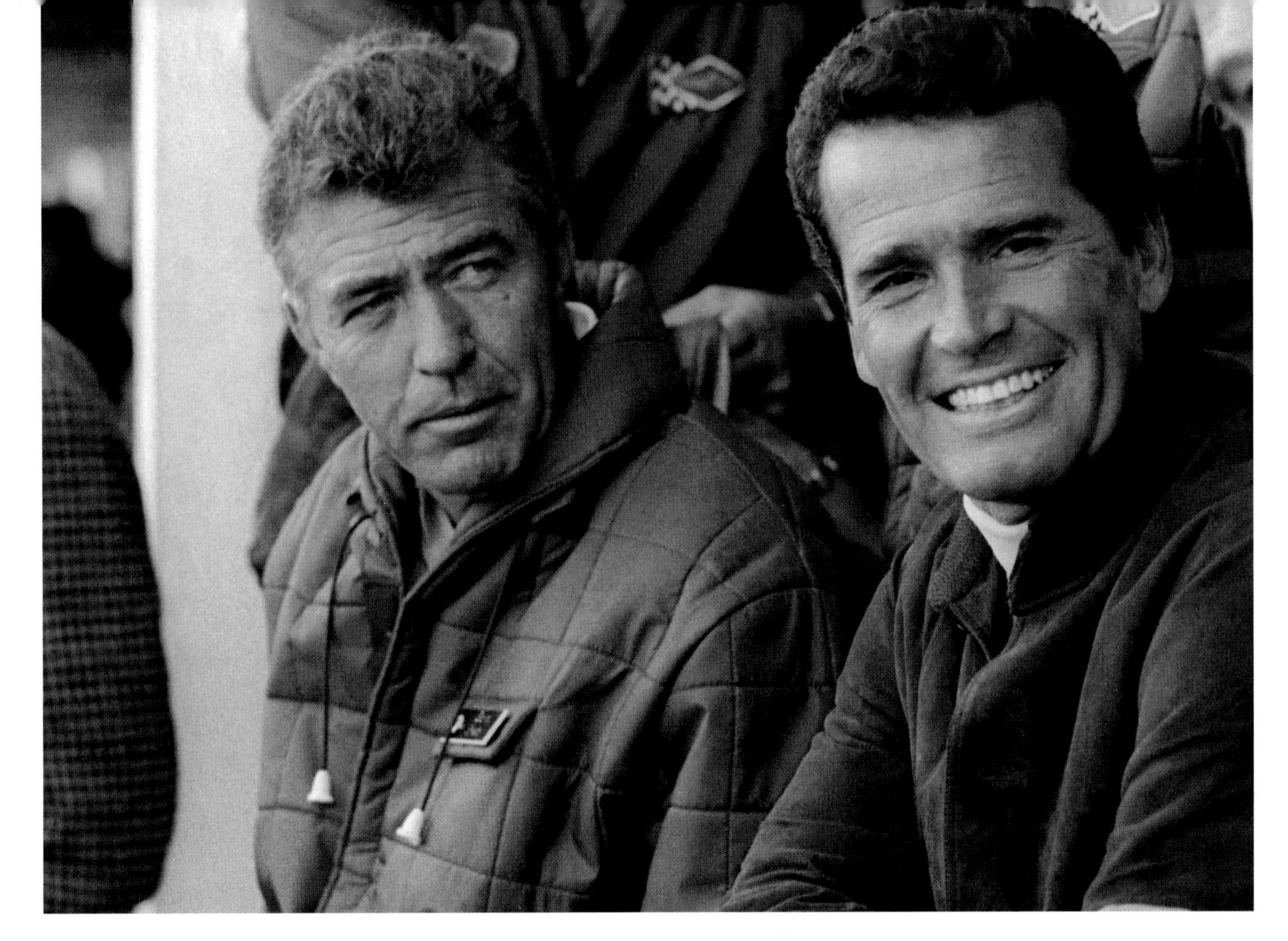

Left: The debut race for Dan Gurney as a driver-constructor. The Eagle used a creaky four-cylinder 2.7-liter Coventry-Climax as a stopgap. It would begin to fly later in the season when the Aubrey Woods–designed Weslake V-12 arrived.

Below: Privateer Guy Ligier would become a constructor after his driving days. Here the Frenchman enters the famous La Source hairpin, named for the hotel. His Cooper-Maserati struggled to sixth, just ahead of Gurney, but neither was classified because of the distance behind the race leaders.

Left: Back in the pits, Graham Hill describes the harrowing scene extricating his teammate Jackie Stewart from his twisted BRM . . .

. . . while (below) Lotus driver Jim Clark explains that his Climax engine had expired on lap one before he could reach the wall of water at Burneville.

F1 MAVERICK

Dan Gurney

Dan Gurney was the All-American racer long before he started the racing team of the same name. You can still find "Dan Gurney for President" stickers on racing toolboxes from the 1960s and 1970s.

Gurney grew up in the Southern California hot-rodding movement, then transitioned to road racing, where he made an instant impression. He was one of the first Americans in Formula One, having joined the circuit in 1959 for Scuderia Ferrari before moving to BRM in 1960.

He had a habit of leaving teams just before they got really good. Ferrari would win the World Championship in 1961 and 1964, BRM in 1962. After a couple of seasons with Porsche, Gurney joined the young Brabham organization, where in 1964 he scored the team's first F1 victory and outpointed team leader Jack all three of their seasons together. Gurney left at the end of 1965, just before Brabham won back-to-back titles.

To Dan that was incidental. He had left Brabham when he did to win a World Championship on his own—with an American car of his own construction.

"In 1966 we both went our separate ways," Gurney told www.PeterWindsor.com. "I followed the trail he had blazed by trying to build, race, and win with my own F1 cars. I have been told that only three men in the history of motor racing have managed to do that. Bruce McLaren and I won races, but Sir Jack Brabham won World Championships. He will be forever in a class by himself."

That first year was a humbling one for Gurney. The chassis was ready, but the Weslake V-12 he'd arranged for—typical Gurney, he was going to do it his way, including engine—was not. But in 1967, the AAR Eagle-Weslake, even with a power deficit and serious reliability issues, was one of the few cars to seriously challenge the DFV-equipped Lotus 49 for speed. When Graham Hill won a debut pole for the 49 at Zandvoort, it was Gurney who qualified second.

Dan's day of days came at the next race on the calendar, the Belgian Grand Prix, which he won a week after his triumph at Le Mans with fellow American A. J. Foyt. He was leading the German Grand Prix with only a few laps to go when an improperly machined half shaft failed. Reliability issues caused him to retire from every race except Belgium and the Canadian Grand Prix, where he finished third, but the point had been made. The Eagle had flown. The American national anthem was played at a Grand Prix, just the way he'd imagined it.

"Standing up there while 'The Star-Spangled Banner' was played was mighty high," Gurney told *Motor Sport*'s Simon Taylor. "I'll tell you something that addresses it a bit. In those days, flying back and forth over the Atlantic in heavy weather got a bit iffy sometimes. I used to say, 'Come on, airplane, don't go down, I haven't won a Grand Prix in an Eagle yet.' After Spa I'd say to the airplane, 'If you want to go down now, it's okay. . . .'"

By most accounts, including fellow American Mario Andretti's, Dan would likely have won one if not several World Championships had he continued driving for top teams instead of designing, building, and racing his own American Formula One car. Jim Clark's father told Gurney that he was the only driver his son feared. But mavericks aren't wired that way. After a long career that saw him take the checkered flag in F1, NASCAR, Indy, Le Mans, Can-Am and Trans-Am events; build championship-winning Indy and IMSA cars; and invent the Gurney flap, which revolutionized wing efficiency, he had no regrets about the path he had chosen. "Genuinely, sincerely," he told us before his passing in 2018, "I feel very fortunate to have done it the way we did."

The All-American racer's beak-nosed Eagle remains the only American-built car to win an F1 race

UNITED STATES GRAND PRIX

October 2, 1966

Watkins Glen

3.78 km (2.35 mi)

Pole Position: Jack Brabham (1:08.42)

Fastest Lap: John Surtees (1:09.67)

Winner: Jim Clark (+1 lap)

Clark in a very different frame of mind after capturing the rich United States Grand Prix at Watkins Glen, the BRM H16 engine's only championship victory and Clark's only victory during the 1966 season after dominating 1965. Lotus boss Colin Chapman (opposite page) tosses his cap in the air as Clark crosses the finish line in upstate New York. It was the fourth straight USGP victory for a BRM-powered car.

KENDALL MOTOR OILS

Above left and right: Clark was followed home by Cooper-Maserati teammates Jochen Rindt (8) and John Surtees (7). Bottom left: Clark enjoys a funny moment during practice with Chapman (right) and the lads. Bottom right: Bob Bondurant (16) holds court in the second Eagle, while team manager Bill Dunne (kneeling) and mechanic Mike Lohman listen. Neither Eagle qualified well or lasted long in the race. Opposite: Denny Hulme confers with Phil Kerr in the Brabham pits.

Clockwise from top left: The BRM H16 featured four separate four-into-one exhausts, one for each bank of cylinders. The 3.0-liter Honda V-12 showed up late in the season and set fastest lap in Mexico. The Maserati was big and old, but one of the revelations of the 1966 season. The four-cam Ford Indy engine never really translated to Formula One, much to McLaren's chagrin.

Honda mechanics burn the midnight oil in the Kendall Garage preparing the cars for Bucknum (14) and Ginther. Neither car would be classified a finisher.

MEXICAN GRAND PRIX

October 23, 1966

Mexico City

5.00 km (3.107 mi)

Pole Position: John Surtees (1:53.18)

Fastest Lap: Richie Ginther (1:53.75)

Winner: John Surtees (+7.88)

John Surtees (7) won easily from pole position, but the victory came too late to close the gap on titlist Jack Brabham. Note the half-buried tires to mark the corners and the proximity of the guardrail. Teammate Jochen Rindt (8) held second briefly before retiring with a broken ball joint. Cooper finished a close third behind Ferrari in the Constructors' Championship.

8
RINDT

Above: In his last F1 start, American Richie Ginther scored a fastest lap for Honda.

Right: Jack Brabham becomes the first man in history to win a Formula One title in his own car.

Above: Unlucky Mike Spence (18) was a Did Not Start after a hub bolt broke in practice, causing the wheel and caliper to fall off and a mighty crash thereafter. He was killed the following May in Indianapolis while shaking down a teammate's troublesome Lotus turbine. The Indy accident would help spur the introduction of wheel tethers.

Left: "After more than two hours and six minutes of hard work in Mexico," said Surtees in his autobiography, "it was good to have the company of the local señoritas on the podium."

F1 MAVERICK

Jackie Stewart

Perhaps no one had a more profound influence on the evolution of the sport than Sir John Young Stewart and the safety campaign he started in 1966.

Stewart himself will tell you that he was not particularly concerned about safety until a wreck at Spa in 1966 left him trapped in his twisted BRM soaking in a pool of gasoline. A single spark would have ended his life.

"I had a big accident myself in '66 at Spa-Francorchamps with the BRM on aquaplaning and really there was nothing to protect the obstacles that I hit," says Stewart. "I hit a telegraph pole, I hit a woodcutter's hut. I ended up in a car that was bent around me, very severely bent. Electrics were still switched on. It could've gone into fire. I was saturated in fuel, there were no marshals, there was no ambulance, there were no medical people there to help me."

It wasn't all the risks of the sport that he resented; it was the ones that he saw as completely unnecessary.

"Racing is too serious a thing to be taken lightly," Stewart explained to the American magazine *Motor Trend* in March of 1970. "I love the sport, but I know all about the money and the safety. I am safety-minded because I love my family. But I also go for safety because I want to be in this game as long as possible."

Stewart's campaign was threefold: he sought to make the tracks, the cars, and drivers' own protective equipment safer.

"I studied every aspect of safety," he continued, "not because I was afraid, but in order to put all the chances on my side. You can't go through life or racing without taking some risks. But your risks must be calculated. If you don't understand that, you are a fool."

He faced massive resistance. It's hard to imagine now, but many throughout the sport attacked him for the changes he was trying to bring about. The old guard questioned his courage, his sanity, even his masculinity.

That he was so blazingly fast was crucial. Anytime anyone questioned his courage, he could point to the stopwatch or his trophy cabinet, which without speaking posed the question *If I'm so much less brave than you are, why am I so much faster?*

If there was residual damage to his reputation, it's that even as a three-time World Champion, he rarely figures in conversations about the best of all time, despite having a higher winning percentage than Senna and Prost and being only a few ticks behind Michael Schumacher, and despite driving at a time when DNFs were far more common and rarely being in the fastest car.

How big a difference did Stewart's safety campaign make? A look back to the time of his accident in 1966 tells the story:

Of the twenty men who scored points that season, ten were killed behind the wheel of a racing car within six years.[1] Another six were seriously injured in accidents they were fortunate to survive, accidents so severe in some cases that several were forced to retire. Most of the remaining four, like Stewart, suffered painful accidents that were a spark away from ending their lives. That's 80 percent of the season's top twenty drivers who were killed or seriously injured over the course of their careers—frontline wartime casualty rates.

No more. Of the nineteen men who scored points during the 2010 F1 season, by contrast, none has died. Only one, Robert Kubica, suffered grievous injuries in a car—and it was a rally car on open roads.

That difference, a difference that has cascaded throughout the sport saving hundreds—possibly thousands—of lives, is attributable to no one more than Jackie Stewart.

FATE OF THE TOP 20 1966 F1 DRIVERS

POINTS	KILLED	SERIOUSLY INJURED	RELATIVELY UNSCATHED
1) J. Brabham	Rindt ('70)	Surtees	Brabham
2) J. Surtees	Clark ('68)	Hill	Stewart
3) J. Rindt	Bandini ('67)	Parkes	Ginther
4) D. Hulme	Scarfiotti ('68)	Bondurant	Gurney
5) G. Hill	Spence ('68)	Arundell	
6) J. Clark	Siffert ('71)	Hulme	
7) J. Stewart	McLaren ('70)		
8) M. Parkes	Bonnier ('72)		
9) L. Bandini	Anderson ('67)		
10) L. Scarfiotti	Taylor ('66)		
11) R. Ginther			
12) D. Gurney			
13) M. Spence			
14) B. Bondurant			
15) J. Siffert			
16) B. McLaren			
17) P. Arundell			
18) J. Bonnier			
19) B. Anderson			
20) J. Taylor			

1. Hulme died behind the wheel of a racing car, but of a presumed heart attack in his fifties at an Australian touring car race, so he's not included.

BRABHAM
1
BRABHAM

CHAPTER 5: 1967

GAME OVER

Walter Hayes had already turned him down once.

Lotus's Colin Chapman had gone to the Ford of England motorsports boss previously to ask him to fund an engine program with Cosworth Engineering, the firm headed by Mike Costin and Keith Duckworth. With the withdrawal of Climax from Formula One, Chapman could see that the game had fundamentally changed. From now on he would have to either build his own engines or purchase them from rivals like BRM and Ferrari. And what were the odds over time that he would get the latest and best-spec engine from a rival on the grid?

The cost of the project was £100,000. That's what Duckworth told Chapman it would take to create the new engine plus four copies. No small sum now, a very large one then. Chapman didn't have it. Hayes wasn't going to provide it.

So here Chapman was, back in front of Hayes to ask him to reconsider.

To his credit, Hayes saw the absurdity of the situation, and the threat to both Lotus and Formula One if it was allowed to continue. Here was the man, Chapman, whom most considered the world's greatest race car designer, building machines for the gentleman, Jim Clark, just as many considered the world's greatest driver. And yet without a satisfactory engine they might be stuck at the back of the grid. How could that be allowed to stand? The Ford man also considered the value to his company should the valve covers on championship-caliber engines say "F-O-R-D" on them.

On second reckoning, £100,000 now seemed like a wise investment. Hayes said yes. He changed the course of F1 history for the next fifteen years. Nye again:

Keith and Mike were brilliant, just brilliant. They cut through all the bullshit and produced something that was small, light, compact, and that could be used as an integral part of the chassis

During this part of the Maverick Era, championships were decided by cars, engines, drivers—and tires. Brabham and Eagle were on Goodyears, most of the other top runners on Firestone. Note the pit board letters scattered on the ground.

because their DFV engine had a fully stressed crankcase and could be used in a structural role as well as providing the motive power.

Cosworth built brilliant Formula Junior engines. They then built brilliant Formula Three engines, brilliant Formula Two engines and ultimately with Colin Chapman of Lotus's encouragement Ford of Dagenham in the UK funded them to produce a brilliant Formula One engine. It was no accident that it won first time out.

The debut of the Cosworth Double Four Valve (DFV) in the back of Chapman's new Lotus 49 at the 1967 Dutch Grand Prix at Zandvoort was everything Hayes, Clark, and Chapman could have hoped for. The season, not so much. After victory in Holland, Clark would place first three more times, but also retire from three events, bringing his season DNF tally to five in what was now an eleven-race schedule. The more clockwork Brabham twins suffered only two DNFs apiece and as a result shaded Clark for the championship. This time Denny "The Bear" Hulme grabbed the honors ahead of Jack.

How superior was the Cosworth-powered Lotus 49?

Starting with Zandvoort, it was on pole at every race—at the Nürburgring by nearly ten seconds. Clark grabbed the top grid position six times, Hill the other two. Clark led every race. He and Hill set fastest lap at six of the nine remaining races. At the 1967 Italian Grand Prix, the 49 looked like it was in a different league entirely. Clark led for the first twelve circuits before suffering a puncture, which cost him a full lap. Thereafter he charged through the field to retake the lead on lap sixty—something previously thought to be impossible at a venue where slipstreaming was crucial—and continued stretching his advantage until he ran low on fuel on the final trip to the start/finish line. He ended up third. It exemplified the 49's first season.

Another noteworthy achievement during the 1967 season came in Belgium, where driver-constructor Dan Gurney took his one and only victory in the short-lived AAR Eagle program. Financed largely by Goodyear and never with an ample budget, Gurney had put together what is considered one of the most beautiful F1 cars of all time, powered by a Weslake V-12 created especially for it. Never quite as powerful as the Cosworth, Gurney nevertheless was able to top the field at Spa and was leading late at the Nürburgring when a half shaft broke.

Gurney's Spa triumph was one of five Goodyear victories that season. Among the major teams, Lotus, BRM, and Ferrari were aligned with Firestone. Brabham, BRM, McLaren, and AAR with Goodyear. Dunlop had Matra.

The combination of the larger, more powerful 3.0-liter engines; better, more rigid chassis; and giant, meaty tires meant that lap records were falling at virtually every track every year. Often in mighty chunks. A comparison of pole times at selected circuits during 1967 with the last year of the 1.5-liter formula tells the story:

	1965	**1967**
Monaco	1:32.5	1:27.6
Spa-Francorchamps	3:45.4	3:28.1
Silverstone	1:30.8	1:25.3
Nürburgring	8:22.7	8:04.1
Monza	1:35.9	1:28.5
Watkins Glen	1:11.25	1:05.48

Traction became the number one focus of every team and designer, in every dimension of performance: acceleration, cornering, and braking. The question on everyone's mind heading into 1968 was:

Where's it going to come from?

Surtees (3) finished the season with a solid fourth.

DUTCH GRAND PRIX

June 4, 1967

Circuit Zandvoort

4.252 km (2.642 mi)

Pole Position: Graham Hill (1:24.6)

Fastest Lap: Jim Clark (1:28.08)

Winner: Jim Clark (+23.6)

Trumpets heralding a massive change. Suddenly, anyone who can afford a Ford Cosworth DFV can contend.

Zandvoort marked the debut of both the Cosworth and Chapman's latest masterpiece, the Lotus 49, with a strong assist from designer Maurice Philippe. "Don't forget," says the great race reporter Pete Lyons, "that [Chapman] attracted a lot of very inventive, like-minded people around him, and generally was not so much hands-on designing the car as he was, 'This is what I want. Draw it up for me and we'll test it.'"

Above: Mechanical troubles during practice left Jim Clark eighth on the grid, but when the green flag waved, the Scotsman steadily sliced toward the front.

Right: In the early going, second qualifier Gurney leads a group including Amon (3), Clark, Rodriguez, and Stewart. This was photographer Pete Biro's first trip to Zandvoort, and when he arrived at the hotel he found he and Goodyear's Larry Truesdale were sharing a tiny room, which Truesadle pledged to remedy. "When I returned from the track, I went to the desk, and the Concierge said, 'Yes, Mr. Biro, we have a different room for you. Come with me.' We went to the lift and he pressed 'P.' Penthouse? Yes. It was amazing, almost the whole top floor of the hotel. I wondered how Larry pulled this off. A few minutes later I hear a key in the door, figuring it would be him. It wasn't. It was Jackie Stewart. He introduced himself (wasn't necessary) and said, 'Helen [his wife] couldn't come this trip and Larry said you needed a place to stay. Would you like some tea?' He rang the desk and had two pots of tea delivered. What a wonderful surprise and a start of a long friendship." Imagine that happening today.

Ludovico Scarfiotti chats with Ferrari team manager Franco Lini (left) and technical director Mauro Forghieri (right). The following race at Spa would be the Italian's last start for the Scuderia.

Above: Now equipped with its twelve-cylinder Weslake engine, the Eagle was perhaps the stiffest competition for Lotus on pure pace.

Left: Chapman confers with Hill in the Lotus pits. Note the other drivers eagerly inspecting the new 49s.

Above: Graham Hill set pole and drove superbly until forced to retire from the lead after eleven laps.

Left: Jack Brabham (foreground) and Ron Tauranac (right) seem amused by something in the rear suspension. Teammate Hulme looks on over Jack's shoulder.

So new was the DFV that Lotus had only one each for the two 49s. Fortunately, Clark's held together for the full ninety laps.

Above: In addition to the Weslake engine, the AAR crew had retrofitted the Eagle with a large number of weight-saving magnesium and titanium components.

Right: Gurney discusses strategy with team manager Bill Dunne.

Opposite: A broken fuel injection metering unit left Gurney by the side of the road. Dunne and mechanic Tim Wall have come to his assistance.

1967

BELGIAN GRAND PRIX

June 18, 1967

Spa-Francorchamps

Pole Position: Jim Clark (3:28.1)

Fastest Lap: Dan Gurney (3:31.9)

Winner: Dan Gurney (+1:03.0)

Once going, Gurney made up for lost time. The Eagle's beak swoops down on the entry to the La Source hairpin.

Clark leads the pack away from the chaotic start. The green flag waved moments after the thirty-second warning, catching several including Gurney off-guard. He hadn't yet put his Eagle in gear.

Clark (21) would run away from the field until forced to pit on lap twelve for spark plug issues that would knock him out of contention. Jackie Stewart (14) took over in the BRM, helped by a Gurney stop for faltering fuel pressure. But once returned to the circuit, the American came storming back, setting fastest lap and overtaking the "Wee Scot" when the BRM H16 developed gearshift issues. *Sports Illustrated* writer Bob Ottum was at Spa that weekend to document Gurney's win in an article entitled, "Apple Pie, Mom and Mr. Gurney." Ottum, a born and bred New Yorker, didn't drive, so he hired Pete Biro to ferry him around. "When Ottum finished his writing, he asked the press chief where the phones were. He had to call his story in to the magazine in New York," Pete recalls. "The press guy handed Ottum an army surplus field phone and told him, 'Go outside and you will find a wire sticking out of the wall to hook up the phone. You then turn the crank to get an operator.'" State-of-the-art reporting in the Maverick Era.

A week after victory at Le Mans, Dan Gurney makes history again at Spa, winning a Grand Prix in his own car.

UNITED STATES GRAND PRIX

October 1, 1967

Watkins Glen

3.78 km (2.35 mi)

Pole Position: Graham Hill (1:05.48)

Fastest Lap: Graham Hill (1:06.0)

Winner: Jim Clark (+6.3)

Once again, mechanical issues hobbled both Lotuses, but Clark (5) and Hill (6) were able to nurse them home to finish 1-2.

6
TEAM
HILL

Clockwise from top left: Kiwi Chris Amon (9) was quickly developing into one of his generation's top drivers. John Surtees (3) delivered Honda its most successful season yet, including a win at Monza and fourth in the final standings. Jean-Pierre Beltoise (22) would help French aerospace firm Matra develop into a title threat in 1968. Many felt BRM's Chris Irwin (17) had World Championship potential, but his career would be cut short by an accident the following spring.

The Lotuses have already disappeared, but third-fastest qualifier Gurney's Eagle was once again "best of the rest," leading Brabham (1), Amon (9), and Hulme (2).

Top left and right: Honda mechanics try to calm Surtees's (3) overheated engine. Bottom left: Gurney's Eagle (11) is one of the few cars with a roll bar high enough to protect its driver. Bottom right: Stewart (7) is one of only a handful of wheelmen using safety belts.

Above: New Zealander Denny Hulme (2) patiently works his way through traffic and will leave the Glen with a five-point lead over his boss going into the season finale.

Left: Jim Clark celebrates as Lotus head Colin Chapman hoists the trophy. Clark would lead every race he started in the 49 and win a season-high four races, but five DNFs would leave him out of championship contention.

MEXICAN GRAND PRIX

October 22, 1967

Mexico City

5.00 km (3.107 mi)

Pole Position: Jim Clark (1:47.56)

Fastest Lap: Jim Clark (1:48.13)

Winner: Jim Clark (+1:25.36)

Chris Amon (9) will start from the number two slot on the grid and finish fifth in the Drivers' Championship. No one would have imagined then that it would be his highest-ever ranking. Hulme (2) won only twice but finished out of the top three just once (South Africa) the rest of the year to clinch his first and only title.

2

Chris Amon's (9) victory at Le Mans the previous year with Bruce McLaren "influenced my career greatly because it was a direct result of that I got offered the Ferrari drive for 1967."

Above: Hemingway once wrote, “There are only three sports: bullfighting, motor racing, and mountaineering; all the rest are merely games.” The prize-giving ceremony in Mexico was held at a local bullfighting ring. Part of the festivities involved winner Clark (helmet) wielding a cape. (They used calves, not full-grown fighting bulls.) Mexican Shelby Mustang driver Freddie Van Beuren showed good form.

Left: In a class by himself. Clark actually stalled the start, causing Gurney to bump into the back of the Lotus, giving it a timely shove. Clark took off. Gurney (15) retired a few laps later having punctured the Eagle’s radiator. *Bernard Cahier/The Cahier Archive*

The magnificent Ford Cosworth DFV engine won its debut race and changed the face of Formula One. Mastermind Keith Duckworth kneels beside Clark.

F1 MAVERICK

Mike Costin and Keith Duckworth

There have been times in F1 history when the teams with the best engines won. Often because those teams, under-standably, refused to supply anyone else. Real advantages in F1 are hard-fought and usually temporary. In 1961, Ferrari drivers came in first, second, and fifth in the championship[1] because Ferrari adjusted to the new 1.5-liter formula better and more quickly than everyone else. The following year, they were nowhere.

But from 1967 to the early 1980s anyone with a checkbook could buy an engine capable of winning races and championships, thanks to a couple of mavericks named Mike Costin and Keith Duckworth, who combined their names and intellects to form Cosworth Engineering. Commissioned by Ford at the behest of Lotus to develop a new engine for the 3.0-liter formula after a disastrous year with the BRM H16 engine, Cosworth immediately reset the F1 hierarchy.

"The biggest explosion was Keith Duckworth producing the Cosworth engine," says Jackie Oliver, who drove Cosworth-powered cars for Team Lotus after Jim Clark's death, then became a customer when he formed the Arrows team in 1977.

"Engines have always dominated Formula One," he continues. "It's 30 percent of the reasons why you can do it and win, and still is, so someone like me, when I wanted to start my own Formula One team, I had thirteen people to make an aluminum monocoque, and I went down the road and bought

1 They conceivably could have finished 1-2-3 had Ferrari not decided to forsake the United States Grand Prix in the wake of von Trips's death.

six engines (from Cosworth) at $25,000 to $30,000 apiece, and I could go racing. There was an explosion of constructors in the early 1970s because there was a race-winning engine available at an affordable price."

The 3.0-liter DFV didn't just win its debut race, it stuck a dagger into the heart of every rival team. Doug Nye:

> **Tony Rudd, who was the chief engineer of the rival BRM team, and who was building rival Formula One engines, told me that at Zandvoort in 1967—when he looked at the Cosworth DFV engine for the first time—and then saw how it performed on track in the new Lotus 49s, he thought to himself, "Well that's it. Game over!" Just like that. That's it. Game over.**
>
> **I've always thought that was a brilliant quote, because it sums up a complete turning point in history. That turning point was confined to Team Lotus for that first season, 1967. Colin tried hard to maintain exclusive use of the engine through 1968 and 1969, but Ford thought otherwise and made it available to McLaren and to the Ken Tyrrell Matra team. That really was the rebirth of Formula One as a kind of Grand Prix racing "Formula Ford," almost everyone using the DFV engine.**

It wasn't just the power of the new unit. The DFV engine also served as a structural member. The 49's monocoque ended at the driver's back. The engine carried the suspension.

"It was Keith's idea that the engine should be a structural member, not Colin's," Costin told *Motor Sport*. "It was held onto the monocoque by two bolts at the bottom and two at the top. It wasn't that big a deal, structurally. The torsional loads going through the engine in heavy cornering were only about 4,000 pounds. Our big-end bolts were much smaller, and stood a load of 10,500 pounds in each one."

Despite being introduced at the third race of the year, the Cosworth nearly propelled Clark to a third championship. Unreliability dropped him from the lead time and again, opening the door for Brabham's Denis Hulme and Jack Brabham. Cosworth engines went on to win the next seven F1 titles.

In all, Cosworth-powered cars captured 155 races and powered twelve F1 Drivers' Champions and ten Constructors'. At the 1974 British Grand Prix, twenty-nine of the thirty-four entries used Costin and Duckworth's engines.

Says longtime F1 mechanic John Dennie, "The biggest innovation in that whole 1967 through the turbo era I think would be the Cosworth DFV. It dominated Formula One through the whole period."

BOSCH
3
SHELL
STP

WINGS OF CHANGE

As 1968 began, Colin Chapman and Jim Clark were looking forward to possibly their greatest season yet. The 49 was finally sorted. Clearly no one had an answer for the Cosworth engine, which Clark had demonstrated with an exclamation point at the season-opening South African Grand Prix, where he steamrollered the field to collect pole, fastest lap, and his twenty-fifth F1 victory, eclipsing Fangio's record of twenty-four.

The team's chronically precarious financial position was improving markedly as well, thanks to a groundbreaking deal with the Gold Leaf cigarette brand. Governments throughout North America and Western Europe had banned cigarette advertising on TV, forcing tobacco companies to look at other advertising venues. As Player's Cigarettes promotions manager Tim Collins told *Motor Sport* in 2015:

[Someone] suggested that we should look at Lotus, so I spoke to Colin Chapman and we began to discuss terms. It all happened fairly quickly, over two or three months, and we didn't talk to anybody else. Besides, Colin offered us a dream team of Graham Hill and Jim Clark, so why would we have wanted to go anywhere other than Lotus?

It wasn't quite so straightforward. Chapman resisted changing the name of the team to Gold Leaf Team Lotus right up until the night before the launch. But in the end he agreed to exchange British racing green for Player's Tobacco greenbacks.

It was a seminal moment in the sport. The floodgates were opened. Soon you would need a major sponsor in order to field a competitive F1 team. There was another effect as well. With

After Clark's death in April, Graham Hill became Lotus's team leader and took his second title.

sponsors came new visual identities. Within seven years only Ferrari would still be flying its national racing colors. That "foreign country" that F1 had been was starting to seem very far away.

There was more good news for Lotus in America. In late March, Clark and Chapman went to Indianapolis to test the new Maurice Philippe–designed Lotus 56 four-wheel-drive gas turbine. The previous year's 500 had been a disaster for Lotus. Neither Clark nor Graham Hill had been able to qualify higher than sixteenth, and neither factored in the race. Now, with a brand new Formula One–style chassis and a dramatic, forward-leaning wedge shape, the planned three-car STP "superteam" of Clark, Hill, and Stewart looked set to dominate. The test only cemented those hopes. On his return to England, Clark told friends he had just driven the car that was going to win the 1968 Indianapolis 500.

A week later he was dead.

Clark's death in a Formula Two race at Hockenheim sent a chill through the F1 community. As his friend Ferrari ace Chris Amon put it, "I wasn't alone in thinking, 'If it can happen to Jimmy, it can happen to me.'"

Derek Bell, then an up-and-coming Formula Two driver, had long admired Clark and was thrilled to meet him that weekend:

> **I'd met him the night before and had tea with him and I even had breakfast with him and (Lotus teammate) Graham Hill and we went to the track together, the three of us in a car, and that was the last I saw of Jimmy. So to meet your hero and then to have him die the next morning was pretty traumatic.**

But the Scot's demise was just the beginning of F1's most deadly season. A month later, former teammate Mike Spence, drafted to replace Clark in that oh-so-promising turbine at Indy, was killed during practice while trying to help sort teammate Greg Weld's car.[1] A month later, Ludovico Scarfiotti, who'd retired from F1 in part because of the death and career-ending injuries to Ferrari teammates Lorenzo Bandini and Mike Parkes the previous year, was killed at the Rossfeld hillclimb in Germany. After three deaths on the first weekend of three consecutive months, there was talk of postponing, at least for the time being, future events on the first weekend of the month. That's how jittery everyone had gotten.

Perhaps it wasn't such an illogical idea after all. On July 7, three months to the day after Clark's crash, Jo Schlesser burned to death in his Honda at the French Grand Prix. While the 1968 season is remembered for these four fatalities in four successive months, they weren't the only casualties. Rising star Chris Irwin was so severely injured at the BOAC 500 the same weekend as Clark's accident that he never raced again. Imagine: five current or former (in the case of Scarfiotti) F1 drivers gone in little more than ninety days.

There was an inherent tension created when so many dollars were flowing into Formula One and so many drivers were being carried out in body bags. The first would not be sustainable without some means of reducing the second. The teams accepted death as part of the sport. Sponsors were not nearly so tolerant. Why invest millions in associating their brand with a top driver, knowing that not only could he disappear tomorrow, but the

---

1 After Clark and Spence were killed and Stewart suffered a wrist injury, the STP "superteam" ended up being Graham Hill, Joe Leonard, and Art Pollard. Leonard seemed to have the race in the bag until a fuel pump failure with nine laps to go.

lasting image of him might be his lifeless form next to the sponsor's crumpled logo?

Stewart's safety crusade suddenly had a lot more support.

From a technological standpoint, the biggest development of 1968 came at midseason with the arrival of wings, and with them serious downforce. Remember how at the end of the previous year everyone was looking for traction? This was one of the ways they found it. Downforce may be the single biggest change to the sport since the introduction of closed-loop lubrication systems.

There's a legitimate question why it took until 1968, two full years after Jim Hall demonstrated the potential in the North American Can-Am series with his seminal Chaparral 2E, for F1 to follow suit. Jackie Stewart thinks he knows why:

> **Not-Invented-Here Syndrome. Colin Chapman was one of the great innovators, but if he didn't invent it, then (in his mind) it couldn't have been right. They just didn't do it. Jim Hall was ahead of the world in that.**

Perhaps that also explains why the early attempts at wings in F1 were so ham-fisted after Hall had essentially provided the blueprint for anyone who wanted to pay attention.

Ferrari's Mauro Forghieri was the first to try, installing hydraulically adjustable wings on his lithe Ferrari 312 for the Belgian Grand Prix. The team abandoned the adjustability feature after a series of failures—Chris Amon went cartwheeling into the trees at Monza later in the year, fortunately without major injury—but soon every F1 car was sprouting wings on the front and back.

Jackie Oliver was drafted in to replace Clark at Lotus and was nearly killed himself at the French Grand Prix when Chapman insisted on mounting an especially large wing on especially skinny struts. Just because. This is how Oliver remembered the incident in *Motor Sport*:

> **There was never any question of going testing with any new bits. Colin would have an idea, and insist it was on the cars for the next race. So there was this giant wing above the back of my car. I was the test rig. Stick it on Oliver's car and see what happens.**
>
> **I looked at this thing up there on stalks, nobody in the team could tell me anything, so I went and asked Chapman what it was all about. "Aerodynamics, lad," he said. "It's the future." I gave one of the struts a push, and it moved from side to side. I said to Chapman, "Is it meant to do that?" He said, "You know when you look out of the window of a Boeing 707 and you see the wings flapping up and down? It's the same. It's got to be flexible so it doesn't break." I said, "Oh, okay," and out I went. There was no, "Go out, do one lap, come in for a check." It was, "Go out and get on with it."**

He did and was lucky to survive the massive shunt that occurred when the wing collapsed whilst Oliver was going flat out past the pits. Nevertheless, by the time of the season-ending Mexican Grand Prix, there were giant skyscraper wings on virtually the entire field.

Lotus did, in the end, win the 1968 title, but there was little joy in the enterprise after Clark's demise. Surprisingly, Hill won just three races, in part because Lotus no longer had exclusive use of the Cosworth engine. Chapman had lobbied Hayes hard to limit its availability to his team. But Hayes saw that it would be in the best interests of both Ford and the sport to make it available to others, including McLaren, Matra, and Rob Walker's privateer Lotus effort.

All three won races.

In fact, every event save one on the twelve-race schedule was captured by a Cosworth-powered team. Only the rain-soaked French Grand Prix went to Jacky Ickx in the twelve-cylinder Ferrari. Ferrari did manage four poles—three of them to Chris Amon—but the New Zealander's notoriously awful luck prevented him from wearing the roses anywhere.

A new force in Grand Prix racing was Ken Tyrrell's Matra team. Tyrrell had had the foresight to sign Stewart after a 1963 test. Tyrrell had recognized the potential of the new Cosworth engine at its debut in the 1967 Dutch Grand Prix and set about organizing a team combining Cosworth engines, Matra chassis, Dunlop tires, and Elf sponsorship.

It was a revelation. In part because the "wee Scot" was fast emerging from Clark's shadow to become the undisputed best driver in the world. Stewart finished second to Hill by twelve points in the title race despite missing two early-season events to a broken wrist. (It's why he missed driving the Lotus 56 at Indy as well.) Hulme finished three points further back in the suddenly transformed McLaren.

In 1969, Tyrrell and Stewart showed that they were just getting started. Stewart won six of the eleven events and won the championship in a landslide, almost thirty points ahead of second-place man Ickx. Jochen Rindt had left Brabham for Lotus but suffered breakdown after breakdown—six in all—and missed Monaco entirely after Chapman once again installed still bigger wings on the now 49B-spec Lotus in Spain and saw both of his drivers crash heavily after the flimsy appendages collapsed at the same point on the circuit. In fairness to Chapman, others experienced wing failures in Spain, prompting the FIA to outlaw high-mounted ones before the next race, Monaco.

Remember we were talking about traction?

Another major trend during the 1969 season was the development of four-wheel-drive chassis. The first 4WD F1 car, the front-engine Ferguson P99, debuted back in 1961. As you might imagine, it offered no great advantage during the 1.5-liter era, but its one great claim to fame was the last-ever Formula One victory by a front-engine car, albeit at a nonchampionship event. BRM followed in 1964 with its P67, which appeared at the 1964 British GP but was withdrawn after qualifying an unpromising last. BRM put it on the back burner while it concentrated on its new H16 engine. Interestingly, BRM included room in the H16 for a second driveshaft should 4WD appear more useful in the coming 3.0-liter "big power" era.

Three teams developed 4WD chassis for the 1969 campaign: Lotus, Matra, and McLaren. Four if you count Cosworth. Keith Duckworth had enlisted the brilliant young McLaren designer Robin Herd to create a 4WD chassis around the DFV engine. We asked Jackie Stewart about them:

Lotus kept it longer than anybody else. Matra: we did testing and we never raced it. Cosworth: Mike Costin and his staff made up a Formula One car with four-wheel drive and that didn't work either. I was one of the few people ever to drive that car, I tested it at Silverstone as a favor. Ken Tyrrell asked me to do it as a

favor to Keith Duckworth, because obviously we were using the Cosworth engine, so it was an easy decision to make.

The four-wheel-drive system that Matra used was a development of the Ferguson 4WD from earlier in the decade. Even when testing showed that there was no real advantage in dry conditions, Stewart thought it was worth pursuing for low-traction conditions.

"I thought we should have a four-wheel-drive car just for rainy days," says Stewart, "just for a wet race."

So what happened?

"In fact, it wasn't even as quick in the wet."

There were several factors working against 4WD. For starters, the increased weight and complexity, two things you don't want in a top-level racing car. But more importantly, advances in tire technology and downforce made it redundant. The designers could achieve the necessary traction through other means. Just in the span of months between when the teams first started designing their 4WD cars and started putting them on the road, they were obsoleted by other developments.

All but Lotus gave up on the concept by the end of the year. Not to worry. The ever-fertile mind of Colin Chapman had something else in store.

Chris Amon has been a sensation, but seven retirements in ten starts will rob him of several wins.

BRITISH GRAND PRIX

July 20, 1968

Brands Hatch

4.265 km (2.650 mi)

Pole Position: Graham Hill (1:28.9)

Fastest Lap: Jo Siffert (1:29.7)

Winner: Jo Siffert (+4.4)

Jim Hall's Chaparral 2E had shown two years earlier at Bridgehampton, New York, that wings needed to be mounted high to operate in clean air for maximum effectiveness and needed to have sturdy supports to be safe. In this case, Formula One was well behind North America's Canadian-American (Can-Am) Challenge Cup.

The great story about the 1968 British Grand Prix is that due to crashes in previous races, Lotus was out of cars. All they had were the two for factory drivers Graham Hill (8) and Jackie Oliver (9). Normally not a problem, except privateer Rob Walker had ordered a new Lotus 49B long before and threatened Colin Chapman with canceling if he didn't receive it in time for their home race. So Chapman struck a deal. He sent Walker Oliver's just completed 49B, and borrowed Walker's older 49 for Oliver. The sad part is that this would probably have been Oliver's day of days. At the start, he burst into the lead ahead of Hill and Walker driver Jo Siffert (22), despite being in the older-spec car. Oliver led until the halfway point, when a plumbing line on his hastily updated Lotus burned through. (It had been routed too close to the exhaust.) Thus, Siffert won in what is considered the last true privateer victory. A fantastic home win for Walker and the first of two GPs Siffert would capture over the course of his career.

Track and spectator safety have evolved a long way by 1968, but a lot of the charm, aesthetics, and sightlines are gone. Note marshall station (right) on the outside of a turn. History does not record who thought this was a brilliant idea.

Clockwise from top left: Endurance ace "Seppi" Siffert wins one for the underdogs. Yellow flag signifies a disabled car ahead. Jackie Oliver hotfoots it back to the pits, not knowing his last best chance of becoming a Grand Prix winner has slipped away.

The aero wars begin. Counterclockwise from top left, Mauro Forghieri had fired the first shot a month earlier at Spa with the midmounted wing on Chris Amon's (5) Ferrari. Already the other teams have followed the Italian's lead. Siffert (22) had the latest Lotus setup with a tall, wide wing in back balanced by substantial canard wings in the front. Honda tried a tall wing on John Surtees's (7) car, which collapsed. It would not be the last.

GERMAN GRAND PRIX

August 4, 1968

Nurburgring

22.835 km (14.189 mi)

Pole Position: Jacky Ickx (9:04.0)

Fastest Lap: Jackie Stewart (9:36.0)

Winner: Jackie Stewart (+4:03.2)

Many consider his drive here in driving rain and dense fog not only Stewart's greatest race, but one of the greatest drives in Grand Prix history. He won by four minutes–plus over Graham Hill.

Left to right: When Jackie Stewart's deal to drive for Ferrari fell through, he and Ken Tyrrell joined forces with Matra to run a Cosworth-powered version of the French machines. Immediate frontrunners, they might have vied more seriously for the title had Stewart not missed two races with a broken wrist. Months later, you can see the splint he still wears. Stewart qualified fifty seconds behind the man Ferrari signed instead, polesitter Jacky Ickx (9). Bruce McLaren (2) scored a historic win at Spa months earlier, but struggled here.

Gurney (14) introduces full-face helmets to F1. Jo Bonnier (center, above) shares a relaxed moment with former Porsche racing boss Huschke von Hanstein after the Swede had withdrawn his privately entered McLaren. British GP winner Jo Siffert (16) retired before half distance. Pete Biro rode to the circuit with Gurney: “I was blown away by how many spectators there were. I asked Dan why there was such a huge crowd even though it was raining so hard. He said, ‘If you’re a racing fan, wouldn’t you want to see the best drivers in the world run in the wet?’”

Clockwise from top: A puncture on lap three dropped Gurney (14) to twelfth after a stop, but thereafter he put on a clinic. Easy camaraderie among rivals: Graham Hill (left) leans in to chat with (left to right) McLaren's Phil Kerr, driver Denny Hulme, Alan McCall, and Honda's John Surtees. Lotus chief Colin Chapman calmly reviews his notes while Bette Hill anxiously awaits husband Graham, whose second place will keep him four points ahead of Stewart in the title chase.

CANADIAN GRAND PRIX

September 22, 1968

Circuit Mont-Tremblant

4.265 km (2.650 mi)

Pole Position: Jochen Rindt (1:33.8)

Fastest Lap: Jo Siffert (1:35.1)

Winner: Denny Hulme (+1 lap)

Left to right: Chris Amon (9) blasts into the lead from second on the grid and has the race in the palm of his hand until lap seventy-three of ninety when his transmission fails. Communication circa 1968: McLaren mechanic Alan McCall informs Hulme he's in first place, Alastair Caldwell explains why, and Tyler Alexander tells him he has an eight-second cushion over BRM ace Pedro Rodriguez. Hulme (1) will lead home a McLaren 1-2.

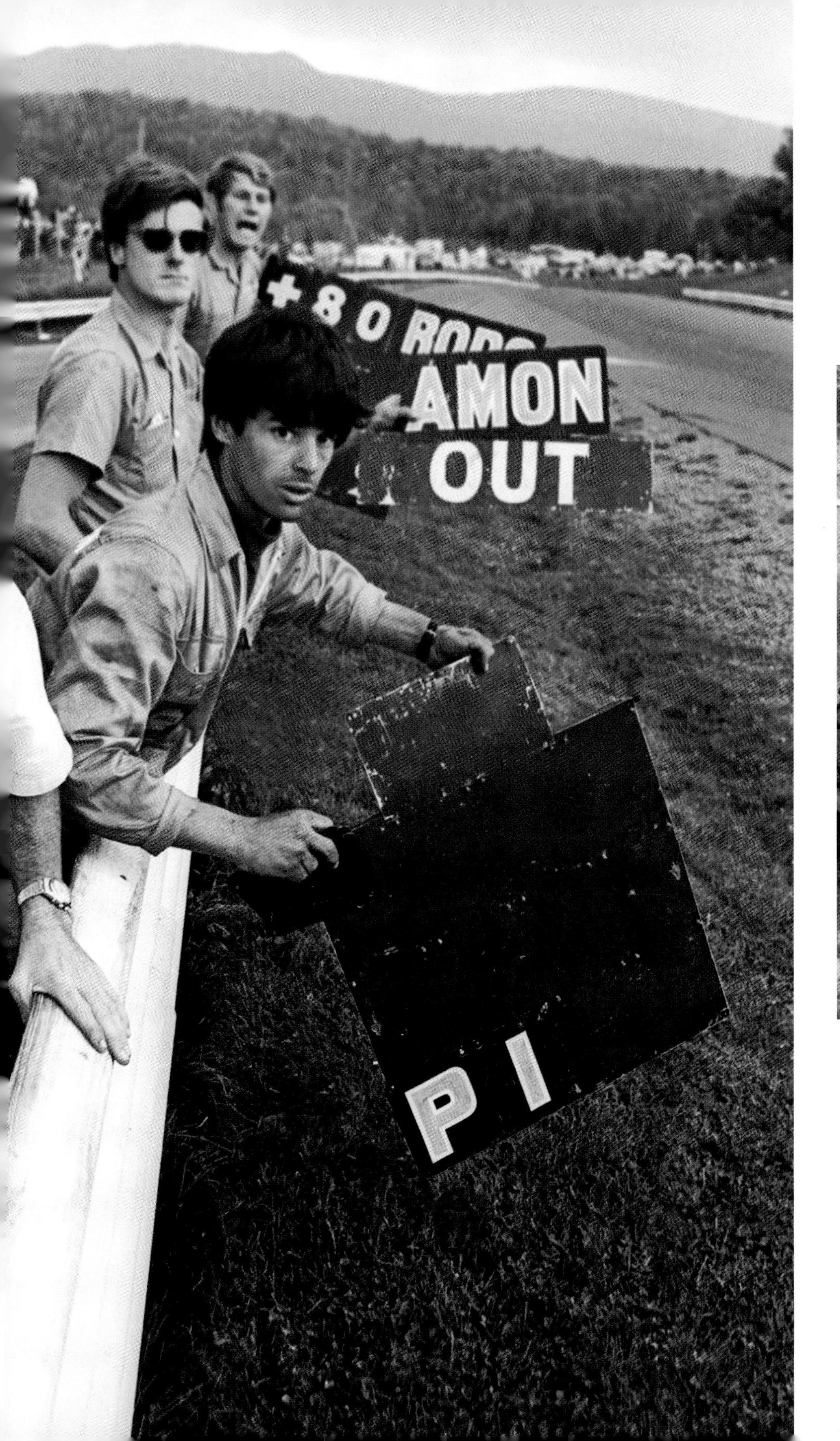
AMON
OUT
PI

Denny Hulme
CHAMPION
FERODO
Roadholder
FORD

Hulme's replacement at Brabham, Jochen Rindt (standing) won pole here; boss Jack couldn't be happier. Out of funds to continue the Eagle project, Gurney (11) accepted a ride from friend Bruce and proceeded to outqualify both McLaren aces and championship leader Graham Hill (3). His storming run will end on lap four.

Left: Helmeted Frenchman Henri Pescarolo (19) will fight the good fight for God and country, but the glorious-sounding V-12 Matras can't compete with the Cosworth-powered ones. Neither he nor teammate Jean-Pierre Beltoise looks particularly pleased.

Below: Final preparation of Hulme's winning Robin Herd- and Gordon Coppuck- designed McLaren M7A (1).

16
OWEN RACING ORGANISATION
REGISTERED DESIGN No.933743 APPLIED FOR

It's doubtful that the winglets on the nose of Pedro Rodriguez's Len Terry–designed BRM P133 (16) are doing very much. The Mexican prepares for battle next to teammate Piers Courage. Former hot rodder Gurney (11) was fascinated by the mechanical side of the sport.

F1 MAVERICK

Jim Hall

Some would ask why the Texan, who never built a single Formula One car, should be considered one of the great F1 mavericks.

Others consider him one of the most important of all.

Hall's first direct involvement with F1 came at the 1960 United States Grand Prix at Riverside, when he ran a surprising fifth as a privateer—his pit crew consisted of his brother Chuck and mechanic Frank Lance—in a car that had no business being in the points, until a stub axle broke in the final laps and dropped him to seventh. A similar performance at the 1962 Mexican GP, when he nearly podiumed in an older four-cylinder car when all the other top drivers had newer chassis powered by Climax V-8s, led to his being invited to join the British Racing Partnership (BRP) team for the 1963 season. Little could Hall know that the team, which had won multiple Grands Prix in the preceding years, was about to go into decline. Hall scored a number of points finishes despite having an aging, underpowered Lotus, then left F1 to concentrate on his new, self-built Chaparral sports cars.

It was with the Chaparrals that Hall pioneered downforce. Others had toyed with the concept dating back to the earliest years of the automobile, but no one had mastered it the way Hall had. Hall turned it into one of the main pillars of performance in every race car from that point forward.

Hall introduced movable wings on the 1965 Chaparral 2C and 1966 Chaparral 2E, which was the fastest if not yet most reliable car in the inaugural season of Can-Am racing. It surprises him to this day that no one in F1 copied his innovation until 1968, but soon every car had wings. They still do. Wings and downforce have been essential to winning in Grand Prix racing ever since. Says Peter Wright, F1's foremost aerodynamics expert, credited with discovering modern ground effect while with Lotus:

> **I think Jim Hall started it all going with the wings on the Chaparral, and basically alerted everybody to the benefits of downforce. And I guess I introduced ground effect in the Type 78 Lotus. Motor racing has been on that groove ever since.**

Chaparral-style high-mounted and/or movable wings were outlawed in Formula One after the near-catastrophic Team Lotus accidents at the 1969 Spanish Grand Prix. So there's no small amount of irony involved in the fact that after being banned for decades, movable wings are now a staple of modern Formula One. The drag reduction system (DRS) was introduced in 2011. It allows drivers within one second of the car ahead to trim their wings for lower downforce and therefore greater speed, just as Hall had proven in the mid-'60s.

In 1978, Formula One copied another Hall downforce innovation from eight years earlier, suction. During the 1970 Can-Am season, Hall shocked the racing world with his revolutionary Chaparral 2J "vacuum cleaner." It quickly proved the fastest car in in the series but was outlawed before it had a chance to contest a full season. Gordon Murray adapted the idea to create the Brabham BT46B "fan car." Unlike the Chaparral, which had constant downforce, the Murray car's downforce was tied to engine speed. Nevertheless, it was a revelation. It won the only race that it entered, the 1978 Swedish Grand Prix—going away—then was shelved by Brabham boss Bernie Ecclestone when the other teams began to mutiny.

The introduction of downforce to Formula One has not been without controversy. Wings and ground effect greatly increased the speeds at which cars could run alone on a track, but the turbulence facing trailing cars has made passing more difficult. Many argue this has reduced the quality of the racing, replacing Rindt-Stewart era wheel-to-wheel action with sometimes tedious processions. The movable wing elements in the DRS were created specifically to address the very issue wings helped create. But carping aside, downforce has led to staggering advances in vehicle performance. And Hall is the man who started F1's obsession with it. Wright thinks he knows why the innovation came not only from outside Formula One, but outside Europe:

> **The thing that's interesting is Grand Prix racing after the war, a lot of it was on very fast circuits. Rouen, Reims, Monza, Spa, places where there were long straights and power mattered and drag mattered. If you read Laurence Pomeroy's (landmark 1959) book, *The Grand Prix Car*, all of his analysis is power-to-weight and power-to-frontal-area. It's all drag, top speed, and acceleration. Nothing about cornering at all, and what Jim Hall did and Chevrolet R&D with their instrumentation (to support it), they said there is a benefit particularly on circuits that don't have very long straights, where you get more from downforce than you lose from drag. That's what he told the motor racing industry.**

When Wright and Hall finally met each other at the 2007 Goodwood Festival of Speed, the Brit approached the man in the Stetson. "I suggested that between us we had wrecked motor sport. He grinned and just about agreed." ■

MOTUL
MOTUL
POLITOYS
MOTUL

CHAPTER 7: 1970–1971

FORWARD, MARCH

As time went on, Ford and Cosworth expanded availability of the DFV basically to any team that wanted one—and just about every team did. By 1970, all save Ferrari, BRM, and Matra had switched to Cosworth power—and BRM and Matra probably would have been better served if they had. Nye again:

> **The fact that it went on to 155 Formula One victories is its own measure of the quality of that thing. It was absolutely epochal change. You had as many as thirty-six or thirty-seven cars being entered for every Grand Prix, because customers could just go and buy a DFV engine off the shelf and bolt it—in some cases—to a complete load of junk and go Formula One racing.**

Only reliability issues had prevented Lotus from winning the championship during the Cosworth's inaugural campaign. Since then, DFV-powered cars had captured four championships in succession:

1968: Hill/Lotus
1969: Stewart/Matra
1970: Rindt/Lotus
1971: Stewart/Tyrrell

So crucial was the Mike Costin– and Keith Duckworth–designed engine that Ken Tyrrell left his very productive partnership with Matra after their 1969 championship year because the French

The "tea tray" March 711 was another Robin Herd design that punched well above its weight, finishing second to Jackie Stewart in the Drivers' Championship. "The 711 front wing was a standard profile," says Herd. "It was elliptical to minimize drag. It worked very well, giving a good range of downforce, enabling the aerodynamic balance of the car to be achieved easily. And it did not suffer problems when following other cars. Its weak point was that at a low downforce setting, when the wing would be relatively flat, the downforce produced would reduce quite a bit as the nose of the car rose. This became an issue in long and very fast corners when understeer would develop on applying power leaving the corner. Niki drove his first F1 race in Ronnie's sister 711 at Zeltweg in his home Grand Prix. The original Zeltweg circuit had more long and fast corners than now, and Niki felt 'power understeer' in very fast corners for the first time. I was told about it!"

aerospace firm wanted the team to replace their Cosworths with engines of Matra's own manufacture. An understandable position for the French concern to take, but Ken knew what he was doing. The Georges Martin–designed 60° Matra V-12 made a mighty roar but would never win a Formula One race.

The problem for Tyrrell was that he found himself with the best driver in Formula One and a championship-caliber engine and no car to put them in.

We'll come back to that in a moment.

For this and other reasons, 1970 would prove to be one of the most curious years in the sport's history. It is remembered as a runaway for Lotus, its new wedge-shaped 72, and star driver Jochen Rindt. But it wasn't as simple as that.

The 72 was the latest stroke of genius from Colin Chapman, the car being designed by Maurice Philippe under Chapman's direction. The core ideas were to increase downforce, reduce drag (in so doing improve acceleration and top speed), and reduce unsprung weight.

Bearing a strong resemblance to Philippe's earlier Lotus 56 turbine Indy car, the 72 achieved its goals in all three areas. The low-drag shape was enabled by splitting the traditionally front-mounted radiator and relocating the new halves to a less draggy position on either side of the cockpit, and replacing the tall, frontal-area-expanding front springs with torsion bars. In back-to-back tests, the 72 was about 10 miles per hour faster than the car it replaced. Unsprung weight was reduced by locating all of the brakes inboard.

It took a while to get it all dialed in. So much so that the introduction of the car was delayed until the Dutch Grand Prix. But once ready for combat, it proved transformative. After winning the German Grand Prix, Rindt remarked, "A monkey could have won with this car today. It's that good."

All was not bliss in Lotus Land, however. Rindt and Chapman clashed throughout the year, Rindt feeling that Chapman, in the pursuit of simple-but-light, didn't leave enough room for safety. For the Italian Grand Prix, Rindt implored Chapman to bring the Lotus 49 instead of the 72 because he felt it would be safer. Chapman refused. Rindt was killed in a Saturday morning crash at the Parabolica when his 72, running without wings, darted left under braking into the guardrails. Rindt's five victories had won him enough points to become F1's first (and still only) posthumous World Champion.

That said, the season wasn't as one-sided as it might have appeared. Jack Brabham won the opening round in South Africa and should have taken several more wins were it not for improbable twists of fate. Who could forget watching him crash out of the lead at Monaco when a backmarker forced him offline heading into the final turn? Likewise, Ferrari for the first time in years had a championship-caliber car in Mauro Forghieri's beautiful 312B, but appalling reliability issues scuppered its chances, Jacky Ickx retiring from five of the first seven races. Thereafter it never finished lower than fourth—and the fourth was a race it led until it developed a fuel line issue. With three victories in the season's final five races, Ickx finished just five points back of Rindt in the standings.

Which brings us back to Tyrrell and Stewart and an ambitious new entity named March. March Engineering was formed by four men whose initials gave it its name: Max **M**osley, **A**lan **R**ees, Graham **C**oaker, and Robin **H**erd. Their announced goal was to build cars for Formulas One, Two, Three, and Ford, plus the

Can-Am, immediately. For a while, the rightly skeptical media said March stood instead for "Much Advertised Racing Car Hoax," but when they launched their first F1 car, damned if Robin Herd hadn't done it again.

One of the questions fans and skeptics alike asked was where the money was coming from. In fact, there wasn't nearly enough. Today, Herd sums up the fledgling firm's F1 experience as "a permanent lack of the finance to compete properly."

> **If you knew the agony of trying to build a proper F1 car for year one in 1970 with £17,500 of capital and £10,000 of STP sponsorship. . . . We were on pole for the first four F1 races,[1] led them all, and won three. Only a tire problem in South Africa cost us a win in all four races.**
>
> **Thereafter a series of unexplained and out-of-character engine-related issues hindered Jackie. His normal reliability would have seen us with the World Constructors' Championship in our very first year, instead of a mere third."**

Part of the problem was that the team, desperate for cash, was spread too thin. Several cars were sold to Ken Tyrrell for Jackie Stewart and François Cevert. The STP money funded a factory entry for Chris Amon and occasionally Mario Andretti. Another car was commissioned by Porsche, in an attempt to retain Jo Siffert's services in the JW Automotive Gulf Porsche 917 sports car team. Part of the problem was that, built on a shoestring and in just three months' time, the March 701 required compromises that revealed themselves as the season went on.

As the shortcomings became more evident, Tyrrell decided to build his own car, to become at last a full-fledged constructor. The Tyrrell 001 wouldn't appear until the last three races of the season, and it wouldn't finish any of them. But it sat on pole at its first race and looked quick elsewhere.

The 1971 season proved how right Tyrrell had been to venture off on his own. Mavericks Ken and Jackie dominated in a way few teams ever have. Stewart won six of the season's eleven races. Teammate François Cevert took the finale at Watkins Glen long after the title had been decided. Ronnie Peterson finished a distant second for Lotus, twenty-nine points back.

So what happened to Lotus, seemingly so dominant just twelve months earlier? Three things. One, the team was still reeling from the loss of the man who may well have been the second-best F1 driver in the world after Stewart. Two, Chapman and the team were devoting a lot of time to the 4WD Lotus 56B turbine F1 car, which went nowhere; Lotus was spread thin too. And three, the increased grip of the 1971-spec Firestones revealed the previously hidden flex in the 72's otherwise standout chassis. Peterson and Fittipaldi reported their findings to Chapman, but to little effect.

"Colin didn't believe us when we said the cars weren't handling," Fittipaldi told *Motor Sport*. "But for the nonchampionship race at Brands Hatch at the end of the year, the one when Jo Siffert died, we had reinforced suspension, a whole new package. The car felt so different. Now we were looking good for 1972."

It was, in fact, an understatement.

---

1 Including two nonchampionship events.

DUTCH GRAND PRIX

June 20, 1971

Zandvoort

4.193 km (2.605 mi)

Pole Position: Jacky Ickx (1:17.42)

Fastest Lap: Jacky Ickx (1:34.95)

Winner: Jacky Ickx (+7.99)

Jacky Ickx (2) and Ferrari began 1971 where they left off the year before, including a dominant win here, but six DNFs in the next seven races meant Stewart (5) would capture his second title, Tyrrell's first as a constructor.

elf
5
Tyrrell-Ford

Left: Denny Hulme (26) wrestled his McLaren M19A to twelfth. Talented Dutchman Gijs van Lennep (30) placed eighth in his Surtees a week after winning the 1971 24 Hours of Le Mans for the Martini Porsche team; a pity the 1972 European F5000 champion never got an opportunity with a top F1 team. “I did eight Formula One races,” says van Lennep. “Finished sixth twice, eighth, ninth, tenth. So it looks quite good, but I never got the right car. My Formula One career was just one-off drives that Marlboro was sponsoring and in sports cars I more or less won everything.”

Below: Stewart’s teammate François Cevert (6) crashed on the twenty-ninth lap.

Ronnie Peterson (16) finished fourth in his STP March. Our man Biro is dressed for the deluge.

CANADIAN GRAND PRIX

September 19, 1971

Mosport Park

3.957 km (2.459 mi)

Pole Position: Jackie Stewart (1:15.3)

Fastest Lap: Denny Hulme (1:43.5)

Winner: Jackie Stewart (+38.3)

The runner-up March 711, Herd's elliptical wing above a bullet nose.

The weekend began bright and sunny. "Mod Scot" Jackie Stewart (left), seated in his Tyrrell, was building an image. "There was something else I needed," he told the *Telegraph* years later. "Headgear to wear before and after my races, because my hair would get matted to my head. I decided a racing driver required something a little more trendy than a country gentleman's cap or a baseball cap, and decided on a black corduroy cap, similar to the one worn at the time by John Lennon." The cars had distinct visual identities too, before effective wind tunnel testing. The winning Tyrrell (11) ran a "sports car" nose at most races.

Clockwise from top: American Mark Donohue's (10) reputation as a driver and engineer was rising so quickly that he was brought in to help "fix" the troublesome McLaren M19A. A beaming Donohue after his stunning third-place finish in his first F1 race enjoys a moment with friend Biro. Earlier in the weekend, he discusses technical matters with Penske crewmember Earl "the Pearl" MacMullan.

Race day is cold and rainy. Jo Siffert (14) splits the two Tyrrells on the front row, then gets the jump on both at the start. The Tony Southgate–designed BRM P160 was the marque's last great hurrah.

Clockwise from top left: The rain clouds force the photographers into wet-weather gear and black-and-white film. Reine Wisell (3) loses his Gold Leaf Lotus 72 on the way to fifth. All three Ferraris finish out of the points, including Mario Andretti (6). Peterson (17) trades the lead with Stewart until backmarker George Eaton moves over on him, knocking the March's wing askew. When fog reduces visibility to the point officials can't see from one marshaling post to the next, the race is red-flagged, the first such occurrence in F1 history.

François Cevert (12) finishes two laps down to Stewart and Peterson. Here he chases Mike Beuttler (19) in his sole factory drive for March.

Wrote *Motor Sport*: “Mark Donohue (10) confirmed what had long been suspected—that he is probably America’s best driver of road-racing machinery.”

Marshals scramble back to position after checking on Jean-Pierre Beltoise's bent Matra. Later, Jackie Stewart enjoys his sixth victory of a championship season.

F1 MAVERICK

Robin Herd

Paul-Henri Cahier/The Cahier Archive

Sometimes fate stands in the way of the success you most want, regardless of how talented you are or how hard you work. Even in Formula One.

Maybe especially Formula One.

Robin Herd is one of the brightest minds the sport has known. At eighteen, the Englishman passed on an invitation to play cricket for Worcestershire to enroll at Oxford, where he graduated with dual degrees in physics and engineering. He was working as a design engineer at Royal Aircraft Establishment (RAE) Farnborough, England's NASA, when Bruce McLaren called him out of the blue and asked him to come design his first Formula One car. Herd, a huge racing fan when he wasn't working on articulated engine fairings for the Concorde, thought it was one of his friends winding him up.

It was one of the smartest phone calls McLaren ever made.

Once at McLaren, Herd commenced work on the McLaren M6A sports car, the first of the "orange elephants" that crushed the competition in the Can-Am and established a large and enduring customer base for the new concern. He also designed the team's first Grand Prix cars, brilliant constructions hobbled by hopeless power units until the team was able to secure a supply of Cosworth engines, whereupon his M7A won the first race it finished. That victory at the 1968 Belgian Grand Prix made McLaren the second man, after former Cooper teammate Jack Brabham, to win a Grand Prix in a Formula One car carrying his own name.

Herd wasn't there to enjoy the victory.

The F1 community was a closely knit one in those days. More like a traveling circus, where everyone knew everyone and side conversations were a form of currency. Keith Duckworth had approached Herd to join Cosworth in late 1967. He needed someone with Herd's abilities to design the new 4WD F1 car he had in mind. With the DFV, Formula One cars now had more power than they could put to the ground. Duckworth was one of the first to see 4WD as the solution.

Herd was torn. He liked being at McLaren, but the team's survival in F1 would depend on obtaining a DFV. Which would only be assured, Herd was told, if he came to Cosworth to work on Duckworth's new car.

"It was a tortuous period, for I wanted to stay at McLaren—of course," says Herd. "And I had promised to say nothing of Keith's approach."

Part of the attraction for Herd was Duckworth's belief that he could convince two-time champion Jim Clark to captain the new team during the 1969 season. There are several, including Herd, who remember Clark in private expressing increasing dissatisfaction with Chapman and Lotus, particularly regarding the fragility of the cars. Jackie Stewart believes his close friend was seriously considering other options, but probably not Cosworth. What is certain is that Herd left McLaren for Cosworth, where work commenced on the 4WD machine early in 1968.

"Being unable to say anything to them," says Herd, "I realized that my best thank-you to Bruce and Teddy for giving me my start was to leave them! It hurt, and they were not happy. To this day I believe that McLaren never knew of the reason for my departure. It was a sore point. I still keep a very kind and lengthy letter from Teddy (a real and largely unappreciated hero in the early McLaren days)."

Thereafter Herd's efforts in F1 were, by his recollection, "always thwarted by one problem or another." Here is his accounting:

> **McLaren: the engine until I left when they immediately won races with my M7 car and said DFV.**
>
> **March: a permanent lack of the finance to compete properly.**

Recorded elsewhere in this chapter were the issues that beset the team in 1970, when Jackie Stewart was carrying the March flag and might have won a fourth title with better reliability. Herd continues:

> **1971: First full season (with) Ronnie Peterson was financially even more difficult, but Ronnie still came second in the World Drivers' Championship despite the extraordinary limitations imposed by our lack of money. Max (a top, top guy) and I were useless at raising sponsorship, yet without making any effort virtually everybody in every category sought to buy our cars.**
>
> **1972: I was commandeered by BMW for their European Championship attack, in which the money existed to perform properly, releasing me from the pain of *our* F1 efforts. And we dominated that EC for several years.**
>
> **1973 onwards in F1 for March was a DFV in the back of an F2 car! Engineered with real ability in the most dire of circumstances by Max, with intermittent remarkable performances.**
>
> **For 1976 I was released by BMW, and Ronnie also rejoined the March F1 team. Poles, led races, and his memorable Monza victory upon the return to a race car of Niki (Lauda) were not enough to stop us selling the team at the end of the year.[1]**
>
> **Then *selling* cars in all formulae (except F1) brought about a new company that was able to do things properly. Indy, of course, was the most important area. But IMSA championships, European championships galore, a Le Mans victory, and other championships throughout the Americas, Australasia, Africa, Europe, and Asia rolled in.**
>
> **I am only sad that there is no racing in the Arctic and Antarctica! And, of course, those Can-Am McLaren days.**

Herd's success in America was extraordinary. At one point in the 1980s, March chassis won five straight Indianapolis 500s.

> **It saddens me to this day, but I was so lucky to have those other opportunities. And to work with truly fabulous drivers and people like Jackie, Ronnie, Chris Amon, Bruce, Denny, John Surtees, Rick Mears, the Andrettis, and others. And similar level nondrivers like Max, Bernie, Roger Penske, Jim Hall, Adrian Newey, and many, many more.**

Starting his own F1 team, victory at Indy, victory at Le Mans, Can-Am championships, IMSA championships, Indy car championships, European championships, and more. All attributable to the extraordinary young designer and cricketer who traded a career in aviation for the highest echelons of motorsport.

But the championship he wanted most remains forever beyond the next horizon.

1 Herd remained to continue to lead March design.

TEXACO
Special
TEXACO

CHAPTER 8: 1972–1973

THE QUINTESSENTIAL F1 CAR

For 1972, Lotus's plump tobacco sponsor asked the team to switch the cars' colors from the red, white, and gold of its Gold Leaf packs to the black and gold of its John Player Special brand. Simple request, but one that would have far-reaching consequences. Overnight, the color scheme was an international sensation, elevating the visibility and perception of both the team (now renamed John Player Team Lotus) and Formula One and spawning black-and-gold production cars around the globe, including a few years later the *Smokey and the Bandit* Firebird Trans Am. Even today, many regard the black-and-gold Lotuses of the 1970s as the defining image of Formula One. Sometimes empires are equal parts substance and cigarette smoke.

The revised Lotus chassis, now designated 72D, was pretty good too. Fittipaldi won five of the twelve races, and in so doing became at twenty-five the youngest World Champion until superseded by Fernando Alonso in 2005. It didn't hurt that this was also the year Jackie Stewart was beset by ulcers, forcing him to miss one race altogether and limiting his form elsewhere, but Fittipaldi drove masterfully. He missed the podium in only four *grandes épreuves*, as they were called in the earliest days of Grand Prix racing—three retirements plus an uncharacteristic eleventh place in Canada due to car problems, one race after the championship had been decided.

Of note is that this was the first year that all tracks on the calendar met minimum safety standards. In fact, the Dutch Grand Prix was cancelled when requested improvements could not be completed in time. It would return the following year.

For 1973, with the season expanded to fifteen races, the championship order was reversed. Fittipaldi started the year with three wins in the first four races but never won again. In part because Chapman curiously refused to impose team orders on Fittipaldi teammate Ronnie Peterson, even though by the time

Designed by Colin Chapman and Maurice Philippe, the Lotus 72 won Constructors' Championships in 1970, '72, and '73.

of the Italian Grand Prix at Monza only Fittipaldi had a realistic chance of catching Stewart. Fittipaldi remembered the crucial moment this way to *Motor Sport*:

> **Colin, Ronnie, and I talk about it before the race and decide we will not race against each other. But near the end, if Ronnie is leading and I am second, Colin will give a signal to tell Ronnie I can come past. So in the race we are an easy one-two and I am waiting for the signal from Colin, and it never comes. I am going crazy, because I still have a chance in the championship. So I start chasing Ronnie, and Ronnie starts racing too. You can't blame him for that, because there was no signal. At the line he beat me by 0.8 sec. After, I went to Colin, very disappointed, and he said, "Well, I decided not to give the signal."**

Fittipaldi began talking with other teams the very next day.

In the end, Fittipaldi and Peterson accumulated fifty-five and fifty-two points, respectively. Stewart, meanwhile, tallied seventy-one to take his third and final title, despite withdrawing from the final race of the season at Watkins Glen after his friend, protégé, and intended successor François Cevert was killed in a practice accident. It would have been Stewart's hundredth Grand Prix.

He retired as the new all-time leader in Grand Prix victories, with twenty-seven.

There were two deaths in Formula One that year. The other was Roger Williamson at the Dutch Grand Prix. Williamson's was a particularly sad commentary on the still-primitive safety systems at work in Formula One. Williamson's car came to rest upside down on the side of the track, the driver conscious, unhurt, and alert, but unable to extricate himself from the overturned car.

The marshals were hopeless. The organizers were worse. A fire safety truck sat beyond the next turn. But because it would have had to drive against race traffic and the organizers elected not to red flag the race, it didn't move. Fans standing on the dunes by Williamson's car surged forward to help—it would have only taken five or six and a good shove to get the March upright—but security forces held them back. Meanwhile, fellow driver David Purley stopped at the scene and ran to his friend's aid. He tried to manage the rescuers, grabbing a fire extinguisher from one of them and putting his shoulder against the stricken car. To no avail. There was, after a damning interval, the telltale whiff of gasoline igniting and the car being consumed in flame. Williamson was burned alive.

The past is not always a quaint place to revisit.

That the Lotuses and Tyrrells did so well that year was in part because the other teams did so poorly. Ferrari, March, BRM, Brabham, Williams, and Surtees all had forgettable years.

The exception was McLaren, which introduced a new model, the M23, designed by Gordon Coppuck, supported by John Barnard. Outwardly, it resembled a Lotus 72. On the track it had the measure of everything else out there. Denny Hulme put it on pole at its very first race. Over the course of the season it captured three wins—one by Hulme, two by American Peter Revson—and seemed destined to improve on that performance.

Perhaps the surprise of the season was the new Shadow entry. Don Nichols was one of the foremost mavericks in the history of motorsports. His introduction to most fans came with the mysterious Shadow Mk1 Can-Am car he towered over on the August 1969 cover of *Road & Track*. Far lower than anything seen previously, it posed the question of whether a two-dimensional car could beat a three-dimensional one.

The project struggled until Nichols landed sponsorship from Universal Oil Products, a company that made unleaded gasoline possible. Unleaded gasoline had become critical to the auto industry with the arrival of new exhaust emission regulations and catalytic converters, which could not tolerate lead.

Nichols hired Tony Southgate to design both a Can-Am car and an F1 car. Southgate had worked for Gurney on his stillborn 1969 F1 Eagle. He moved on to BRM, where he gave the Bourne firm in 1971 one last season in the sun. In 1973, Southgate's Shadow DN1 scored two third placings amidst a flurry of retirements.

As 1973 came to a close, it had been nine full seasons since Ferrari had won a World Championship, and there was little to indicate that streak was about to come to an end.

Mauro Forghieri had other ideas.

American Peter Revson (8) had his best season in Formula One in Gordon Coppuck's M23 McLaren, winning twice and finishing fith in the title chase.

UNITED STATES GRAND PRIX

October 8, 1972

Watkins Glen

5.435 km (3.377 mi)

Pole Position: Jackie Stewart (1:40.48)

Fastest Lap: Jackie Stewart (1:41.64)

Winner: Jackie Stewart (+32.27)

On the rostrum, team owner Ken Tyrrell celebrates with Jackie and Helen Stewart.

Counterclockwise from top left: The season went to Emerson Fittipaldi and a rejuvenated Lotus, but here at the Glen, Jackie Stewart (1) led home a Tyrrell 1-2 ahead of François Cevert (2). The team entered a third car for Frenchman Patrick Depailler (3), who finished seventh. Derek Bell (31) tried his best with the underpowered Tecno PA123, but the car DNFed in all five races it started. Ronnie Peterson (4) finished fourth.

Above: Sam Posey (34) acquitted himself well in a one-off ride in a Surtees TS9B, twelfth and first among the independents.

Top right: Newcomer Jody Scheckter was a revelation in a third McLaren, running fourth until a late spin.

Right: Jacky Ickx (7) likewise won one race, but the Ferrari 213B2 was beginning to show its age.

Above: On François Cevert (2) becoming his teammate, Stewart told *Motor Sport*, “We knew it was a matter of, ‘Who’s the best French driver available?’ and Ken asked me to keep an eye on François. I thought François was the best.” After a couple of seasons together, Stewart felt he had championship potential.

Right: Denny Hulme (19) won just one race (South Africa) but four straight podiums, including third here, to put him third in the final standings.

MONACO GRAND PRIX

June 3, 1973

Circuit de Monaco

3.278 km (2.037 mi)

Pole Position: Jackie Stewart (1:27.5)

Fastest Lap: Emerson Fittipaldi (1:28.1)

Winner: Jackie Stewart (+1.3)

The latest Derek Gardner–designed Tyrrell (5) is all the racecar Stewart needs. In Monaco, he ties Jimmy Clark on the all-time list with twenty-five victories. But Stewart (left) is hiding a secret only he, Ken Tyrrell and Ford's Walter Hayes know: he's planning to retire at year's end.

Above: Stewart's main rivals for the title will be Lotus aces Emerson Fittipaldi and Ronnie Peterson (2), here being chased by McLaren's Denny Hulme (7) and former McLaren mechanic Howden Ganley's (25) Iso-Marlboro.

Opposite top: It will be a lost year for Ferrari, with only one podium for team leader Ickx and Arturo Merzario (4), here running against Emerson's older brother Wilson (7) in the Gordon Murray design that will spark Brabham's revival.

Opposite bottom: Jean-Pierre Jarier (14) and Carlos Pace (24) command their March and Surtees platforms. Cevert (6) will start and finish fourth.

MAZ
lampes et apparei
lampe
auto
HEUER
4

GOODYEAR
STP
STP
STP
STP
STP

Bond Oxo
24
SURTEES

elf
elf
6

Opposite and above left: Jackie and Helen Stewart enjoy another bottle of Moët and another meeting with Monégasque royals Prince Albert and Princess Grace.

Above right: Colin Chapman (center) will let his two drivers Peterson (right) and Fittipaldi race the season without team orders, helping Stewart to the title.

UNITED STATES GRAND PRIX

October 7, 1973

Watkins Glen

5.435 km (3.377 mi)

Pole Position: Ronnie Peterson (1:39.6)

Fastest Lap: James Hunt (1:41.6)

Winner: Ronnie Peterson (+0.668)

It was to have been Jackie Stewart's one hundredth and final race. But a crash during Saturday morning practice claimed the life of friend and teammate François Cevert (6).

Stewart was convinced Cevert simply lost control of the ultrashort-wheelbase Tyrrell over unforgiving bumps. Of Derek Gardner's Tyrrell 005/006, Stewart told *Motor Sport*, "I reckon I was at my peak in my last year, but I remember Emerson [Fittipaldi]—who was driving the Lotus 72—saying, 'I don't know how you drive that car . . .' He and I were fighting for the championship, so a lot of the time he was watching my car from behind, and he was right: it was a handful." Tyrrell boss Ken (right) was grooming Cevert to be the team leader in '74. The remaining cars for Stewart and Chris Amon (29) were withdrawn.

Ronnie Peterson (2), right and above, won a race-long battle with newcomer James Hunt (27). So closely fought was their battle that Hunt quipped afterward to the *New York Times*, "I got up nose to nose going around the first turn . . . but coming out of the turn, I decided to back off and not try to pass. He looked fiercer than me." Hesketh, Hunt's team, was one of the last old-school, rich-guy privateer teams. The team's only advertising was the patch on Hunt's overalls, "Sex: Breakfast of Champions."

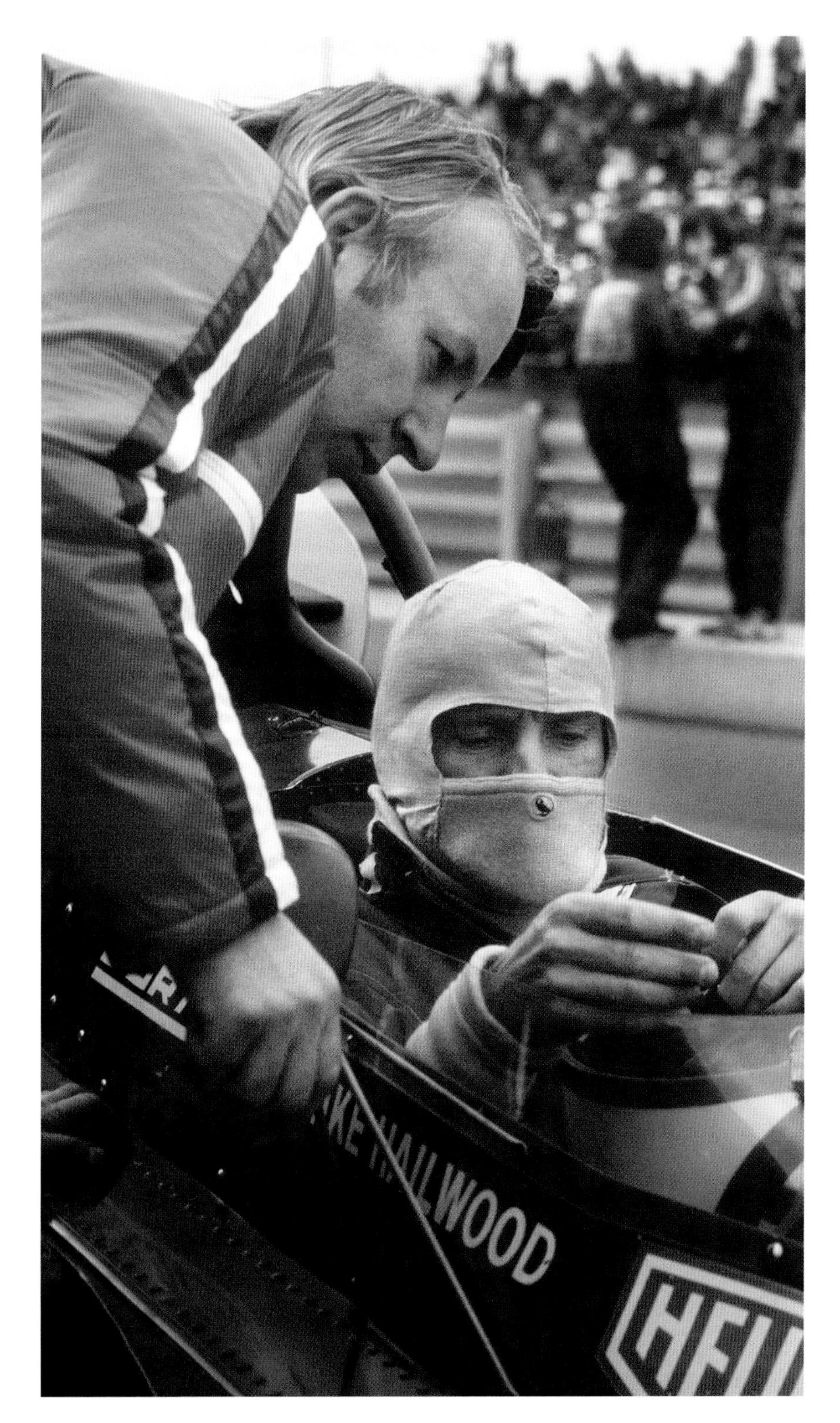

Above: Two-time World Champion Graham Hill (12) had formed his own Embassy Hill team, using customer versions of Tony Southgate's Shadow DN1.

Left: The underfunded Surtees team made it difficult for Mike "the Bike" Hailwood (seated) to repeat the success of his boss, John Surtees (standing). Surtees remains the only man to win World Championships on two wheels and four.

The team's fortunes steadily improved, especially as Ecclestone gave more and more responsibility to brilliant young designer Gordon Murray, seen here conferring with driver Carlos Reutemann (7) at the 1976 Long Beach Grand Prix.

F1 MAVERICK

Bernie Ecclestone

If Colin Chapman was the front man for technical innovation in the Maverick Era, the man who may have been the most responsible for the sport changing from what it was to what it is is Bernard Charles Ecclestone.

Ecclestone was a driver before several accidents convinced him that his best opportunities lay outside the race car. He started managing other drivers in the late 1950s, notably Stuart Lewis-Evans. Later Ecclestone managed Austrian Jochen Rindt, who was torn between remaining with Brabham for 1969 and accepting an invitation from Chapman to join Lotus. Ecclestone told *Motor Sport* that he advised his client, "'If you want to win the World Championship, you've got more chance with Lotus than with Brabham. If you want to stay alive, you've got more chance with Brabham than with Lotus.' It wasn't a bad thing to say—it was a matter of fact. That was what the pattern was, for whatever reason; people did get killed in Lotuses."

In 1971, Ecclestone became a team owner when he purchased the Brabham team from Ron Tauranac. A sign of his maverick personality revealed itself when it came to deciding which people to keep and which to let go, when he singled out upstart designer Gordon Murray.

Together Murray and Ecclestone would win a number of races and eventually championships, but it was when Ecclestone formed the Formula One Constructors' Association in 1974 with fellow owners Colin Chapman, Ken Tyrrell, Max Mosley, Frank Williams, and Teddy Mayer that he really found his métier and transformed the sport. Rising to chief executive in 1978, he controlled F1's television rights, which propelled it to

After giving up on becoming a driver himself, Ecclestone began to manage others, including Austrian Jochen Rindt (8), who went on to become 1970 World Champion for Lotus.

new heights and made Ecclestone one of the world's wealthiest men. A worldwide television audience overnight made Formula One attractive to multinational corporations, and the money flowed in. We asked Ecclestone how the changes came about:

When you look back at the sport during the Maverick Era, what drove the major changes?

It could all be attributed to one very simple thing: a lot more money arrived in the sport.

How did the money get there, and how did it change the sport?

Basically, because manufacturers and a lot of larger companies came in and made more money available. And the minute you do that, whoever it's available to will spend it—in my opinion, not perhaps in the right way, but they spend it. And obviously the people who've got the money normally have got one ambition: to win. Not thinking long-term or anything, but they want to win. And that's what happens.

Where did the money come from? Are we talking about the first major sponsorships, like Gold Leaf with Lotus in 1968, or other types of backers?

People coming in who bought teams and invested in teams. *[Ecclestone purchased Brabham in 1971—Ed.]* Drivers who had friends that had a little money and sort of bought a seat for them. Plus the fact that I generated quite a lot of money, which went to the teams. But not really in that period, because it wasn't until the 1980s that we really started making a lot of money.

When he bought the Brabham team in 1971, it wasn't clear it would even survive. Here Emerson's brother Wilson Fittipaldi (30) wrestles with the Ron Tauranac- designed BT34 "lobster claw."

If sponsorship became prevalent in the 1970s, what changed in the 1980s?

Television. Worldwide television, which attracted people. We did a lot of things early on, but really it wasn't until the 1980s that it really caught on. And the other thing was, when I think we were most successful was when everybody had the same engine, the DFV (Cosworth) and the Ferrari. And it was a lot better. Now we've got—well, we don't want to talk about now! Things have changed.

Why were things better when you had the DFV and the Ferrari engines?

Genuinely different people. People owned the teams, like Colin Chapman and Lotus and Teddy Mayer with McLaren. We all owned our own teams. I owned Brabham. And it was an awful lot different. We could make decisions. What was good for the sport in general didn't hurt us and we could (proceed accordingly). . . . But nowadays it's all completely different. It's very corporate.

Talk a bit of the balance between the sport and entertainment. That changed during the Maverick Era as well.

Very much so. Very, very much so. People are always saying about the good old days and they don't even know when they are, but anyways. . . . People were there because they liked the sport and wanted to win. Didn't have massive egos, nobody was in it for any reason other than to win races if they could.

Designer John Barnard told us in the 1960s the driver was perhaps 50 to 60 percent of the equation. Today, the driver is about 15 to 25 percent of the equation. Do you agree that the role of the driver has changed? And if so, how did it happen?

The technology. The amount of money that's floating around. This allows the engineers to spend and makes the cars very, very sophisticated. Now I think you could take one of the guys at the back of the grid or more or less at the back and put him in one of the cars at the front of the grid and he may do just as well. And the opposite; you set one of those stars at the front, put them at the back, and they'd be in the same position. So in the end the answer is exactly what I said earlier: it's the amount of money that's come into the sport.

In the 1960s you had technology that people could see that made the cars different. Today it's largely invisible, and if you're not a PhD, it's a little hard to understand. What is the role of technology in F1, and how has it changed?

It's what I've been saying for a long time: nobody cares what's hidden. They don't see it and don't care. They want to see guys racing. Today, all the money that's being spent, or most of it, goes into things that are hidden, that people can't see. So it's not something fantastic for the [fans].

Is there a cure?

No. It doesn't matter how much money comes into the sport, it's where the money is spent. If we [can't] find a good way to make the technical regulations so it doesn't matter how much money you want to put into the business, it ain't gonna help. Because you can't.

Safety changed tremendously during the Maverick Era. How important was safety to the sport going from where it was in the 1960s to where it is today?

Well, I think it's one of those things that happened (where) we couldn't keep losing people. And that's why [Dr.] Sid [Watkins] and I got together [in 1978] with the intention of making sure that if the inevitable accident happened, at least the drivers would be safe. [FIA president] Max Mosley got behind testing the cars and making sure the cars were much, much safer. Me and Sid, our position was making sure if there was an accident and if the guys got hurt, they could be looked after.

Half your collection of vintage F1 cars are from the 1960s through the 1980s. Is there anything special about that era compared to others?

These are cars that I've got a history with them. I've got the car that won James Hunt the championship and from when John Surtees won the championship. Those are the sorts of cars I like to collect. Maybe if I was still around in twenty years I'd be collecting the cars we've got today.

By the early 1980s, the Murray/Ecclestone tandem began to dominate, winning World Championships in 1981 and 1983. A big factor was Nelson Piquet (5). But over this period, Ecclestone began to concentrate more on his duties as the top man in Formula One, bringing giant success—and profits—to the sport.

GOODYEAR
HEUER
12
Agip
GOOD YEAR
Agip

CHAPTER 9: 1974–1976

RED TEAM RISING

Emerson Fittipaldi was perhaps the first great driver Chapman let slip away. It may have been the costliest personnel decision he ever made. The Brazilian took his talents and his Texaco money to McLaren and immediately won the 1974 World Championship. Lotus immediately went into a swoon.

The title was contested primarily between three teams: McLaren, Ferrari, and Tyrrell. Now Lotus's lead driver, Ronnie Peterson won three races—the same number as Fittipaldi—but six retirements in the fifteen-race schedule left him fifth in the final standings. He only broke into the top five after the ninth race and never rose any higher.

The title chase was a close-fought thing through the first eight rounds. At that point, Fittipaldi led new Ferrari man Niki Lauda by a single point and Lauda's teammate Clay Regazzoni by three. Jody Scheckter, the new Tyrrell team leader after Stewart and Cevert were gone, was eight points back. Three races later, the deck was reshuffled. Regazzoni now stood atop the standings ahead of Scheckter, Lauda, and Fittipaldi, all of them separated by just seven points. Thereafter an appalling string of DNFs put paid to Lauda's and Scheckter's title hopes; the Austrian failed to finish any of the last five races. That left Regazzoni and Fittipaldi deadlocked at fifty-two points headed into the season finale at Watkins Glen.

In the end, it was a decidedly dramatic if unheroic finish to a Grand Prix season. Both of the main protagonists struggled. Fittipaldi soldiered home in fourth. Regazzoni came eleventh after several stops. It may not have been obvious at the time, but Regazzoni's last best hope of a World Championship was gone.

It was a euphoric moment, by contrast, for Team McLaren. Bruce's firm took both the Drivers' and Constructors' titles after

You can't keep a good scuderia down. Ferrari had last won a title in 1964 but was now about to embark on a run of four Constructors' Championships in five years.

nine years in the category. Difficult to appreciate today is just how few people were involved in the accomplishment. Team manager Alastair Caldwell:

I always like to tell people that I've got a nice photograph of the McLaren team—complete—outside the factory at the end of 1974 when we won the World Championship, we won Indy, we won the Formula 5000 championship, we won some Formula Two races with Scheckter. We built all the cars. We built five Grand Prix cars, because there were two teams. We built the Indy cars. We built the 5000 car. We built the Formula Two car.

The whole factory's outside and it's thirty-four people. That includes two tea ladies. There was almost more tea ladies than anybody else. Two tea ladies, an accountant, a receptionist, you had the works manager. . . . Thirty-four total employees to do all that and win all the races.

But if Fittipaldi was most deservedly the new champion, Niki Lauda was the new fastest man in Formula One. After years of struggling with inferior machinery, Mauro Forghieri's 312B3-74 was the newest chariot of the would-be gods. The Austrian put it on pole nine times. If they could find reliability, where might they finish in 1975?

First, it turns out. With a reliable car at last—he'd finish the 1975 campaign with just one DNF in fourteen starts, after suffering eight the previous season—Lauda won the championship going away. Once again he sat on pole nine times, finished first in five races, and set two fastest laps.

Lauda's cause was aided slightly at the Spanish Grand Prix on the Montjuich circuit when Fittipaldi refused to race because of the danger. As the reigning champion, the Brazilian had become a leader in track and driver safety issues. He'd done an inspection of the circuit a few days earlier and found guardrail sections that were just propped in place. Unbolted. When the organizers refused to act, Fittipaldi said he would do the opening lap, then retire the car. When he followed through on the threat, Jean-Marie Balestre and the FIA commission—which had declared the track safe—revoked his license and suspended him for three races.

Fittipaldi got on a plane and flew home to Switzerland. Fittipaldi told *Motor Sport*:

When I landed at Geneva airport, there was a TV crew waiting to interview me, I assumed because I'd walked away from the race. What I didn't know, what they wanted to ask me about, was Rolf Stommelen hit the barrier and was launched into the crowd. He had broken legs, wrist, and ribs, and four people in the crowd were killed. We wasted four lives for nothing. Montjuich was never used again and, of course, I heard no more from Balestre about my ban.

As always, progress on safety in Formula One came slowly and was paid for in blood. For a long time almost every safety change came about in reaction to tragedy. A small sampling:

Driver:	**Accident:**	**Action:**
Lorenzo Bandini	1967 Monaco Grand Prix	Discontinue use of hay bales.
Jochen Rindt	1970 Italian Grand Prix	Have medical team at races.
Jo Siffert	1971 Race of Champions	Require piped oxy-gen supply.
Mark Donohue	1975 Austrian Grand Prix	Recess helmet visors.
Ronnie Peterson	1978 Italian Grand Prix	Station medical director in safety car.
Elio de Angelis	1981 Practice Session	Ban flexible skirts.

Lauda and Ferrari looked set to repeat in 1976 and were well on their way to doing so until the German Grand Prix. At that point, Lauda led the title chase with fifty-eight points to Hunt's thirty-five. The Austrian's accident there would trigger one of the great comeback stories in sports, well-covered in a number of books and the 2013 Ron Howard film *Rush*. Lauda missed the next two races after Germany. He was back in the car for the Italian Grand Prix at Monza. At the final race of the year, in Japan, it rained heavily. Lauda took the start but then decided to retire. The team offered to say the car broke. He said no. His decision was his decision. Hunt thereby won the World Drivers' Championship. Ferrari took the Constructors' title.

These were heady times for the McLaren team. It also won the Indy 500 that season for the second time as a factory, third overall.

To crank up the drama in *Rush*'s cinematic retelling of the Hunt-Lauda battle, the filmmakers portrayed the pair as bitter rivals. They were, in fact, good friends. The movie men also left out a lot of the humor that was still part of the scene then. McLaren had arrived several days early at the Fuji finale. When Lauda walked over to say hi to James, he found that the radiator and engine intakes on the McLaren were covered with a fine mesh screen. McLaren, which had arrived in Japan several days earlier, explained that there were so many loose pieces of rock and gravel on the circuit that they had found it necessary to install ballistic screen to protect the radiators and injectors. Lauda immediately went back to Ferrari, which then spent half a day going into Tokyo to locate the necessary screening.

It was all a ruse.

There was no problem with rocks at the circuit, and by the time Ferrari had obtained their screen, McLaren had removed its own. Simpler times.

Lauda's accident had one more consequence that would change forever the character of the sport: for 1977 the Nürburgring and the other extralong circuits, like the 5-mile Charade and old 8.7-mile Spa, where it was difficult to provide adequate marshaling, were dropped or shortened.

1974 saw a short-lived resurgence of American makes, with Mario Andretti (55) behind the wheel of the Parnelli VPJ4 and Mark Donohue coming out of retirement to pilot the Penske PC1. Both entrants would fold their tents by the end of the 1976 season.

UNITED STATES GRAND PRIX

October 6, 1974

Watkins Glen

5.435 km (3.377 mi)

Pole Position: Carlos Reutemann (1:38.97)

Fastest Lap: Carlos Pace (1:40.6)

Winner: Carlos Reutemann (+10.73)

A season of change. Brabham hadn't won a race since Jack retired, but Gordon Murray's BT42 was a revelation, propelling Carlos Reutemann (7) to three wins.

Watkins Glen saw Emerson Fittipaldi (above) clinch the championship, breaking a tie with Ferrari's Clay Regazzoni heading into the final round. If anything, Regazzoni's teammate Niki Lauda (12) seemed a bigger reason for the team's newfound success, but DNFs in the season's final five races wasted his early-season brilliance. That kind of thing happened often. "Back in the days when I was covering racing, a 50 percent finishing ratio in a 200-mile race was perfectly normal," says Pete Lyons, who covered F1—exquisitely—in the mid-1970s for *Autosport* and *Autoweek*. "You just accepted it. I highlighted somebody one year; they had a finishing record of 54 percent in the season's races, and that was pretty good. They won the championship." Fittipaldi's teammate Denny Hulme (6) won the season opener, but thereafter had only one podium and decided to hang up his helmet at the end of the year.

Above: The very tidy McLaren M23 (5).

Left: A year after his last race, Jackie Stewart (dark glasses) confers with new team leader Jody Scheckter (center) and Tyrrell designer Derek Gardner (right).

Some of the Glen faithful give a shout out to now-broadcaster Stewart (top photo) while others root on his South African replacement Scheckter (bottom).

UNITED STATES GRAND PRIX WEST

March 28, 1976

Long Beach

3.251 km (2.02 mi)

Pole Position: Clay Regazzoni (1:23.099)

Fastest Lap: Clay Regazzoni (1:23.076)

Winner: Clay Regazzoni (+42.41)

Clay Regazzoni scored a rare grand slam: pole, fastest lap, and victory while leading every lap.

Above: New to the calendar for 1976 is the United States Grand Prix West through the streets of Long Beach, California.

Left: Dan Gurney won the support race for Grand Prix legends, including Juan Manuel Fangio (left) and Denny Hulme (right).

The support race showed just how much F1 technology had changed during the Maverick Era. Counterclockwise from top left: Fangio drove his front-engine 1954 Mercedes W196. Jack Brabham (24) was reunited with the rear-engine Cooper that began the sea change. Maurice Trintignant (33) competed in period-correct headgear.

Right: Defending World Champion Niki Lauda (1) brought his Ferrari 312T home second. The Austrian had four wins and two seconds in the season's first six races.

Bottom left: Chris Amon (22) came eighth in the Ensign.

Bottom right: Ronnie Peterson (10) qualified sixth for March, finished tenth. Tyrrell's Patrick Depailler (4) finished right behind the two Ferraris.

UNITED STATES GRAND PRIX

October 10, 1976

Watkins Glen

5.435 km (3.377 mi)

Pole Position: James Hunt (1:43.62)

Fastest Lap: James Hunt (1:42.85)

Winner: James Hunt (+8.03)

James Hunt (right) needed to win here to keep his title hopes alive by outscoring defending World Champion Niki Lauda. He did so by winning from pole and setting fastest lap, heading to the season finale at Fuji just three points in arrears. Jody Scheckter (3) had little love for Derek Gardner's most audacious design, the six-wheeled P34, but he scored one victory and four seconds, including here at the Glen.

Marlboro

Opposite and bottom left: When Gordon Coppuck's McLaren M26 struggled initially, the team continued with the updated M23 (11), still a force to be reckoned with in James Hunt's hands.

Left: The crew, led by Teddy Mayer (looking at clipboard), waits for their man.

Bottom right: Hunt enjoys the fruits of the weekend's labors.

Reliable aero data is still hard to come by, so teams still experiment with very different aero packages. Irishman John Watson's Penske PC4 (28) uses a wedge-and-canards nose similar to the Lotus 72 and McLaren M23. American Brett Lunger's Surtees TS19 (18) deploys a sports car-style nose. Arturo Merzario's Williams FW05 (20) and Jacques Laffite's Ligier-Matra JS5 (26) split the difference, with wing sections for downforce and fairings intended to smooth airflow over and around the tires. Even Mario is having difficulty making the Lotus 77 (5) stick. The new rolling ground plane in the Imperial College wind tunnel will help Lotus, then Williams make major breakthroughs—and begin the great homogenization of body shapes.

F1 MAVERICK

Mauro Forghieri

When we asked 1979 World Champion Jody Scheckter to what he attributed Ferrari's stunning resurgence from 1975 through 1983, a period during which Ferrari won six of nine Constructors' Championships and three Drivers' titles, he responded with two words:

Mauro Forghieri.

He is not alone in his esteem for the Italian engineer. Forghieri had come to Ferrari in 1960 and was put in charge of all motorsports activities the following October.

He was twenty-six.

"I was scared," Forghieri told www.F1i.com. "And I told Ferrari so, but he reassured me by saying he was behind me. He taught me that you never have to feel defeated beforehand."

His talent manifested itself quickly, through designing the Ferrari 158 with which John Surtees won the 1964 championship. As time went on, his maverick mindset showed itself more and more. Forghieri was the first to put a wing on a Formula One car. At the 1968 Belgian Grand Prix, wrote *Motor Sport*'s Denis Jenkinson, "Ferrari came out with an elaborate aerofoil mounted high above the gearbox like a miniature Chaparral." Not just a wing, but a movable one like the Chaparral, although activated by the transmission rather than a separate pedal. Ever the skeptic, Jenkinson posited that any benefit to this aerodynamic apparatus was "purely psychological."

Apparently it had a beneficial effect on Amon's psyche; he put the Ferrari on pole by *3.7 seconds*.

Despite his inventiveness, the later 1960s were dry times for Ferrari. Although the various V-6 and V-12 engines sounded glorious, they struggled against the all-conquering Cosworth. Which is why Forghieri commenced to build the flat-12 "Boxer" engine. Amon, a Forghieri fan but impatient for a car he could win with, left at the end of 1969. He could sense the potential of the Boxer, but it kept blowing up during testing.

"Ferrari's problems were ongoing, and I honestly believed I couldn't get anywhere in F1 without a DFV," Amon told *Motor Sport's* Simon Taylor. "So I told Ferrari I'd changed my mind [about continuing]. It was the biggest mistake of my life, but frustration does that to people. I said to the Old Man, 'You know how things have been, and I can't go on putting all my effort into this.' 'All right,' he said, 'but I'll win a Grand Prix before you do.' He was right."

Forghieri's flat-12 engine would put Ferrari back at the sharp end of the grid for more than a decade. Chapman's new wedge-shaped, hip-radiator, torsion-barred Lotus 72 grabbed all the attention and the championship in 1970, but the more conventional-looking 312B was arguably its equal. Only horrible reliability in the first half of the year kept Jacky Ickx from mounting a stronger challenge. As it was, from the French Grand Prix on, Ferrari won five of eight poles and set six of eight fastest laps—including the last six races in a row.

His 312T, which debuted in 1975 and was in its fifth iteration during the 1980 season, was the dominant car of its lifespan, scoring twenty-seven wins and sixty-one podiums in just ninety races. The T stood for *trasversale*; its transverse gearbox could be located ahead of the rear axle for a lower polar moment.

Forghieri's record is unassailable. From 1975 through 1983, Ferrari won six of nine Constructors' Championships

(1975–1977, 1979, 1982–1983) and three Drivers' titles (1975, 1977, 1979). Had Niki Lauda decided to race in the season-ending Japanese Grand Prix in 1976, it might have been four.

Forghieri spoke about the nature of Formula One during the Maverick Era in a 2013 www.Petrolicious.com interview:

> **In that era—say from roughly 1962 to 1980 or 1984—racers had to be men before they were champions. Do you understand what I mean? Drivers ate with mechanics and technicians; it helped maintain a friendly, familylike atmosphere. Today, there is too much money involved, and sponsors have destroyed the spirit of the championship.**

Ferrari would not win another championship until Ross Brawn and Michael Schumacher arrived on the scene in the late 1990s.

Forghieri (right) takes notes as driver Lorenzo Bandini (left) describes what the Ferrari is doing.

John Player
John
Player
Special
6
Valvoline
Valvoline
GOODYEAR

CHAPTER 10: 1977

SOMETHING FOR NOTHING

The single greatest advance in vehicle performance during the Maverick Era was downforce. It began in earnest with wings (thank you, Mr. Hall) and progressed from there.

But the key to the next great advance in downforce was the development of better wind tunnels. Wind tunnels are inherently artificial. Developed originally for aircraft, they differ from real life by having the aircraft stationary and having the wind moving.

When racers and manufacturers started using them to determine the aerodynamic efficiency of vehicles, they simply sat the vehicles on the wind tunnel floor and blew air past them.

This introduced distortion in at least two areas that people hoped would have made no difference. One, in the real world, the road was moving in relation to the vehicle. Two, the tires were rotating. Turns out both things matter. Especially with a Formula One car with exposed tires. This only became apparent in the mid-1970s with the introduction of moving ground or floor planes. That's right. Now when they turned the air on in the wind tunnel to, say, 100 miles per hour, they were able to have the "road surface" (actually a large conveyor belt) move at the same speed. Tony Southgate was one of the premier designers of the period and one of the first to understand and exploit this new development:

When wind tunnel testing you are after the most accurate performance figures and the best that can be recorded about your new race car. That way you can calculate the on-track performance of the new car. Wind tunnel testing did not get going bigtime in F1 until the 1970s (in the UK). Until then the car's designer was responsible for the aero shape, basically producing aesthetically pleasing shapes. Wind tunnel models were quite basic at the beginning, but with the advent of the moving floor plane the model had to become much more realistic, featuring suspension, full

The World Championship-winning Lotus 79 was the team's second ground-effect car. "We should have won the championship with the 78 in 1977," said aerodynamicist Peter Wright, "but we had engine problems."

water and oil systems, etc. The result was very accurate downforce and drag forces plus the very important center of pressure or pressure distribution to the front and rear axles.

The moving floor was introduced in 1975. I was the first in the UK to develop a new design using it. The car was the Shadow DN5, which when it first appeared was aerodynamically the best car on the grid.

The greatest reason for this was that the center of pressure was completely different when measured with the floor moving, 10 to 15 percent less on the front axle, so I simply reengineered the distribution by creating larger front wing sections and downforce-generating nose shapes. The wing sections were also at an advanced level.

The comparison was very easy to check; you simply switched the floor off when running the tunnel to get the old figures.

Imagine designing a race car suspension and not realizing the engine should be 10 to 15 percent farther fore or aft than it was. Imagine plotting the trajectory of a lunar mission and not only being 10 to 15 percent off, but not realizing it until your man was on his way to the moon. That's the way it'd been for racing designers prior to moving ground planes.

Race car builders had been putting their designs in the wind tunnel for years, only to get to the track and find that the cars often didn't behave the way they expected. This was famously the case with the Ford GTs of the mid-1960s. When testing at Le Mans, Gurney said, "You need to fix this, the front wheels are lifting off the ground on the Mulsanne Straight." "Nonsense," one of the engineers said, "This car was tested in the wind tunnel. There's no lift." Whereupon Gurney invited the engineer to ride with him for a lap. When he got out of the car, the now very ashen-faced engineer turned to the other Ford people in the pit and said, "We need to fix this. The front wheels are lifting off the ground."

Moving ground planes made wind tunnels much more reliable for race car development.

The problem with downforce was that it usually came at a great cost in drag. Jim Hall introduced movable wings to his cars when he realized that fixed spoilers and air dams cost almost as much speed on the straightaways as they provided in the turns.

Thus began the search for "free" downforce. Using the air in such a way that it didn't incur a severe drag penalty. One solution was the Chaparral 2J "vacuum cleaner" of 1970, whose powerful fans created constant downforce with minimal drag. It was quickly outlawed but not forgotten. When Southgate went to work for Lotus in the mid-1970s, one of the first things Colin Chapman asked him to explore was a way to achieve fan-driven downforce within the existing F1 rules. It never went beyond the idea stage. (It would take until 1978 for Gordon Murray to crack the code, as you'll read in the next chapter.)

The next great advance came when Peter Wright and others went to the Imperial College wind tunnel to measure the effectiveness of the new Lotus 78. The side pods on the wind tunnel model kept sagging, giving inconsistent results, so they added card stock to keep them an exact height off the surface. The card stock served as side skirts, and the downforce numbers went through the roof. Lotus was exploiting the Bernoulli Effect, which describes the decrease in static pressure as airflow speed increases. The shape of the underside of the side pods promoted it. Massive downforce with relatively little drag.

The results were so staggering and the cause so easy to keep hidden that Lotus launched a disinformation campaign to distract the other teams from the side pods. Their newfound speed, Lotus leaked to selected pressmen, was due to a revolutionary new transaxle . . .

You would think that the first ground-effect car would have dominated. It did and it didn't. Andretti's Lotus 78 took seven poles in the season's seventeen races, one more than McLaren's James Hunt. And he registered four wins, also more than anyone else. But a series of DNFs caused in part by Chapman making a special deal with Cosworth to run more powerful but unproven development engines gave the once again impeccable Niki Lauda and the Ferrari 312T2B the Drivers' and Constructors' titles. Lauda left the team with two races to go—Maranello politics again—but had already clinched his second World Championship.

Jody Scheckter finished seventeen points aft of Lauda in the blue-and-gold Wolf, which had been the surprise of the early season before a rash of DNFs midyear. In one eight-race stretch, Scheckter failed to finish six times.

In other news, Alan Jones piloted the Shadow to the marque's first and only F1 victory. What was impressive about it was that Don Nichols' upstart team had now won in every category in which it had competed: F1, Can-Am, and Formula 5000.

At Lotus, there was a fair argument for just bulletproofing the 78 for the following season, but Chapman decided to pull out all the stops and develop a new car, the 79, and forego the development engines. In retrospect these were both excellent decisions.

How important had that moving ground plane been in discovering ground effect? This story from Peter Wright provides an indication. He told *Motor Sport*:

We heard that when the type 78 came out, Ferrari built an equivalent version and tested it in a tunnel in Italy. I'm not sure which one, possibly Pininfarina, but without a rolling road, and they said, 'Ah, it doesn't work.' So yes, if you don't have a rolling road, you will definitely get the wrong airflow conditions underneath the car.

More than Ferrari had failed to grasp where the Lotus's advantage lay.

UNITED STATES GRAND PRIX WEST

April 3, 1977

Long Beach

3.251 km (2.02 mi)

Pole Position: Niki Lauda (1:21.65)

Fastest Lap: Niki Lauda (1:22.75)

Winner: Mario Andretti (+0.773)

Second-row qualifier Jody Scheckter's (20) Wolf WR1 rockets past first and second qualifiers Niki Lauda (11) and Mario Andretti (5). But it's Lotus's day. Mario will become the first American to win a Grand Prix on home soil and score the first victory for the new ground effect Lotus 78.

THE MOVIE
ADULTS ONLY
"SATAN WAS A LADY"
"TEENAGE SEX KITTEN"
MARIO
25 2

PROFESSIONAL TV SALES · SERVICE RENTALS
GINO'S Beauty SALON
LIQUOR
Marlboro
Marlboro
TEXACO
Marlboro
1
GOODYEAR
FINA
7
MARTINI BRABHAM
FINA
John Player Special
5
TOYOTA
YOU ASKED FOR IT. YOU GOT IT.
INSTRUMEN

Above: Shadow would have a star-crossed season. Many felt it had a future champion in Tom Pryce, killed senselessly in South Africa when a marshal ran across the track. But later it scored its first and ultimately only F1 win when it convinced another future champion, Alan Jones, here turning down Linden Avenue, to give F1 one more try. "Pryce was killed at Kyalami, and [team manager] Jackie Oliver came on the phone," Jones told *Motor Sport*. 'What are you up to, Alan?' 'Nothing much.' 'Come and drive for Shadow.' 'Well, trouble is I've got this contract with Surtees.' 'Let me handle that,' said Jackie. I don't know what happened, but he did handle it, and I became a Shadow driver for 1977. [Shadow owner] Don Nichols was a bit different—anybody who wears a black hat and a black cape is a bit different—but Alan Rees was a good team manager, he made things happen. We had a podium at Monza and a couple of fourths. And I won the Austrian GP."

Left: Mario (5) was fortunate to escape the first-turn accident that launched defending World Champion James Hunt's aged McLaren M23 (1) high into the air. Amazingly, Hunt soldiered on to finish just out of the points in seventh. As part of his duties at Long Beach, lensman Biro was in charge of the photographers. Friend Dale von Trebra asked him where he should shoot the start. "Outside of the first turn," said Biro. That's where von Trebra captured this iconic image. *Dale von Trebra*

CD-2
STEWART-WARNER
INSTRUMENTS
CD-2
LIQUOR
TV
RENTALS

The brainchild of former travel agent Christopher Robin Pook, who was convinced Southern California could support a Monaco-like race through the streets, the Grand Prix of Long Beach drew large crowds. Converting the streets into a racecourse was an enormous undertaking, but the event helped revitalize the city and remains a fixture to this day, albeit as an Indy car race since 1984.

F1 MAVERICK

Peter Wright

There was a time when F1 careers could start like this:

> **I did engineering at [Cambridge] University, but I contacted Tony Rudd at BRM during my second year, and asked him if I could come and work for BRM. And he said, "No, you don't want to do that."**
>
> **I said, "Yes, I do."**
>
> **He says, "Oh, sod. I suppose you better come see me."**

Rudd offered Wright a "summer vacation," what nowadays would be called an internship. Wright dug into his work there, and Rudd offered him a job as his personal assistant. He started full-time in 1967. He was twenty-one. Formula One during the Maverick Era.

The timing was auspicious. The following year BRM, like the rest of F1, was concentrating more and more attention on downforce. Something Wright was especially suited to, because he'd specialized in aerodynamics and thermodynamics at Cambridge. So when Rudd was asked to develop BRM's capabilities, "Tony just pushed the whole lot across his desk at me one day," Wright remembers. "He said, 'Wright, you can deal with all this.' John Harvey came up from the Imperial College and said, 'I think you guys need a wind tunnel.' And Tony said, 'Oh, yeah, I suppose. Yeah, Peter, go have a look! Find out what that's all about!'"

Wright spent crucial time testing out new ideas in the Imperial College wind tunnel, which was named for land speed record holder Donald Campbell. The 5-by-4-foot tunnel was suitable for scale models, not full-size cars, and its moving ground plane was still years away. But it was the best wind tunnel around.

It was Rudd who encouraged Wright to look beyond the wings then beginning to sprout on race cars around the world.

"Tony Rudd said, 'I don't like wings. I don't think they're a safe, nice thing. They shouldn't be on a racing car. Find another way of doing it,'" says Wright. "That's what [inspired] me to try and figure out a way of using the whole body of the car to create downforce."

Wright spent time in the Imperial College wind tunnel developing what he described in his excellent 2001 book *Formula 1 Technology* as "stubby, airfoil-section side panniers." Basically, airfoil tanks between the BRM's front and rear wheels. The initial tests were inconclusive, and then there was a regime change at BRM that saw Rudd leave for Lotus. Wright went to Specialised Mouldings, which was doing work on composites.

While there, Wright developed the graceful airfoil-section supplemental fuel tanks for Robin Herd's March 701. "But that was all without the benefit of wind tunnels, it was just off the top of my head, my concept of aerodynamics," says Wright. As with the panniers on the BRM, there was no clear gain in downforce, but Mario Andretti remembers under certain conditions where suspension loading brought one of the tanks in close proximity with the road surface there seemed to be a sudden, marked gain in traction.

Fast forward to 1976. Rudd is still at Lotus. Wright has just moved there, and Chapman has tasked both of them, in conjunction with designer Ralph Bellamy, with exploring new low-drag downforce systems for the upcoming Lotus 78. So

Wright and Bellamy went off to the same Imperial College wind tunnel, with its newly installed moving ground plane, armed with a quarter-scale model of the 78. By now, Wright had sensed that having a moving ground plane and rotating wheels was essential to generating effective results from wind tunnel testing.

We set up a very fundamental research program, we said, "What do we want ahead of the front wheels that will create the most downforce? Do we want wings, do we want a full-width nose? What do we want?" And we saw immediately that wings, as they approach the ground, worked better and better. Which was the first clue.

Then they looked at the center section of the car. Part of the concept of the 78 was to have a very narrow chassis, so Bellamy needed to add more fuel tankage and cooling.

All right. "So, why don't we make some streamlined side pods?" Airfoil-section side pods, put some fuel in them and put the radiators in them. And back we went to the tunnel.

Suddenly they were getting wildly inconsistent readings. Wright noticed the side pods were sagging and wondered if they needed to be propped up to their intended height.

We braced them and put some cards along to close the gap between the edge of the side pod and the floor, just leaving a tiny gap, and bingo! The results were so dramatic we didn't believe them. We had to do it about three times.

Wright, Tony Rudd, and Ralph Bellamy created the first ground effect race car. *Courtesy of the Revs Institute; Eric della Faille Photograph Collection.*

What they'd improvised simply to keep the side pods from drooping was what we now know as skirts. These prevented the massive suction created by the ground effect from bleeding into the atmosphere. Another innovation pioneered by Jim Hall, on the Chaparral 2J "vacuum cleaner."

Developing skirts that worked was the other half of ground effect. So once you have the aerodynamics right, then you've got to make the skirts work. That was a really fun time, because every time you made an improvement to skirts, the drivers came in and said, "Bloody hell!" They went a second a lap quicker.

A new age in downforce was born. It took the better part of a decade, but that was nothing to discover the racing equivalent of El Dorado. Downforce without the cost. Today, downforce is a fundamental design consideration of every major type of racing vehicle, from Formula One to Le Mans to Top Fuel dragsters and NASCAR stock cars.

TOYOTA
Valvoline
Valvoline

CHAPTER 11: 1978

MARIO'S YEAR AT LAST

Mario Gabriele Andretti's Formula One dreams began in 1954 watching Ascari and Fangio, winners of seven of the first eight World Championships, dueling at Monza. Now he was back at Monza, on the grid for the 1978 Italian Grand Prix, starting from pole, with one hand on a championship of his own. So superior was Colin Chapman's ground-effect Lotus 79 that only the 1967 Daytona 500 and 1969 Indianapolis 500 winner's great friend and teammate, Ronnie Peterson, was still in contention with three races left, and "Super Swede" Peterson was twelve points back. Furthermore, unlike 1973, when Lotus teammates Fittipaldi and Peterson raced to the end, there were team orders in place, meaning Mario would win the title barring a catastrophe.

Peterson, thirty-four, had agreed to the terms and honored them. When friends would point to races Peterson might have won, as if to say maybe he should have ignored the agreement, he would shut them down. A deal was a deal. Besides, Peterson said, it was Mario who'd done the lion's share of the development. The American, now thirty-eight, was a major reason the car was in a position to win. Mario had earned his number one status. My time will come, said Peterson.

Only sometimes one's time never comes.

The start of the race was chaotic. The rear of the grid was still forming when the starter gave the signal to *go*. Big mistake. Too many cars, too little space. Peterson speared into the barriers and sat trapped in his burning car, his legs badly damaged. As was too often the case back then, it was not the officials but fellow drivers who pulled him from the flames. Had we learned nothing since Roger Williamson? Peterson died of an embolism the following day.

Mario Andretti (5) started the season with the trusty Lotus 78, but when the 79 arrived, it would carry him to his first and Chapman's final World Championship.

Andretti:

The 1978 Italian Grand Prix in Monza had huge significance for two reasons:

First, I was back in my native Italy, in the exact place where the dream began for me. Monza is where I saw my first-ever race at age fourteen.

Second, this race was going to determine the Formula One World Champion. It would either be me—or my teammate and best friend Ronnie Peterson. At the start of the race, there was a horrific crash.

I won the World Championship that day . . . Ronnie Peterson died. It should have been the happiest day of my life. My lifelong dream had come true. I was World Champion. But Ronnie was dead. The combination of triumph and tragedy was unbearable.

So dominant was the new Lotus 79 that season that Andretti and Peterson still finished one-two in the Drivers' Championship, despite Peterson missing the final three races. Lotus won the Constructors' title going away. Ferrari, a distant second. Lotus won half the season's sixteen races, took eleven poles, and set six fastest laps. What Ralph Bellamy, Tony Rudd, and Peter Wright had theorized in the Imperial College wind tunnel was now proving itself the future of Formula One.

Carlos Reutemann had replaced Lauda at Ferrari and finished what could only be a disappointing third for Forghieri and the Prancing Horse crew despite four wins. Lauda, now ensconced as team leader at Brabham, came fourth.

For drivers like Jody Scheckter, who looked like a championship contender at Walter Wolf Racing when the Lotus 78 arrived on the scene, there was now the unwelcome realization that they wouldn't stand a chance without a ground-effect car of their own.

"You'd do twenty laps," Scheckter remembers with a chuckle, "and [the Lotuses] would be two seconds or quicker than you straight away, and from then on, that's what it stayed. And after, they'd say, 'Oh, look how [the Lotus driver] drove. He's so fantastic, he doesn't slide the car or anything.' Thanks a lot."

Which brings up another big change that ground effect introduced: the cars didn't move around anymore. Throughout the history of the sport, part of the thrill of spectating was watching different drivers' techniques through the turns. Before the advent of wide tires, all the cars "drifted" through corners. Even when slicks came in, there were still drivers like Jochen Rindt, Ronnie Peterson, and Hans Stuck Jr. who cornered in dramatic tail-out fashion. But ground effect worked best when the car was pointed as straight as possible; the great, graphic slides disappeared. And by their nature, ground-effect cars were more upset following other cars, so overtaking dropped off dramatically. That quickly, the great spectacle that was Formula One became a lot less spectacular. And it's never recovered since.

It was Lauda and Brabham who—briefly—posed the greatest threat to Lotus's newfound hegemony. As soon as Brabham recognized why the Lotus was so fast, they realized that not only did they need to build a ground-effect car of their own, but that even if they did so, its aerodynamics would be compromised in a major way by the girth of their flat-12 engines.

The team's South African–born designer, Gordon Murray, still just thirty-one, applied his trademark lateral thinking to the problem: an ingenious workaround of the F1 rule prohibiting movable aerodynamic devices. The resulting car was not just competitive with the Lotus; it was demonstrably faster. It won its one race, that year's Swedish Grand Prix, going away. After

Sweden, winning driver Niki Lauda was just eleven points behind Andretti with eight GPs still on the calendar.

The other teams were up in arms. Colin Chapman was furious. He led a protest of the new Brabham, just as McLaren had protested the BT46B's inspiration, Jim Hall's Chaparral 2J "vacuum cleaner," eight years earlier, but this time to no avail. The Brabham may have exploited a loophole in the regulations, but it exploited it well. The BT46B, the FIA affirmed, was perfectly legal.

Then, just as suddenly as it appeared, it was gone.

Brabham owner Bernie Ecclestone explains his thought process:

> **Well, it took us, Gordon probably told you, a couple of months really to develop that. Went through a lot of problems. Somebody like Chapman could have probably done it quicker, because we learned and then they would have learned from us what not to do or what to do. We would have had an advantage maybe for another couple of races, then everyone would have caught up. And the cars then would've been so quick, it would have been dangerous. So I thought the best thing to do (was to) save people spending an awful lot of money to get where we were and take the risk to withdraw it, so we withdrew it. Gordon wasn't at all happy with the fact that I withdrew the car, but never mind. That's what we did.**

Furthermore, the FIA already had announced it intended to close the fan car loophole for the following season, which meant even if the advantage remained through the end of the year, that was it.

What undoubtedly influenced Ecclestone's thinking more was his still-solidifying role as head of the Formula One Constructors' Association. He'd just been named the group's chief executive. He was the point person for the increasingly lucrative television rights that over time would make him and the other team owners extremely wealthy men. Alienating the other owners would risk more in the long run than winning a few races might gain in the short.

Thus, Mario Andretti had his first Formula One World Championship.

Colin Chapman had his first Constructors' Championship since 1973.

Few who watched the black-and-gold Lotus 79s slash across the racetracks of Europe and beyond that season, wheeled by Super Swede and Super Mario, could imagine it would be Chapman's last.

UNITED STATES GRAND PRIX WEST

April 2, 1978

Long Beach

3.251 km (2.02 mi)

Pole Position: Carlos Reutemann (1:20.63)

Fastest Lap: Alan Jones (1:22.21)

Winner: Carlos Reutemann (+11.061)

Reutemann will win here, edging Andretti, and finish third in the championship.

Pete Biro was one of the original staff members of the Long Beach Grand Prix Association. When he learned of plans to hold a victory banquet Dinner in the just-completed exposition hall of the Long Beach Convention Center (circular building) , he said, “Good luck. You won’t have the winning driver there. Soon as the flag falls and they get out of their cars, they’re off to the airport for the first flight home.” But Pete had his own maverick moment. “I had to do something,” Pete says. “They had sold out the banquet. I went to the Ferrari chief engineer, Mauro Forghieri, whom I had gotten to know at the Mexican Grand Prix a couple of years earlier. He was dating the daughter of my friend Fred van Beuren, and I was staying at the Van Beuren home. I told Mauro the problem and we came up with the following idea. He would have the chief mechanic drive the Ferrari right into the dining area, right between the tables, accompanied by the entire Ferrari crew. The problem was, however, that it was against the law to fire an engine inside the building, and if I asked my boss, Chris Pook, he would have to say no. I have to tell you, when that Ferrari lit the tires and came into the room at 10,000-plus rpm, it raised the hair on everyone’s neck!”

MONACO GRAND PRIX

May 7, 1978

Circuit de Monaco

3.312 km (2.057 mi)

Pole Position: Carlos Reutemann (1:28.34)

Fastest Lap: Niki Lauda (1:28.65)

Winner: Patrick Depailler (+22.45)

The 1978 season will be remembered for the dominance of the new Lotuses and multiple wins by Ferrari's Carlos Reutemann and Brabham, but at Monaco a very different winner prevailed. The Grand Hotel Hairpin is one of the most famous turns in racing—and also one of the slowest.

In six seasons, Mauro Forghieri's 312T series Ferraris won 27 races, three Drivers' Championships, and four Constructors' Championships. It is considered by some measures the most successful F1 design ever.

Patrick Depailler (4) scores a brilliant first win, one of only two in a career that will be cut short by a testing accident two years later. Reutemann (11) started from pole but had to pit for repairs after colliding with James Hunt's McLaren. For a while, John Watson (2), Depailler (4) and Watson teammate Lauda (1) ran in a train until about half distance when the Irishman went straight on at the chicane. "Niki was not only one of the finest drivers with whom I have ever worked, but also as good-humored and pleasant as any," says March maverick Robin Herd. "Considering he is up against Ronnie (Peterson), Jackie (Stewart), and the like, that is some compliment."

Above: On the season, Andretti (5) would win six races and Peterson (6) two, the Swede often dutifully following the team leader home.

Right: Biro captures midrace action from the roof of the Loews Hotel, Andretti leading third-place finisher Jody Scheckter's Wolf (20) and Alan Jones' Williams (27).

UNITED STATES GRAND PRIX

October 1, 1978

Watkins Glen

5.435 km (3.377 mi)

Pole Position: Mario Andretti (1:38.11)

Fastest Lap: Jean-Pierre Jarier (1:39.55)

Winner: Carlos Reutemann (+19.739)

Newly crowned champion Andretti (5) thrilled the home crowd by putting his Lotus on pole and into an early lead ahead of Reutemann and Jones.

Top left: Ultimately, Reutemann (11) put his Ferrari on the victory stand and closed the points gap to Peterson, who had been killed at the previous race in Italy.

Top right: Two-time champ Emerson Fittipaldi's (14) fifth place here would deliver Fittipaldi Automotive's highest-ever championship placing, seventh.

Bottom: Brett Lunger (23) soldiered up from twenty-fourth on the grid to finish thirteenth in Mo Nunn's handsome Ensign.

F1 MAVERICK

Paul-Henri Cahier/The Cahier Archive

Gordon Murray

Bernie Ecclestone remembers that when he bought Brabham in 1971 from Ron Tauranac, "Tauranac told me I should get rid of [Gordon Murray] and keep everybody else. So I kept Gordon and got rid of everybody else."

As usual, Ecclestone the master contrarian made the right choice.

Murray went on to become one of the greatest change agents in the sport, despite the fact that Brabham was in those years typically much smaller than the other major teams. "We were giant-killers," Murray told *Motor Sport*. For his final three years in F1, Murray left Brabham for McLaren, where his cars were untouchable, including in the 1988 season, when his MP4/4 won fifteen of the year's sixteen races. Over the course of a twenty-year F1 career, Murray's cars won fifty-six F1 races, five World Drivers' Championships, and three World Constructors' Championships.

The South African innovated in every aspect of the sport. Materials, where he was the first to use carbon fiber as a structural material and carbon brakes (although not the first to do a complete carbon-fiber monocoque). Strategy, when he calculated that a car designed to carry half a fuel load would cover a Grand Prix distance faster than a car carrying a full one even with the midrace pit stop this would necessitate. And performance technology, of which there was no better example than his 1978 Brabham BT46B "fan car."

The fan car was a direct reaction to the introduction of ground effect. Murray:

When ground effect was discovered in the mid-to-late 1970s by Chapman [and] Lotus, we were at a huge disadvantage because by the time people looked at the geometry of the venturis down the side of the car, the Cosworth V-8 being a 90-degree V-8 was perfect, because you could sweep the primary pipes up out of the way and you could have a really good-shape diffuser and venturi, whereas our flat-12 was right in the middle of where you needed to be. I said to Bernie, "We're sunk, really, because we'll never get a venturi past that engine."

So he reread the regulations. And found a loophole big enough to drive a Brabham through.

I was quite good in those days at finding loopholes in the regulations. I reread Article 3.7 in the FIA book, which said that anything whose primary purpose was to have aerodynamic influence on the car had to be fixed and not movable.

I stared at "the primary purpose" and I spoke to a couple of lawyers and I said, "If I've got two functions, what's the primary purpose?" They said the one that had the biggest influence.

That's when I hatched the idea of cooling the car with a fan and having 55 percent of the (air) going through the radiator, which could be measured, and the other 45 percent sucked the car down to the ground. I never ever pretended it didn't suck the car down, but its primary purpose was to cool the car, that's why the car never got banned.

The idea was to create a large area underneath the existing BT46 that would be sealed to the road surface with skirts. The fan, which was attached to the engine, would evacuate the air underneath the car to create massive suction. How much suction? "We couldn't measure it. We could calculate it," Murray says. "I know even at half revs the car would hold itself upside down on the ceiling."

The resulting car, renamed BT46B, was completed in just three months, in time for the Swedish Grand Prix, eighth of the sixteen races that year. Three months in which Murray and fellow designer David North did about one hundred design drawings, made all the parts, built them, put them on the car, and went testing. The fans alone went through three iterations, from glass-reinforced nylon to cast magnesium to hubs machined from solid aluminum. The skirts were just as complicated.

Somehow they made the deadline.

"Right up until a week before Sweden we were still breaking fans and fan hubs and all sorts of things," Murray remembers.

Once there, it was all the other teams who were going to pieces.

> **Chapman immediately went on a mission to get the thing outlawed . . . because he could see his championship gone. Nobody was going to beat this thing. He got Ken Tyrrell and various other team owners rallied around. They got drivers to say that the car was throwing stones out the back, which of course it didn't, the fan efflux is only 58 miles an hour.**

The cars didn't look dominant in practice, but only because Murray had told Lauda and teammate John Watson not to showcase their advantage. "We kept saying to the drivers, 'Don't go flat out. If you do, it will just make it worse for us if we're first and second on the grid.' But they couldn't go slow. Lauda kept saying to me, 'I'm trying to go slow, but I'm still doing these times.'"

When qualifying came, Murray made a split-second decision to insure the cars didn't set laughably fast times: he sent Lauda and Watson out on full tanks. And they *still* qualified second- and third-fastest.

During the race, Lauda hung back a while for appearance's sake, then disappeared into the distance. Clearly, if the cars continued to be reliable, Lauda would be the clear favorite for the title.

Then Bernie the contrarian flipped the script again, voluntarily withdrawing his giant-killer from the remaining races. "Bernie Ecclestone was just getting powerful in those days," Murray explains, "and taking over control of the racing [as head of] the Formula One Constructors' Association. And basically, [the other team owners] wrote to him and said, 'If you continue to race the car to the end of the year—because the FIA had said you can race it until the end of the year and then we'll change the regs—that's the end of the Formula One Constructors' Association.'"

Bernie decided that concession was the better part of valor, and the BT46B was no more. But it lives on as one of many examples of Murray's genius and ingenuity.

So why did the South African native leave the sport twelve years later after winning both the Constructors' and Drivers' Championships at McLaren three straight years?

Basically, because the Maverick Era was long over by then. As Murray told *Motor Sport*:

> **The days of real technical innovation in F1, with big steps forward overnight, were rapidly disappearing, because of the increasing levels of regulation. Young engineers joining F1 now don't know any different, and for them it must be great, but it didn't appeal to me as much as the days when it was more sports- and engineering-driven. Now it was just all business.**

A business that was, thanks in many ways to Ecclestone, stronger than ever. And a sport growing less and less sporting with every passing year.

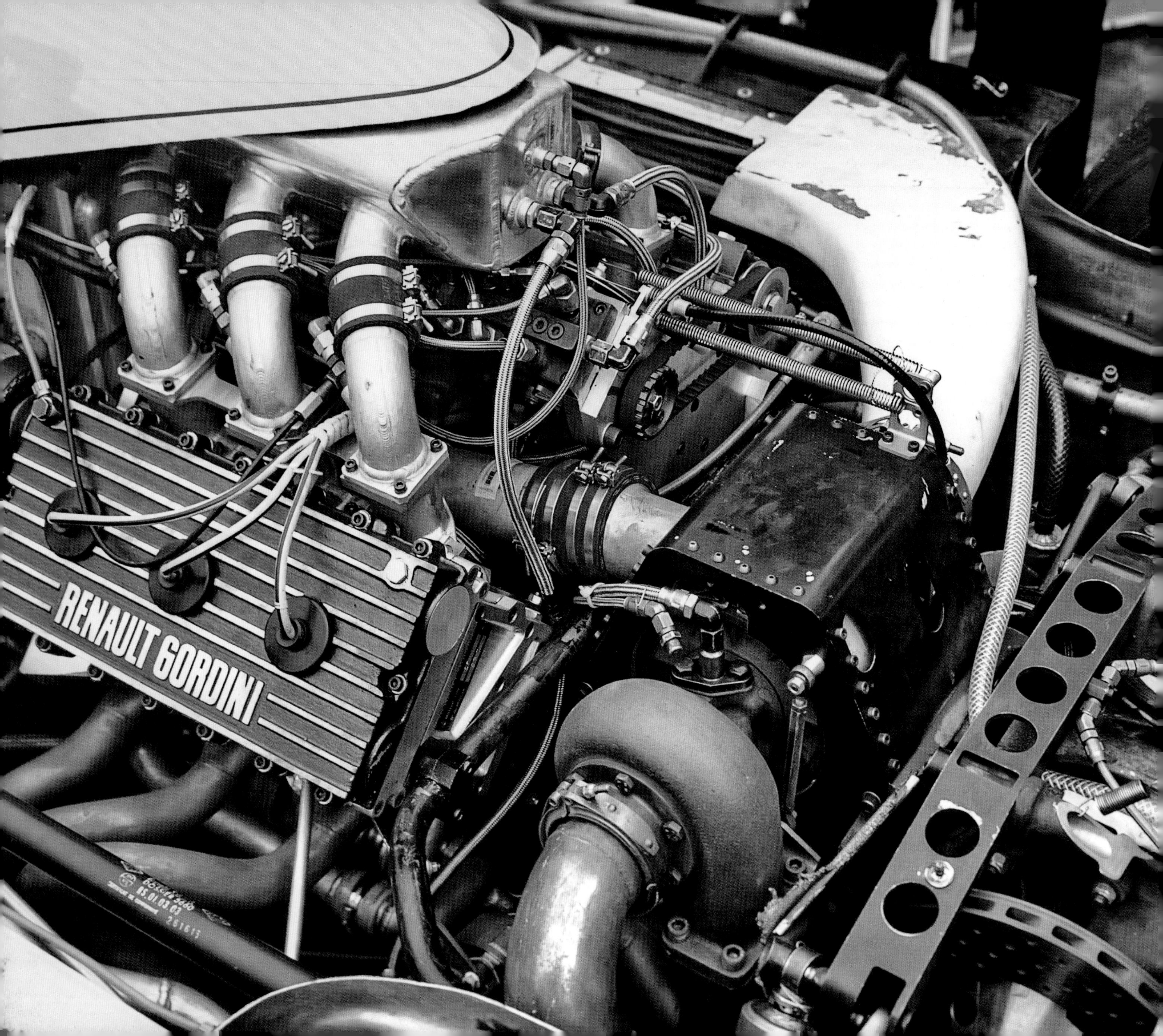
RENAULT GORDINI
05.01.03.03
261613

CHAPTER 12: 1979

PARLEZ-VOUS TURBO?

On the surface it was Ferrari's year. Anybody could see that. The Scuderia captured both the Drivers' and Constructors' crowns. Joy in Modena. South African Jody Scheckter and Canadian Gilles Villeneuve each won three of the season's fifteen races and finished in that order in the points. Scheckter became the first (and is still the only) F1 titlist from a non-European, American, or Australasian country.

But it was two other teams, Williams and Renault, who pointed the way to the next horizon. The new ground-effect Williams FW07 initially was dismissed as a poor man's Lotus 79, but in short order insiders were forced to see the 79 as a poor man's FW07. That's how good Patrick Head's new car was. Introduced at the fifth race of the season with some technical issues still to be solved, it won six of the season's final eight events. Driver Alan Jones finished third in the championship.

Head tells us how they were able to one-up Lotus at the end of the next chapter.

Even more influential in the long run was the screaming yellow lawn dart that won the July 1 French Grand Prix at Dijon. This was the ultimate French victory. Gallic car (Renault), Gallic engine (ditto), Gallic driver (Jean-Pierre Jabouille), Gallic tires (Michelin), Gallic fuel (Elf). In front of an overjoyed French crowd.

But even more significant, this was the first time a turbocharged engine had won a Formula One race. (It was also the first F1 car, thanks to Michelin's entry into the sport to challenge Goodyear,[1] to use radial tires.) Renault had debuted its 1.5-liter forced induction

1 Firestone had left during the 1975 season, leaving Goodyear as the sole major tire supplier.

According to the rules, turbocharged engines could have only half the displacement (1.5 liters) of naturally aspirated cars. It didn't matter. Renault proved they could develop gobs more power and other teams soon followed suit. *Paul-Henri Cahier/The Cahier Archive*

V-6 two years earlier at the 1977 British Grand Prix at Silverstone. It lasted sixteen laps. For quite some time after that, it appeared to be an exercise in futility. That first season, the car retired in each of the four races at which it appeared. The following year Jean-Pierre Jabouille DNFed or was unclassified in ten of the fourteen races he started. Ken Tyrrell started calling The Renaults "yellow teapots" because seemingly at every race they would boil over, and steam would come pouring out.

Slowly but surely it got better. In 1979, now with two cars at every race, one for Jabouille and one René Arnoux, the Renaults sat on pole six times, set two fastest laps, and had that breakthrough win at Dijon.

Renault would have to wait until 2005 to win a Formula One Constructors' Championship, but it had changed forever the course of F1 engine building, the heart and soul of the sport. In short order, turbocharged cars came to dominate so completely that, in the mid-1980s, F1 started awarding the Colin Chapman Trophy, a consolation prize for achievement among normally aspirated cars. In just a few short years, Renault engineers Francois Castaing, Jean-Pierre Boudy, Bernard Dudot, and others had changed not just Formula One but motorcars in general in a way few had ever done before. Castaing said:

> **[Dijon 1979] was the turning point for Formula One because everybody, all our colleagues in Formula One, said, "Next year we are going to be turbocharging our engines." And that's the way it happened.**
>
> **Long story short, we turned the opinion of everybody on [turbos], not only for Formula One or for Le Mans, but for production cars. Until then, there was no market for making turbochargers. Overnight it became a big market and now it is a gigantic one.**

Like Jochen Rindt and Ronnie Peterson, Villeneuve, waving to the crowd, didn't score a lot of wins in his too-brief career, but his drives were always memorable, including here where he sat on pole, registered the fastest lap, and took the checkered by almost thirty seconds over teammate Jody Scheckter, who later in the season would capture his first World Championship.

UNITED STATES GRAND PRIX WEST

April 8, 1979

Long Beach

3.251 km (2.02 mi)

Pole Position: Gilles Villeneuve (1:18.82)

Fastest Lap: Gilles Villeneuve (1:21.20)

Winner: Gilles Villeneuve (+29.38)

It's hard to explain now how much excitement Canadian Gilles Villeneuve (12) generated with his tail-out, never-say-die attitude at a time when, because of ground effects, it was thought sideways driving was a thing of the past.

F1 MAVERICK

Ken Tyrrell

Anybody who builds a six-wheel car—and wins with it—has to be one of our F1 Mavericks.

But that's only a part of what made Ken Tyrrell so special.

"In a time when motor racing was conducted with integrity and passion, one unique character graced the stage of Formula One. His name was Ken Tyrrell." So begins the film *Ken Tyrrell: Surviving Formula One*, produced by longtime Tyrrell driver Jackie Stewart's son Mark. Tyrrell was known as a kind, sometimes blunt, and almost unfailingly honest man who, with his wife, Norah, created a family-like atmosphere within his team. Amazingly, Stewart and Tyrrell trusted each other so implicitly that for most of their relationship together, their "contract" consisted of a handshake.

When Tyrrell decided to go F1 racing in 1968, he forged an improbable partnership between French missile-maker Matra, Ford's Cosworth engines (despite the fact that Matra had its own engines), and Dunlop tires. It achieved immediate success, winning three races that year and scoring the team's first—and Matra's only—World Drivers' and Constructors' Championships the following year.

When the French concern insisted on using its own engines in 1970, Tyrrell decided to forego its backing and fielded March-Cosworths before deciding early in the season to build his own chassis. The resulting Tyrrells, designed by Derek Gardner and built in a converted hut in Tyrrell's timber yard, won championships in 1971 and 1973 and provided a formidable challenge in 1972, despite lead driver Stewart's battle with ulcers. (This was on the heels of Stewart's battle with mononucleosis in 1971. "I was so exhausted at the end of the 1971 season," says the Scot, "that I never even went to pick up my World Championship trophy. My wife did it for me.") Stewart retired at the end of 1973, withdrawing from what would have been his hundredth and final F1 start at Watkins Glen when friend, teammate, and would-be successor François Cevert was killed in practice.

"The aftermath of it was really awful," said a shaken Tyrrell. "I came close to giving up motor racing in the few weeks after the accident."

Thereafter, the team was never quite so competitive again, although it continued to run near the front for a time, most notably with Stewart's replacement, Jody Scheckter.

Perhaps Ken's most iconoclastic moment came when Gardner proposed a new design based on an idea he'd been dying to try for more than a decade: a car with six wheels instead of four.

Like the first Tyrrell, the car was built in utter secrecy in Tyrrell's timber yard.

The Tyrrell P34 was introduced in September 1975, complete with four tiny (10-inch) front wheels, and began racing partway through the following season. Over the course of two campaigns, the P34 won once and finished on the podium often enough that despite a rash of retirements Tyrrell ended up third in the 1976 World Constructors' Championship. Thereafter the car's viability began to ebb, in part because tire-maker Goodyear needed to focus on fending off a new radial-tire challenge from Michelin and could devote fewer resources to updating the P34's special 10-inch tires.

Others had looked into a six-wheel approach as well, including March, Ferrari, and Williams, but all of them put four wheels in the back and none of them raced. Robin Herd reckons the March 2-4-0 was the most profitable car the constructor ever made; Britain's Scalextric offered a slot car version that became so massively popular that the royalties helped fill March coffers.

Not long after, the FIA decided to permit only cars with four wheels and the six-wheel wonders were consigned to history's dust heap. Perhaps the biggest blow to the team's fortunes came with the arrival of turbo engines in the late 1970s, which Tyrrell steadfastly resisted using. Said Stewart in his biography, *Winning Is Not Enough*, about Tyrrell's later years:

> **He continued to run his F1 team during the 1990s but became increasingly disenchanted and at one stage raged against the introduction of the turbo engine. "It's unnecessarily expensive," he declared, "and beyond the reach of ordinary individuals, so it's turning the sport into the exclusive domain of the major car manufacturers . . ." And he would yearn for the relatively recent past, when almost every F1 car used the 3-liter normally aspirated Ford Cosworth engine, which was affordable so private entrants could compete on a level playing field; the result was probably the most exciting and competitive era in the history of F1 racing.**

It seems only fitting, then, that the last victory for a Cosworth-powered car happened in the back of a Tyrrell at the 1983 Detroit Grand Prix. In 1999, Tyrrell sold his team to British American Racing and one of the last great forces of the Maverick Era was gone.

"This sport would be a better sport by a million miles," says Stewart at the end of *Ken Tyrrell: Surviving Formula One*, "if there were more Ken Tyrrells in it."

LUB
PIT
PACIFIC
El Paso
AKAI
AKAI AKAI
Marlboro
ALBILAD
GOOD YEAR
Leyland
Vehicles
GOOD YEAR
saudia
27

CHAPTER 13: 1980

SUDDENLY IT'S 1962

For those who had been around F1 in 1962, 1980 seemed to have stolen its plot. In 1961, Ferrari had ruled the roost. So superior was the 156 that the championship, for all intents and purposes, was between Ferrari drivers Phil Hill and Wolfgang von Trips. The Scuderia won both the Constructors' and the Drivers' World Championships.

In 1962, Ferrari did a face plant.

Fast forward to 1979. Ferrari wins both championships again. And once more it is nowhere the very next year. This time, too, it's engine-related. Turns out Mauro Forghieri's exquisite Ferrari boxer engine that has powered a Prancing Horse renaissance has one crucial shortcoming.

It's a boxer engine.

As Formula One teams now began to pour unprecedented resources and technical focus toward aerodynamics, for this was where the biggest performance gains were to be found, they realized that the game now was to make ground-effect tunnels as wide as possible for maximum downforce.

They also realized this was a lot harder to do with a fat, wide boxer configuration than to arrange one's pistons in a taller, narrower V. It's the very reason Gordon Murray had developed the BT46B fan car, to work around the fat Alfa flat-12.

The Williams team didn't run the table, but they might as well have. Alan Jones and Carlos Reutemann finished first and third in the Drivers' Championship and scored almost twice as many points as runner-up Ligier in the Constructors'. Jones won five times during the fourteen-race campaign. Only once during the eleven races he finished did he end up off the podium, at Zandvoort, where Williams's critical downforce advantage was negated by damaged skirts, all that low-pressure air escaping.

Designed by Patrick Head, Frank Dernie, and newcomer Neil Oatley, the Williams FW07 dominated the 1980 season. Like the Lotus 78 and 79, it benefited from extensive development in the Imperial College wind tunnel.

Brabham driver Nelson Piquet won to close within two points of the Australian. By edging Jones in the next race in Italy, Piquet actually took a one-point lead. But Jones captured the final two races and the championship as Piquet failed to finish either.

Brabham's ascent was engine-related as well. After struggling for several years with that Alfa Romeo flat-12, the team had acquired Cosworth engines, and the BT49, built in just six weeks, was a clear winner.

The year 1980 also saw the debut of a young French driver at McLaren, Alain Prost. Gordon Coppuck's M29 and M30 did not provide an outstanding showcase for his talents, but a new chassis by John Barnard would.

The season highlighted for many a changing of the guard in F1 that was almost complete. The great teams of the past were mostly gone or superseded. Cooper, Matra, BRM—consigned to the history books. Lotus and Tyrrell from this point forward would slip further and further away from the top tier. Brabham and McLaren remained, but these were no longer the Brabham and McLaren of Jack and Bruce. In 1981, Ron Dennis would begin buying out all of the original shareholders and reform the company in his own image. McLaren and Williams would dominate F1 over the following two decades. We asked Williams technical director Patrick Head why his team was able to do so well for so long:

> **I think we had a great passion for racing, and also for winning, possibly maybe also a contempt for losing. We engaged engineers with ideas and, I hope, were open to ideas from all within. A great workforce, many very skilled artisans, always seeking better ways to manufacture components.**
>
> **We reinvested every year in better equipment; in the first ten years Frank and I took very little out of the company and invested as much as we could afford in facility.**

No longer would the old ways of doing things suffice. The names had changed. But the passion remained.

The Maverick Era is ending, and the guard is changing—dramatically. The sharp end of the grid at Long Beach now features a Brabham (5) on point, beside René Arnoux (16) in the Renault turbo, followed by Patrick Depailler (22) in the Alfa, Jan Lammers (10) in the ATS, and eventual World Champion Alan Jones (27) in Patrick Head's brilliant Williams.

Marlboro
22
Marlboro
27
elf
16
elf
15
29
4

UNITED STATES GRAND PRIX WEST

March 30, 1980

Long Beach

3.251 km (2.02 mi)

Pole Position: Nelson Piquet (1:17.69)

Fastest Lap: Nelson Piquet (1:19.83)

Winner: Nelson Piquet (+49.212)

Winner Nelson Piquet will have a breakout season in Gordon Murray's ingenious BT49, collecting his first three victories and finishing second in the championship behind Jones.

Left: 2019 Motorsports Hall of Fame of America inductee Linda Vaughn was a fixture and crowd favorite at Long Beach from day one.

Right: Piquet was joined on the podium by Emerson Fittipaldi (left) and Riccardo Patrese in Jackie Oliver's Arrows. Arrows would match but never surpass Patrese's second place here, and Fittipaldi Automotive would only once beat Emerson's third.[1] Over the course of the Maverick Era, starting a team became exponentially more expensive and risky. Arrows founder Oliver: "Someone said to me about four or five years ago, 'The grids are too small in Formula One. Why on Earth don't more people do it? So, why have we only got ten teams?' And I said, 'Because they went bust.' They said, 'Well, not many went bust.' I said, 'Well, how many teams do you think went bust trying to do Formula One from 1970 until today?' And he said, 'Five or six?' I said, 'How about sixty-seven?'"

1 Fittipaldi finished second at the 1978 Brazilian Grand Prix in front of his home crowd.

Paul-Henri Cahier/The Cahier Archive

F1 MAVERICK

Sir Patrick Head

There was a time when people wondered whether Frank Williams belonged in Formula One. Throughout much of the 1970s it looked like his team would be a perennial also-ran. Then, things changed. Suddenly, starting in 1979, Williams was a frontrunner, and it stayed that way for nearly twenty years. From 1980 through 1997, Williams won seven Drivers' and nine Constructors' Championships.

One of the biggest reasons was the arrival of Patrick Head. Remember, 1979 was the year following the championship-winning debut of the groundbreaking, ground-effect Lotus 79, a car many, including almost certainly Colin Chapman, thought would rule the sport for the foreseeable future as his 72 had done earlier. More puzzling still, at a glance the FW07 seemed little more than a 79 impersonator.

But it sure didn't perform like one. We asked Head how he and Williams were able to leapfrog Lotus so quickly and so comprehensively that Chapman's firm never again won a World Championship. In fact, in 1979 Lotus dropped to fourth in the Constructors' Championship and never placed higher than third (1984, 1986, 1987) in its remaining fifteen years in existence. Head:

> **Lotus, or Colin Chapman, was strong on ideas, but no good at interactive development, and the Lotus 79 of 1978 had a poor chassis, of thin aluminum skins riveted without adhesive (I think), and was not very stiff when new, but became "soft-er" when the rivets started moving a bit. It also had inboard**

rear brakes that were not well cooled, often overheating during races and limited performance, plus, and maybe the most significant, a relatively short side pod (underside) that did not extend forward far, thereby requiring the car to have a large front wing to achieve aerodynamic balance.

Really, the car was not developed at all into 1979 as their efforts went into the Lotus 80, which was a failure for a number of reasons, mostly a curved skirt system which did not go up and down smoothly and would jam readily, resulting in a bouncing that became known as "porpoising." It also had a similar chassis construction to the 79.

The FW07 design aerodynamically came out of a week in the Campbell tunnel at Imperial College,[1] at which it was clear that the side pod worked much better with no disturbing wing in front, so we lengthened the side pod so that the car was balanced without a front wing, although we often used a small neutral profile for trimming.

The FW07 also had a bonded aluminum honeycomb chassis, as the small cross-section indicated that chassis stiffness would be a problem.

The FW07 also had outboard rear brakes (as at the front), which were well cooled and allowed a bigger airflow volume out from the back of the car.

Lotus had to retire the Lotus 80; the skirts were too big a problem, and the Lotus 79 was undeveloped from 1978 so was outdated. The pace of F1 development was high even then.

A new generation, inspired by mavericks like Cooper and Chapman and Forghieri, had come along with the express purpose of beating them. And Patrick Head was fast proving to be one of the best at beating the best.

1 The same moving-ground-plane wind tunnel where Peter Wright and Tony Rudd developed ground effect for the Lotus 78 and 79.

Marlboro
8
UNIPART
UNIPART
UNIPART
UNIPART
parmalat
LONG BEACH-CHICAGO

CHAPTER 14: 1981–1982–?

END OF AN ERA

The 1981 and 1982 seasons were two of the strangest on record, in part because of the ongoing battle between FISA and FOCA for control of the sport. The Fédération Internationale du Sport Automobile (FISA), headed by Jean-Marie Balestre, was Formula One's governing body as a subcommittee of the FIA. The Formula One Constructors' Association (FOCA), headed by Ecclestone, represented the teams. The main points of contention were the amount of money the teams were receiving, the technical regulations, and the perceived bias on the part of FISA in favor of the manufacturers involved in the sport, mainly Ferrari, Alfa Romeo, Talbot-Ligier, and Renault. The conflict spilled out onto the races themselves. The first major conflict was at the 1980 Spanish Grand Prix, which was forced to run as a nonchampionship event. The following year the FOCA teams threatened to form a rival series under their own "World Federation of Motor Sport" banner, but the two sides reached an agreement after a single "outlaw" race had been run. Things remained heated in 1982, when the majority of the FOCA teams boycotted the San Marino Grand Prix.

The laurels in 1981 were split between the Brabham and Williams teams. Nelson Piquet won the World Drivers' Championship in part because the two Williams drivers, Alan Jones and Carlos Reutemann, between whom no love was lost, took points from each other. Jones was the nominal number one, but it was Reutemann and Piquet who went into the final race at Caesars Palace—replacing a financially troubled Watkins Glen—separated by a single point. Neither driver was in top form, but Piquet's fifth place allowed him to edge Reutemann by a single point. Jones was third, helping Williams to the Constructors' crown. In all, seven drivers won races.

Technically, the most significant advance during the 1981 season was the introduction by designer John Barnard of a full carbon-fiber monocoque in the McLaren MP4/1. It would

John Barnard would usher in a new era of performance with his super-rigid composite chassis McLaren MP4/1. "Really, the carbon monocoque was born because I was trying to get the absolute maximum surface underneath the car to create downforce."

revolutionize not just Formula One performance but safety as well, and the other teams quickly followed suit.

The following year saw an even more balanced distribution of success. In all, eleven drivers scored wins. The driving force behind this seeming parity was the loss during the season first of Gilles Villeneuve, killed at Zolder, and then Didier Pironi, who suffered injuries in Germany from which he never fully recovered. Both Ferrari drivers were favorites to win the title, and Pironi was the clear points leader at the time of his accident. In the end, Finn Keke Rosberg grabbed the World Drivers' Championship for Williams, while the four different men who drove for Ferrari accumulated enough points for the Constructors' trophy.

The open warfare between the organizers and the teams and the increasing division within the fields between the haves and the have-nots—turbos versus normally aspirated, giant factory teams versus independents—made it feel like the end of an era. But just as surely as an era ends, so another begins. The period from 1958 through 1982 had seen change unlike any before or since. Not just to the cars and the tracks but to the people and the sport itself. The *idea* of Formula One.

Peter Manso wrote two books that serve as exquisite time capsules of the F1 of the late 1960s and early 1970s. One is *VROOOM!!*, which consists of interviews with ten of the top drivers circa 1968 to 1969. Four were dead within three years. Only Ickx, Moss, and Stewart are still with us. The other book is the bestseller *FASTER! A Racer's Diary*, written with by many accounts the era's greatest driver, Jackie Stewart. We asked Manso to compare the drivers of that time with the drivers of today. Were they the same or different?

"The drivers were different as people, as sensibilities back then," says Manso. "There was an ethic that was embraced that amounted to a code that was more the stuff of a person's spine, essential and real, than what we have today, be it with race drivers or artists or the neighborhood handyman who came to repair your lowly kitchen sink."

Not only the drivers had changed, but the teams and the team principals. Today the teams are much larger. Where once they consisted of a handful of people, now they're in the hundreds. Prior to the 2018 United States Grand Prix, Mercedes driver Lewis Hamilton explained on the *Good Morning America* TV show, "There's a big team behind me. It's a different kind of sport. There's 1,800 people to build those two cars." Almost all of them specialists or with very specific areas of responsibility.

There are not that many because there have to be. There are that many because there *can* be. Colin Chapman could have used a hundred people but, in the early days, could never afford to. The economics of the sport have changed entirely, mainly due to Bernie Ecclestone and the TV contracts that have opened the floodgates to millions and millions of dollars in sponsorship. According to *Forbes*, the most recently public Ferrari F1 budget was $571.1 million.

There were still great mavericks in the sport bringing forth an ever-expanding collection of new ideas for how to win. Gordon Murray, John Barnard, Patrick Head, and others were every bit the innovators and mavericks as were forebears such as Chapman, Hall, Cooper, and Duckworth. But now the sport was less about finding new areas to explore than finding loopholes within an ever more constrictive rulebook to exploit. Even Murray's brilliant pit stop innovation today has been codified into mandatory stops to change tires that the regulators have made sure need to be changed.

In the end, it is up to you to decide whether the Maverick Era is any better or worse than the eras that preceded and followed it.

The only thing for certain is that we will never see its like again.

How crazy was the 1982 World Drivers' Championship? It was decided in a parking lot in Vegas, and the guy who finished second in points missed the last five of the season's sixteen races.

UNITED STATES GRAND PRIX WEST

March 15, 1981

Long Beach

3.251 km (2.02 mi)

Pole Position: Riccardo Patrese (1:19.39)

Fastest Lap: Alan Jones (1:20.90)

Winner: Alan Jones (+9.19)

The introduction of ground effects tunnels changed the shape and proportions of Formula One. The introduction of tall, narrow turbocharged engines changed them further. The Williams FW07 dominated from its introduction in 1979, and defending champion Alan Jones's FW07C (1) won here on its way to capturing a second straight World Constructors' Championship.

Nelson Piquet in the Brabham BT49C (5) will squeak by the two Williams aces to take the Drivers' title. Neither the French Ligier JS17 (below left) nor Renault 20B (below right) yet have that kind of reliability, but from midseason they'll win seven straight poles. Doug Nye: "Initially we called the [Renault turbo] the steam kettle because it would boil its way into retirement after very few laps in every race, all Puffing Billy, because it was just hopeless. It wasn't until the French Grand Prix in 1979 that they suddenly came on song. Then it was obvious that they had 650 to 700 horsepower, and it would survive race distance, whereas the Cosworth engine by that time was producing around 470 to 480 horsepower. It was just the passport to success, if they could make them reliable."

CAESAR'S PALACE GRAND PRIX

September 25, 1982

Las Vegas

3.650 km (2.268 mi)

Pole Position: Alain Prost (1:16.35)

Fastest Lap: Michele Alboreto (1:19.63)

Winner: Michele Alboreto (+27.292)

Diana Ross lends star power to a podium featuring third place man Eddie Cheever (left), winner Michele Alboreto (center), and runner-up John Watson.

At the Caesars Palace finale, Williams's Keke Rosberg (above) and McLaren's John Watson (7) were the only two contenders who could grab the crown, and all Rosberg had to do was finish sixth or better to leave Watson in the cold. Rosberg finished fifth and Watson second behind surprise winner Michele Alboreto (3). It was Tyrrell's first win since 1978. The outcome ensured that Ferrari's Didier Pironi, whose career ended in a Hockenheim crash, would keep the runner-up spot in the title chase. Despite the musical chairs following Pironi's crash and Gilles Villeneuve's death earlier in the year (that's Mario Andretti pinch-hitting in the #28 Ferrari in his final F1 start), Ferrari still won the Constructors' Championship with the dominant turbo V-6 126C2. Another sign of the changing times: fourteen of the season's sixteen poles went to turbocharged cars.

Paul-Henri Cahier/The Cahier Archive

F1 MAVERICK

John Barnard

In addition to designing several of Formula One's most successful cars, the London native introduced two technologies that transformed the sport. At McLaren in 1981, he introduced with the McLaren MP4/1 the first carbon-fiber composite chassis, a giant step in performance and safety. At Ferrari later in the decade, he pioneered semiautomatic gearboxes, which have since been adopted by almost every high-performance road car. They can shift better and faster than even the best drivers can do manually. Barnard began his career in 1968 at Lola, where he helped design, among others, the cigarette-box T-260 Can-Am car. In 1972, he joined McLaren, helping the team win its first F1 and Indy 500 titles. After penning the first Indy car to win with the turbocharged Cosworth DFX engine, the Vel's Parnelli Jones VPJ 6, he designed the ground-effect Chaparral 2K "yellow submarine" with which Johnny Rutherford won the 1980 Indy 500 and Indy car title, and revolutionized Indy car construction. Many consider the 2K the prototype for every Indy car that followed. Barnard then returned to F1 with McLaren, Ferrari, Benetton, and Prost, where in addition to the aforementioned technologies he produced multiple World Championship winners. We asked him how he came to develop the innovations he did and how he views the sport today.

What do you see as the major technological changes during the Maverick Era?

First, the transition to rear-engine—actually mid-engine layout. Cooper started that. Then I suppose you got the wings on suspension [in the late 1960s]. Which was the correct way to do it, but unfortunately, people didn't do it in a well-engineered way, and wings came off, and it all got very dangerous. So that was banned. Which is a shame. I hate banning things because of poor engineering. Then [in 1977] Renault introduced the turbo engine, and Lotus started the whole ground-effect thing. That really opened up a whole new area for us.

I took it to Indianapolis with the Chaparral. I'd seen the Lotus 78, which was probably the first Formula One car with proper ground effect. They had a wing on the side and I think brushed skirts initially. And then they did the 79. I don't know what the launch dates were, but the Chaparral was only a little way behind the 79 in coming out. *[The 79 debuted at the midpoint of the 1978 season, the 2K in early 1979—Ed.]* I remember some people said, "Oh, you've copied the shape of the Lotus 79." But, in fact, I hadn't seen the 79 when I did the Chaparral. It just seemed to me you had to use the whole of the underside of the car, take the whole diffuser and ground-effect undersurface to the rear of the car, as far as you could go really.

Then around about 1980 I did the carbon monocoque. A proper, full-carbon monocoque. *[Developed at Project 4, it became the McLaren MP4/1. —Ed.]* Lotus were playing around with a kind of hybrid version, but I did the carbon monocoque to give myself the opportunity to have maximum ground effect. Really, the carbon monocoque was born because I was trying to get the absolute maximum surface underneath the car to create downforce.

How did going from aluminum to carbon fiber make it possible to increase the surface area under the car?

My requirement was to make the chassis narrower so I could maximize the width of the tunnels. When you make the chassis narrow, you lose the geometry that is going to give you torsional stiffness. I started thinking, how do I make a narrow chassis without losing torsional stiffness?

I contemplated thin steel sheet. That's fine, but it gets heavy. I got into the carbon through visiting an aerospace plant, and I thought, well, that's the answer. It's a fundamentally stiffer material than aluminum, and it's fundamentally lighter, which is nearly everything you do in a racing car. But it was all aimed at giving me a narrow chassis to improve the ground-effect capability of the car.

Is there a simple way to quantify how much the carbon fiber allowed you to increase the Venturi area versus aluminum?

To pop figures off the top of my head is not easy at this stage—it's so long ago. But in terms of total what I call ground-effect area, I certainly increased the width of that by something like 40 percent. I should point out that having done the carbon chassis built around a Cosworth V-8, it was only about eighteen months later that I started working on a car with a turbo engine designed around the chassis (so the tunnels could be even wider). And that's when we came up with the Porsche turbo.

I had a package in my head where I could make the engine narrower than the Cosworth V-8, which we did. I sat down with Porsche, with a whole raft of requirements and specifications. In doing that, I was able to increase the aerodynamic surface under the car, as I say, it must have been by 40 percent. I know the numbers that we were getting from our [wind tunnel] model at the time were lit up. Our downforce was climbing massively because of the narrow chassis—and the [narrower] engine to go with it.

Really, about 1982 was the time when we really got to grips with the downforce created from underneath the car [with ground effect]. And of course, then Ferrari were falling further and further behind in that area and started playing politics and fundamentally got the rules changed and brought in the flat-bottom cars in 1983. That put lots of our work in the dustbin, which was a huge disappointment.

Is it possible to compare the significance of advances? On a scale of one to ten, is ground effect an eight?

Ground effect was a big jump in cornering power—and cornering power that wasn't too costly. For example, up until the time we had honed our ground-effect cars, Renault had a turbo engine with probably 150 horsepower more than the Cosworth, in race trim. But in order to use that 150 horsepower, they were running more wing.

You can bolt on a big wing and make more downforce. That's great, but then you're going to increase your drag. They weren't getting their downforce without paying for it. With the ground effect, we were getting downforce and not paying for it. Then, at the end of 1983, when we started using the TAG-Porsche turbo engine, we would have probably been racing with at least 300 horsepower more than a Cosworth. I'm talking race trim; the horsepower jump in qualifying with some of those turbo engines was just astronomic, because they (mostly BMW) used to build an engine that would last for about four or five laps and that was it. The thing would virtually melt after that. But of course with the change in regulations that year to flat-bottom cars, we lost a lot of the downforce. If we'd been left alone to continually develop the ground effect and the turbo engine, we'd have had cars that were just mind-blowingly fast around corners and down straights.

Advances that couldn't happen until other advances did.

When I started in the business in 1969, carbon composites weren't even on the horizon. So that was one thing that came along and allowed us to do things. And if you look at where it's got to today, everything is carbon now—suspension and everything.

Electronics is another big thing that's happened. If I think back even up to 1983 or so, the electronics on the Formula One car was next to nothing, really. We didn't have all these onboard logging systems. If we had a logging system at all, it would be so big and clumsy, you'd never be able to race with it.

The mid-1980s was when it all kicked off with the electronics. Partly because of the turbo engine, because controlling the engine required electronic control of the fuel injection and all the rest of it to get the best out of it. Along with that you started collecting data, and it wasn't long before we started having onboard data collection systems with transducers and everything all over the suspension, measuring suspension travel and all that kind of thing.

Up to that point, the information we had as designers was very, very limited. It was based on trial and error, on some experience, on a few basic numbers that we would use for working out suspension strengths and so on. But when the electronics came along, then you're getting information back that is just a *huge* step forward.

What kinds of information?

Ride height, for a start. Actually monitoring damper travels and so on. We would know very closely the ride height of the car as it went into the corner, through the corner, out of the corner, down the straight. It was hugely important.

Now you've got traction controls and launch controls and all the rest of it that are literally taking [control] away from the driver. Taking away the drivers' skillset if you like.

Bruce McLaren said he became a constructor because the driver's role was shrinking. How do you see the driver/car equation from the 1960s till today?

I didn't really start in it till 1969, but in the 1960s and early 1970s, I would have said the driver was certainly 70 percent of the equation. You watch a guy like Jim Clark. Whatever he got in, he was quick or quickest, and that was his talent.

I go back to the 1980s where we're dealing with people like (John) Watson, Lauda, Prost, and so on. Watson was quite capable of beating Lauda, for example. I've seen him drive around the outside of Niki at Long Beach and win the race. The problem with John was that he used to struggle with the setup of the car through the practice [sessions]. He would be more finicky, I suppose, to get the setup 100 percent the way he liked it, and unfortunately he would take that to an extreme where he never left himself time to go out there and just do a banzai qualifying lap and put himself further up the grid. But in race trim, he was just as quick, say, as Niki.

And then, of course, along comes Prost and you put Lauda and Prost together, and again you come back to the qualifying issue. Prost nearly always outqualified Niki, because Prost just had those few tenths of a second available to him in qualifying. But again, you come to a race, and there was not much to choose. To me anyway you were still talking 40 to 50 percent driver back then.

I think it's even less now. Twenty percent? Difficult to put a number on it. There is still a difference in drivers. Qualifying is where you'll see it. Hamilton most times can pip [Valtteri] Bottas by two or three tenths. That's just him. That's his ability to drive a car fast. But that's kind of all you're looking at really. If you took somebody else on the back of the grid and put him in one of those Mercedes, they would be there or thereabouts, but Hamilton would still pip them by three or four tenths.

Was the Maverick Era unique from a technology standpoint?

The innovation in the cars from that period was far greater than it is today and greater than it had been up to that point. Because the British teams did not have the ability to develop the engine. Until Cosworth came out with their V-8, Ferrari were the engine people, and everything they did was concerned with the engine. The British teams, because they didn't have the engine facilities and capability in their locker, were forced to develop the car, the chassis, and the aerodynamics. So lots of interesting steps were taken to the point that people like Ferrari started to get left behind.

If you were twenty-one today, would you still get into motorsports?

I'm sure if I was twenty-one now, I would have the same absolute, total immersion in cars and racing cars that I had then. How I would get into it now, I'm not so sure.

We were lucky. People like myself, Patrick Head, people like that, we started at Lola's. Eric Broadley never got all the credit he should have. Because Eric was responsible for an awful lot of people getting into racing and learning the business from the ground up, and I think that's important.

We did everything. We did Formula Fords, Can-Am cars; you were able to deal in all kinds of different types of car and get involved in the building, testing, and running of them.

I think Formula One now is so big that the opportunity to get involved in all these different areas of the car just isn't there. There are just too many big departments. You're in suspension, or you're in gearbox, or you're in electronic controls.

But I'd probably still try and do it.

Levi's

AFTERWORD

NIKI LAUDA

When Andreas Nikolaus Lauda decided he wanted to get into Formula One, he took out a massive bank loan he could only pay back if he succeeded. The Austrian knew exactly what he was doing. He went on to win three World Drivers' Championships (1975, 1977, 1984) and famously walked away from a potential fourth when he declined to participate in the rain-soaked 1976 season finale at Fuji, handing the title to friend and rival James Hunt. That was the year he was badly burned in a crash at the Nürburgring and given last rites. Six weeks later he was on the grid at Monza. He retired at the end of the 1979 season but was lured back in 1982 by McLaren, for whom he won his final championship two years later. He remained in racing as an adviser or team manager for Ferrari and Jaguar. Today he is the always-candid nonexecutive chairman of the Mercedes AMG Petronas F1 team. We spoke to Lauda early in 2018 about how the sport has evolved from the Maverick Era to the present day.

During your career you've seen lots of technology arrive in Formula One. Which has had the biggest impact on the sport, good or bad, and why?

For me in 1984, when the TAG Turbo was introduced in the McLaren. The situation was as follows. In 1982, I came back from nowhere with McLaren and I lost the championship that year against Rosberg, because I thought we were never going to win against the turbocharged cars,[1] and I never really pushed hard. When Villeneuve got killed in Zolder and Pironi got hurt in Hockenheim, it was too late for me to react and to go quick with the normally aspirated car, and Rosberg won the championship. He was always second, third, and so on.

Therefore, [for 1983] I went to Phillip Morris myself in Lausanne [Switzerland] and said to these guys, "In your contract with McLaren it is written that if there is a better engine available, you will use the turbo (that is, better) engine, because the TAG Turbo was already developed for McLaren. And as we were not winning anything, I said, "Put an engine in my car." I was called back by Ron

1 Because of the departure of the favored Ferrari drivers, it was one of the strangest title campaigns on record. The sixteen events were split among eleven drivers. Five, including Lauda, had two wins. None more. Keke Rosberg took the prize despite winning just one race, outstripping his rivals based on his Williams' greater reliability. Lauda, whose McLaren retired often, finished fifth, fourteen points back.

Lauda began his F1 career with March in 1971 and went on to win championships with Ferrari and McLaren.

Dennis, [who said], "Are you nuts? We are running the team and not you. If you do this once again, you're going to be thrown out."

I didn't let go. I pushed and pushed. Because [designer] John Barnard would have never put a car on the racetrack if he wasn't sure this design he had developed was as reliable as he wanted it to be.

Anyway, as the year was so boring, I forced them with Marlboro money, and at Zandvoort we had for the first time the turbo engine in my McLaren. When I came to the circuit and I looked at the car, I said, "This wing in the back looks a bit small." Barnard said, "Shut up, you have no idea." Because all of the turbo cars had twice as big a wing as I had. So then I went down the straight at Zandvoort [at, like, 350 kilometers per hour], I can't remember, but through the corners my car didn't work.

I said to John, "We have a problem with the rear wing." Anyway, to make a long story short, the last race, which was in Kyalami [South Africa], I was leading the race against all the other turbos because the car was so good, the engine was so good. Unfortunately, my generator broke in the race. So I was right to push them as hard as I could to start developing the [turbo car] the year before. Because if we would have started in [1984], no way would we have been finished. Whereas we did the other half season [in 1983 developing] this turbo thing and the wing, I really had a competitive car.

The only problem was this stupid, nice friend Prost turned up [for 1984], and then we both had this incredible car.[2] And these cars in these days were half a second quicker than anybody else. So the biggest fight I had with the turbocharger was the question with Prost to win by half a point the championship. So this was for me the most difficult car to drive. Because [with] the turbo power we had 1,200 horsepower for one lap [in qualifying trim and because the supersticky qualifying tires only lasted for one lap], then 600 to 700 [horsepower] for the race, because of the fuel flow and what you've got in your tank. This was for me the most exciting and best-ever combination, no question.

During the time you were in Formula One, were there technologies that were banned that you think should have stayed or vice versa?

Frankly, I would have loved if [the turbos] would have stayed[3] because we would have kicked everybody. . . . The Turbo Era was the most exciting car to drive because of the power difference [between qualifying and the race]. All the rest was in these days difficult. If you ask me, I would have loved to race today because no risk whatsoever, forty, fifty million being paid a year, and the cars, some of them, drive like Formula Three cars. The rule changes for last year were different, because afterwards the cars got more difficult to drive. But beforehand, the year before, it was easy in a way. They had power steering, everybody could drive it, and that was it. It was the worst Formula One for me, in 2016.

Have you seen the balance change between how much is the car and how much is the driver in deciding success?

You cannot divide this at all because you always need a driver and you need a car. But to drive on the limit in all these cars is always the same. There's the best driver in the world who can do it better, and the worst is two or three tenths slower. So to be on the limit is the same problem. But the operation of the car, to operate it, is ten times easier today. All you do is, you have power steering, and you drive—click, click, click [that is, you turn on the different

---

2 Lauda is referring to the not completely welcome arrival at McLaren of a very fast young Alain Prost, fresh from the Renault F1 team.

3 The FIA banned turbochargers starting with the 1989 season. They were reintroduced for the 2014 season at 1.6 liters displacement.

systems]—and then off you go. All anybody has to do. Only have to concentrate to keep on the limit and go quicker. In my time, with gear changes, you missed one gear and the engine blew up.

What do you think Formula One needs to recapture that excitement for the fans? What are the core ingredients?

The core ingredients to be exciting: get rid of all these stupid rules we all introduced. Start with five-places-back for gearbox, engines, ten-place grid penalties; all this manipulating the sport. We have moved away from basic racing, where you see how the drivers fight with the cars to their physical limits and then make mistakes, or not. Which makes the difference. All this is drifting away.

At the moment we are driving in a very boring Formula One time. Five years ago it was better. I think this Formula One boring time will continue until [the Concorde Agreement] is over in 2020. People are less and less interested. Not because the racing is boring. The whole attraction of Formula One is gone.

We all complain about this Halo bullshit, but if you look at the thing and what it does, the attraction is gone. You should see at least a human being sitting in the car driving, then you see maybe in his head movements how hard it is. But you don't realize. You don't even see it. Lewis did a lap in Bahrain or somewhere—six-tenths quicker than the others—and I don't even see it. Me, and I know what to look at. I don't even realize it. When I see the lap time, I'm like, "Fuck, he's quick." All this is going wrong.

Look at the [Moto GP] motorbikes. The motorbikes are still going as they were always going. Attractive. Aggressive. You see what these guys do. Why did we change Formula One around so stupid? We keep going backwards and backwards and backwards. Motorbikes are still exactly the same as one hundred years [ago], and they're still as attractive as at the first day. But why? Because they don't change the rules over time. The FIA doesn't get involved in making everything safe, putting Halos on the thing. They keep the basics going. We are destroying slowly the basics. We are going in the direction of, I don't know, a playground for . . . how are these things called? What the kids play? Computer games.

How much of that do you think is the circuits?

The circuits, it's a combination of having runoff areas everywhere and no more close guardrails where you see how quick they go. All of this development goes hand in hand. Circuits. Cars. Halos. All this is going, step by step, small steps into the wrong direction, I think.

If you could take a car from today and race it on one racetrack that you raced on in the 1970s to capture that excitement, where would you go?

Nürburgring. Nordschleife. But it can't be. If you ask me this question, I give you that answer. But you cannot go back and make it more dangerous. You can't go back. But we have to stop all these extra things we load onto Formula One in little steps to make it completely. . . . The only excitement today is the start [of the race]. At the start, they're all going into the first corner, the tires smoke, they go forwards and backwards and [at that moment] you think, ah, something unexpected will happen. After the start, more or less, most of the races are not interesting anymore.

PETE BIRO

1933–2018

Pete Biro passed away shortly before F1 Mavericks was completed. Away from the track, Pete was a professional magician. He brought a magician's mindset to his photo assignments, always looking for an unexpected angle and inventing shots that left other photographers mystified as to how he'd gotten them—the very definition of magic. He will be deeply missed by his many friends in both communities.

My uncle, Edward Biro, was an amateur photographer and electronics whiz working for Bell Telephone. When I was about nine years old, he gave me the first of my cameras. I think it was some kind of folding camera. I started taking photos around the neighborhood, chased a few fire trucks, and took photographs of my friends playing baseball and members of the family.

After I graduated from high school, I was immediately drafted in the US Army, and luckily, during the Korean War, I went to Germany and wound up in the G2 (intelligence section) of the First Division. While in Germany I took a class in darkroom work and learned how to process and print my own film.

When I came home in 1952, I discovered sports cars. Before I went away, I had a 1932 Ford, but my dad sold it while I was gone. Looking for a sports car I wound up buying an MG TD. I paid $1,100 for it, had it for two years, and traded it for a Triumph TR2, getting $1,100 for it. Gee, I had a car for two years and got all my money back when I got rid of it. With these cars I went on a lot of rallies and started going to sports car races, and of course I brought my camera along with me.

When the digital age started to creep in, I immediately bought a digital camera, but it wasn't very good. I eventually wound up going through ten different cameras until the technology and quality reached the point where the photographs were as good as if not better than film cameras.

To put this book together I started digging through piles of photographs, boxes of slides, stacks of pictures in filing cabinets, boxes in my garage, you name it I had it, but it was in no particular order, since I am not a very organized person.

In the beginning, I was contacted to supply photographs to *Road & Track* for a story on the Barneson Special, a custom-made sports car with a big Chrysler engine. I spent an afternoon taking pictures of the car, sent them to the magazine, and got $80 for a couple hours' work. I said to myself, "This is a business I should get into." Up to then I had been working in the sign-painting business painting signs on windows, walls, trucks, and midget race cars. You name it, I painted signs on everything. One time I painted the numbers and sponsor names on A. J. Foyt's race car for the Daytona 500.

Following the Barneson story, *Road & Track* assigned me to cover the Pebble Beach road races. I was excited and when I got to Pebble Beach, I picked up my pass and started taking pictures in the pits. All of a sudden I heard my name over the public address system. I reported to the office and it turned out John Bond, owner of the magazine, wanted my pass back because he had a guest he wanted to give it to.

Following that, a couple of us got together (John Kelly, John O'Donnell, and Fred Amundrud), and we decided to start our own magazine. That way we could assign the photo passes and give them to ourselves, and no one would be able to take them away. We named it *Sports Car Pictorial.*

We published this magazine for five years to the day, and as we were going to the printer with that edition, I told the guys, "We only have $30 in the bank." We decided to quit publishing and sold it to *Autoweek* for one dollar.

By that time David E. Davis Jr. had discovered my work and was giving me assignments for *Car and Driver.* In addition, I was shooting for *Hot Rod*, *Motor Trend*, and *Sports Car Graphic*. I also got some dream assignments from *Sports Illustrated*, most notably coverage of A. J. Foyt at his ranch in Houston.

Working with David E. Davis Jr. was unbelievable. We traveled all over, went to Europe, had great times, met a lot of great people, and luckily we were there in 1967 when Dan Gurney won both the Belgian Grand Prix and Le Mans. Sadly, however, the magazine lost most of my film from Gurney's two historic wins.

There are a lot of photographs that I've made that will not be in the book. Often I would send all the film to advertising agencies, they would select what they wanted, and sometimes

photograph by Tim Considine

they would send the film back to me, but other times it just vanished into their files never to be seen again. So, I hope you enjoy looking at these pictures as much as I did making them.

One of the great assets of this kind of life, traveling to all the races, was getting to meet, know, and become friends with so many of the drivers and other members of the press. I count Dan Gurney, Phil Hill, Bruce McLaren, Denny Hulme, Jackie Stewart, Bobby Unser, Tony Adamowicz, Sam Posey, A. J. Foyt, Richard Petty, David Pearson, and many others as good friends.

Looking back at the fifty years I spent on the road with a camera, I would do it all over again; probably the only thing I would change would be my socks and underwear.

INDEX

Gulf
Gulf
MERCEDES-BENZ
batteries
FINA
OP s.P.